Black Swan Start-ups

D0809577

Sami Mahroum

Black Swan Start-ups

Understanding the Rise of Successful Technology Business in Unlikely Places

Sami Mahroum
INSEAD Abu Dhabi Campus
Abu Dhabi
United Arab Emirates

ISBN 978-1-349-84647-4   ISBN 978-1-137-57727-6 (eBook)
DOI 10.1057/978-1-137-57727-6

Library of Congress Control Number: 2016939256

© The Editor(s) (if applicable) and The Author(s) 2016
Softcover reprint of the hardcover 1st edition 2016 978-1-137-57726-9

The author(s) has/have asserted their right(s) to be identified as the author(s) of this work in accordance with the Copyright, Designs and Patents Act 1988.
This work is subject to copyright. All rights are solely and exclusively licensed by the Publisher, whether the whole or part of the material is concerned, specifically the rights of translation, reprinting, reuse of illustrations, recitation, broadcasting, reproduction on microfilms or in any other physical way, and transmission or information storage and retrieval, electronic adaptation, computer software, or by similar or dissimilar methodology now known or hereafter developed.
The use of general descriptive names, registered names, trademarks, service marks, etc. in this publication does not imply, even in the absence of a specific statement, that such names are exempt from the relevant protective laws and regulations and therefore free for general use.
The publisher, the authors and the editors are safe to assume that the advice and information in this book are believed to be true and accurate at the date of publication. Neither the publisher nor the authors or the editors give a warranty, express or implied, with respect to the material contained herein or for any errors or omissions that may have been made.

This Palgrave Macmillan imprint is published by Springer Nature
The registered company is Macmillan Publishers Ltd. London

*This book is dedicated to my parents
who have thrived all their lives
in unlikely places.*

Foreword

Unicorns, which are start-ups with valuations exceeding US$1 billion, have become a worldwide phenomenon. A decade ago, all unicorns were from the USA. Nowadays they hail from every corner of the globe. They come from Europe but also from emerging markets, Israel, Korea, Indonesia and, above all, India and China.

This tectonic shift is part of the ongoing rebalancing of the wealth of nations. Emerging markets are no longer (only) low-cost factory locations but the home of some of the largest ever tech initial public offerings (IPOs) (e.g., Alibaba) and the largest ever "score" of venture capital. Years ago the investment arm of South African firm Naspers invested around US$40 million in an unknown Chinese start-up called Tencent. Today that stake is worth US$40 billion. This "score" is by far the largest ever, more than that managed in Google by legendary venture firm Sequoia, for example.

The shifting wealth of nations is today more than ever about tech, start-ups and venture capital. This century will witness an increasing number of rising tech stars from emerging markets and from the margins of the start-up world. For example, Edinburgh, Scotland, known more for its annual music festival than its tech companies, has given rise to two unicorns, FanDuel and Skyscanner. But this trend, as this book will show, is also evident in other traditionally peripheral places such as Bergen,

Tallinn, Lahore, Amman and Dubai. The major news is that successful tech start-ups can rise up now from anywhere around the globe – and emerging markets are a big part of this story.

The Emergence of Less Likely Places

While Europe is slowly losing its technology icons – the latest to fall being Nokia, now in the process of reinventing itself with its 2015 acquisition of Alcatel-Lucent – the emerging markets are becoming ever stronger in innovation and technology. Some of their companies are already world leaders in their respective sectors.

This is the real news: the emerging markets and the periphery of mature economies are no longer low-cost, low-technology-intensive countries. It is no longer a matter of trade and financial flows, but of countries and regions betting on innovation and technology. And their bets far exceed the usual European perception.

In 2015 the four so-called BRICs (Brazil, Russia, India and China) alone accounted for 43 % of the world's population, 21 % of world gross domestic product (GDP), and 20 % of direct foreign investment (nearly US$205 billion). In less than a decade, trade among these nations increased tenfold to surpass US$200 billion. These four countries are respectively already the seventh, eighth, tenth and second world economic powers. China already has as many companies as the UK (33) in the Financial Times (FT) Global 500, which is composed of the world's 500 largest companies by market capitalisation. The same trend can be observed with India and Brazil, which, with ten each, are already ahead of Spain, with nine companies in the top 500.

Other countries, such as Singapore, are unseating the major western financial centres, particularly those of Switzerland. Singapore is in fact the first emerging economy to join the select club of triple-A countries with the top international credit rating. Chile, Turkey and Mexico are already members of the Organisation for Economic Co-operation and Development (OECD). The greatest concentration of millionaires is in Qatar, ahead of Switzerland (in fact, Qatar has the highest GDP per capita in the world). Similarly, the world's biggest airlines are now those of emerging market countries, with the United Arab Emirates in the lead. All seek to acquire iconic assets and, above all, to acquire knowledge with the aim of providing services within their respective countries. Thus, in 2015 the Fosun Group bought Cirque du Soleil in order to round out its offering of entertainment for China's middle class, after buying Club Med, also in 2015, and having bought a stake in travel agent Thomas Cook.

From Raw Materials to Killer Apps

But above all we are seeing a wave of technological expansion. We are no longer dealing with countries with cheap labour full of raw materials but with economies that are downloading so-called technological 'killer apps' at breakneck speed. In 2015, the world's biggest supplier in the telecommunications industry is no longer an American, French or Swedish company but a Chinese one (Huawei). The world's largest producer of personal computers (PCs) is no longer American but Chinese (Lenovo). One of the world's most research and development (R&D)-intensive companies is Korean (Samsung), which since 2013 has also been ahead of its Finnish and American competitors as the leading producer of mobile phones and devices. We are witnessing an unprecedented tectonic shift. The spread of technology is accelerating as never before, in space and in time, as Diego Comín points out.[1]

A clear case in point is that of South Korea. In the 1960s, South Korea was poorer than Spain or any Latin American country.[2] In 2015, it surpassed them all in terms of GDP per capita, to say nothing of its performance in education (equal with Finland in the OECD's PISA reports). In 1963, Korea exported goods at a value equivalent at current prices to slightly more than US$600 million, comprised mainly of agricultural and fishery products. In 2015, it exported more than US$600 billion worth of goods, mainly electronics, machinery, chemical

---

[1] See Diego Comín, Mikhail Dmitriev and Esteban Rossi-Hansberg, "The Spatial Diffusion of Technology," Harvard University, Boston College and Princeton University, March 2013 (unpublished). http://www.dartmouth.edu/%7Edcomin/files/SDT.pdf

[2] For a comparison between Spain and Korea, see one of the chapters in the book by Javier Santiso, *España 3.0: Necesitamosresetear el país, Barcelona*, Planeta, 2015.

products and shipping technology. The giant Samsung Group consists of more than 80 companies and employs over 380,000 people around the world. In 2013, it even surpassed Apple, selling more smartphones and generating more profits than its California-based rival.

Until recently, innovation, particularly corporate innovation, was largely a western story. Multinationals from OECD countries designed, produced and sold innovative products. Gradually another model established itself: innovation was still conceived in the West, but it was produced in emerging markets. This is Apple's model with iPods and iPads, which are partly produced in Taiwan, Korea or China. Now we are seeing a third model emerge, in which innovation is not just produced and sold from the emerging markets, but increasingly also being conceived in them.

New Companies from an Old World

This shift is bringing about an accelerated reordering of world company classifications. The classifications of the most innovative companies produced by Boston Consulting Group (BCG) or Forbes tell a similar story. BCG's Top 10 is headed by Tencent and also features a Taiwanese company (Mediatek), a Mexican one (AméricaMóvil), another Chinese one (China Mobile), two Indian companies (Bharti Airtel and Infosys) and one South African company (MTN). In the Forbes list, too, Tencent features in the Top 10 (again ahead of Apple and Google), and other names include Brazil's Natura Cosméticos and India's Bharat Heavy Electricals.

The world of the Internet has always been dominated by US multinationals. However, Tencent now has a market capitalisation of US$45 billion, ahead of eBay and Yahoo. From Moscow, Yuri Milner is revolutionising the rules of digital venture capital, hitherto dominated by California-based funds. His company, Digital Sky Technologies (DST), owns mail.ru, one of the successful Russian start-ups listed on the London Stock Exchange at a valuation of more than US$8 billion. His venture capital fund is one of the few with holdings in Facebook, Zynga and Groupon. In 2011, Milner launched a second fund, DST Global 2, at a valuation of US$1 billion, an unheard-of size in Western Europe. From Singapore, telecommunications operator Singtel also launched its own venture capital fund in 2011, with more than US$250 million, in order to accelerate the acquisition of technology start-ups. All these initiatives show, as if further proof were needed, the extent of the emerging Asian countries' commitment to carving out an ever bigger space for themselves in the world of start-ups and venture capital.

This phenomenon is not confined to Asia. The case of Naspers, a South African multinational in the digital world, is a prime example: it obtains more than 70 % of its revenues from the African continent but has also made many acquisitions in emerging markets. The 45 % stake in Tencent which it bought in 2011 has increased in value by more than 3100 % since then: so the biggest "score" in the history of the Internet belongs to a fund based not in California but in South Africa. Naspers has also invested US$390 million in Russia's mail.ru and holds 91 % of Brazilian start-up Buscapé, for which it paid more than US$340 million. In Eastern Europe it bought Tradus for more than US$1 billion in 2008. Since 2010 it has continued its buying spree in Latin America, acquiring the Argentine start-up DineroMail, the continent's biggest online-payment firm, and Olx.com, in 2011, for nearly US$145 million. Naspers now has a presence in 129 countries; with annual revenues of approximately US$4 billion, it has 12,000 employees and has become one of the main investors in emerging market start-ups.

We still tend to think of Silicon Valley as the all-powerful global centre of innovation and technology. However, since 2013 China has occupied second place as a global venture capital hub. There are more start-ups per capita in Israel than in any other country in the world: there, venture capital per capita has reached a record of more than US$140, double the US$70 figure for the USA.

Brazil already has a more powerful ecosystem of start-ups and venture capital funds than Spain does: in 2015 Brazil already has several venture capital funds with more than US$100 million for investments exclusively in Brazil (Spain has no fund of this size dedicated exclusively to investing in Spain). Brazilian media group RBS launched e. Bricks, a fund of more than US$100 million, to invest in Brazilian Internet companies. The major California-based funds have now set sail for this new El Dorado: Redpointe.ventures closed a US$130 million fund to invest in Brazilian start-ups. European funds are on the move, too; in 2012, London-based venture capital fund Atomico landed in Brazil.

In 2013, Amadeus, another major European fund, closed a US$75 million fund with the South African telecom company MTN to invest in start-ups in emerging markets, including African markets, such as Kenya and South Africa, where there is also considerable movement. Telefónica for its part made a massive commitment to emerging markets, particularly those in Latin America, by means of a network of accelerator funds in eight Latin American countries (Wayra) and venture capital funds in three of them (Amerigo). Mexico's América Móvil also invested in start-ups in 2013, including the UK's Shazam, in which it acquired an 11 % stake for around US$40 million, proposing to spread the Shazam app throughout the region.

Spanish groups have not been idle either, particularly BBVA, which set up a US$100 million venture capital fund to invest in the USA and also, occasionally, in Latin America. In 2013, it took part in an investment of more than US$20 million in SumUp, a German financial services start-up. Santander did likewise with Sweden's iZettle in 2013. Both banks are supporting these European start-ups in their internationalisation, opening paths to the emerging markets of Latin America.

This leads us to imagine that, in addition to having executives based in Spain to cover the Spanish market, these European start-ups, oriented by Spanish banks towards Latin America, could also use Spain as the headquarters for executives responsible for developing new markets or, in any case, Latin American markets (in the case of iZettle they are in London, and in the case of SumUp they are in Berlin). Why not imagine Spain (Madrid and Barcelona) becoming a hub for European start-ups looking to enter Latin America (and viceversa, a gateway to Europe for start-ups from Latin American and other emerging markets)?

From Copacabana to the NASDAQ: The Silent Latin American Revolution

Technological change, beyond commercial and financial change, is evident in China, India, Korea and Singapore. But it also encompasses other regions of the world. Specifically, there has been a silent revolution in certain Latin American economies. In several countries in the region we are seeing an extraordinary flowering of entrepreneurship and an unprecedented boom in multinationals that now extends well beyond Mexico and Brazil, the two dominant regional powers.

For example, in 2010, when it joined the OECD, the Chilean government launched Start-Up Chile, an ambitious and determined programme which has already brought more than 1000 start-ups to Chile, leading to the emergence of a "Chilecon Valley" in the Southern Cone. In 2013, Brazil launched Start-up Brasil, and Peru followed suit in 2014. Colombia for its part has promoted one of the continent's most ambitious programmes for digitalizing the economy. Through its Ministry of Information and Communication Technology (ICT), it has launched a powerful digitalization programme. These countries are thus leading the wave of expansion in the region towards innovation, and let us not forget Mexico, which has succeeded in carving out a place for itself in the aerospace industry, with a powerful cluster in Querétaro.

In just a few years these activities have begun to bear fruit. Chile has succeeded in putting itself on the world start-up map: in 2010, its acceleration programme received some 100 applications, leading to the selection of 22 start-ups; in the latest round, nearly 1600 projects were presented, of which around 100 were selected. A key aspect is that 80 % of them came from abroad; one in every four start-ups selected comes from the USA, with others coming from India, Spain, Russia and the UK, as well as neighbouring South American countries. However, the most powerful and unexpected effect of this programme has been to arouse the entrepreneurial appetite of the Chileans themselves. Of the 100 or so start-ups selected in 2013, 19 were Chilean – and the figure increased further in 2014 and 2015. In barely 5 years, the programme has launched nearly 1000 start-ups. Meanwhile, Chile's venture capital industry has also grown, with no fewer than six new funds being launched in 2013, which will contribute some 125 million euros for financing new start-ups.

As in Brazil and Colombia, Chile's public institutions have played a key role in promoting this boom. In Chile, the Corporación de Fomento de la Producción de Chile (Corfo, or Chilean Production Development Corporation, a government body) is a key instrument. In Brazil, the driving force is split between the powerful BNDES (Brazilian Development Bank) and Financiadora de Estudos e Projetos (FINEP, or Funding Authority for Studies and Projects, a government organisation for funding science and technology). In Colombia, the Ministry of ICT (through Apps.co) and the Banco de Comercio Exterior (Bancoldex, or Bank of Foreign Trade, a state-owned bank that also acts as an entrepreneurial development bank) are the prime movers of these changes. Admittedly, the continent still has a long way to go before it can join the ranks of the world's most innovative regions: not a single Latin American company appears among the world's 100 most innovative companies as identified by Thomson Reuters.

Some of the region's technology companies, for example, Chile's Sonda, already have annual revenues exceeding US$1 billion. This Latin American wave has only just begun: in 2013, in a Financial Times–Telefónica Global Millenials survey carried out in 27 countries, young people in Latin America led the responses of those seeing themselves as technological leaders. In Colombia, 27 % of young people surveyed were identified as technological leaders, just ahead of Peru (26 %), Chile (22 %), Mexico (21 %) and Brazil (18 %). All these countries surpassed the USA (16 %), the UK (13 %), Germany (12 %) and Spain and France (6 % each). In other words: the youth of Latin America is being pushed along on a wave of technological expansion that is much stronger than what we are seeing in Europe.

Clichés about Latin America abound. We continue to see the region as one big open-cast mine, brimming with raw materials and populist uprisings. And in part, this is indeed still the case. But we would do well to take note of the other Latin America that is emerging: thrusting, innovative and disruptive. We should not be surprised to see before long a Latin American start-up leap from Copacabana to the NASDAQ. In fact, it has already happened: MercadoLibre has leapt from the shores of Mar de Plata, and another called Globant, also from Argentina, took the leap in 2014. Others will soon follow, from Brazil, Chile and Colombia. We should not be surprised by this. Nor should we harbour any doubts about whether it will occur. Perhaps in the future the next Google will come from Rio de Janeiro. After all, the creator of Kinect, Microsoft's star product, is Brazilian.

In Conclusion

The book that follows represents an invitation to a journey towards many remote towns where start-ups are now being nurtured. I underline Latin American examples in order to stress other geographies that complement those envisaged in the detailed case studies that will follow. They show that Europe is also in the picture, and the trend extends far beyond the usual suspect cities of London and Berlin; other geographies are part of this wave, Asia, of course, but also the Middle East and Africa. The journey does not end in the towns and countries mentioned herein. More will come as part of this newly emerging and shifting world, also in terms of innovation, firms and technology.

IE Business School, Madrid, Spain   Javier Santiso

Acknowledgments

I start off with an acknowledgement of the generous financial support I have received from the Abu Dhabi Education Council (ADEC) to embark on the project which has resulted in the 11 cases studies constituting most of the material for this book. Support for the idea behind the project from a public entity in Abu Dhabi, an economy better known for oil and gas than technological entrepreneurship, is indicative of the change this book seeks to explore, which is the surge of interest and activity in technology start-ups from less likely places.

Another word of acknowledgement is due to my colleagues at INSEAD, who have allowed me the space and freedom to pursue this idea as part of the school's research programme in Abu Dhabi. This has allowed me to draw on the support of my colleagues at the INSEAD Innovation & Policy Initiative, an applied research programme which I lead at INSEAD. I mention here the research assistance provided for some of the case studies by Yasser Al-Saleh, Pascale Balze and Mohamad Fakhreddine. I would also like to acknowledge the support and assistance provided with a visit to Finland by Dr Petra Turkama and her insightful comments on the Finnish start-up scene.

There is one person in particular whose research assistance and case-study writing have been most instrumental in the completion of this book – Ms Elizabeth Jane Scott. Liz was a Research Fellow on my team, and not only did she provide enormous help with the researching and writing of the original case studies, but she continued to send me relevant information and updates on various case studies months after she had left her job at INSEAD and gone back home to Brisbane, Australia. I feel hugely indebted to her for helping me get this work done.

Another person whose support I would like to acknowledge is Ms Shellie Karabell, whose help was instrumental in helping me tell the stories in a reader-friendly and accessible way. Shellie was also very helpful in raising questions about the different stories as they were told.

I also want to acknowledge the support and assistance I received from Allen Gomes, who helped me at various stages with editorial and language issues and who also raised very useful questions as he read through the various chapters.

On the academic side, I'd like to acknowledge the peer-review support I received from Robert Hassink, Professor of Economic Geography at the Department of Geography, Kiel University, Germany, and Professor Robert Huggins, Chair of Economic Geography at Cardiff University, the UK. I would also like to thank Professor Javier Santiso, IE Business School, who has shown an enormous interest in this work and agreed to write the book's foreword.

Last and not least, I would like to take this opportunity to express my deep gratitude for the support and time made available to me by my wife – Gawieh Haymour – and two young daughters, Julia and Sophie. Much valuable family time was spent by me working on the book, and I am indebted for that time to my lovely family.

Contents

List of Figures

List of Tables

1

Introduction

For much of the last three decades, the world of business and economic development has been dominated by the Silicon Valley Paradigm. This paradigm stipulates that high-growth technology companies most likely emerge under the particular framework conditions that govern the business environment of Silicon Valley. These include, for example, the abundance of risk capital, a culture of risk taking, the availability of a deep pool of highly skilled talent and the presence of large communities of foreign-born graduates and entrepreneurs, in addition to strong university–industry links and other factors. Considering the rapid emergence in Silicon Valley of numerous high-growth, high-tech start-ups that have gone on to become globally dominant, it is easy to see why this region has come to dominate attention and perceptions about what is most important for start-up success. With a population of less than three million, Silicon Valley generates a GDP of around US$210 billion (or US$70,000 per capita), with 45 % of households claiming an income over US$100,000. On a per capita basis, Silicon Valley counts among the richest areas of the world—in the same league as countries like Norway and Singapore.

© The Editor(s) (if applicable) and The Author(s) 2016
S. Mahroum, *Black Swan Start-ups*,
DOI 10.1057/978-1-137-57727-6_1

The remarkable success of this region has made it a model to be copied by aspiring regions around the world, from the Silicon Plateau in Bangalore, India, to the Silicon Gulf in the Philippines, from Ireland's Silicon Bog to Israel's Silicon Wadi. Academically, a lot has been written about the Silicon Valley phenomenon. A quick search on Google Scholar for the two words 'Silicon Valley' (in quotation marks) returns over 161,000 hits, excluding patent citations. As early as 1984, innovation guru Everett M. Rogers wrote (with co-author Judith K. Larsen) his seminal work *Silicon Valley Fever*, and in 1985, AnnaLee Saxenian, a scholar based in Silicon Valley, compared Silicon Valley with (Boston's) Route 128, exploring whether the two regions embodied a formula for start-up success or if they were merely the results of exceptional historical serendipities (Rogers and Larsen 1984; Saxenian 1985). In fact, Saxenian had already tried to answer this question in an earlier work titled 'The Genesis of Silicon Valley' which ascribed the regions' success to both historic serendipity and industrial organisation factors (Saxenian 1983), two important explanations I will touch upon subsequently in the next chapter.

Over the following three decades, the phenomenon of Silicon Valley fever went global—with its particular elements and structure achieving almost the status of a theory stipulating that if a region is able to assemble a number of core factors that recreate certain conditions found in Silicon Valley, technology businesses will thrive. And yet, despite the hundreds of Silicon Valley type experiments around the world and the thousands of pieces of literature devoted to the topic, as recently as 2015 and 2014, we are still asking how Europe can create its own Silicon Valley, how India can create its own Silicon Valley, and whether China can create its own Silicon Valley.

Meanwhile, a growing body of evidence has shown that successful technology businesses can emerge in places far removed from Silicon Valley or any initiatives inspired by it. From Australia to Zambia, successful technology start-ups are emerging at an international scale. In some places the trend has been so strong that books are being written about it. In *Start-up Nation* (2009), Dan Senor and Saul Singer details the successful stories of technology start-ups coming out of Israel; in *Startup Asia* (2011), Rebecca Fannin gives an in-depth analysis of a similar growth trend in China and India, and in *Startup Rising* (2013), Christopher M. Schroeder documents the same phenomenon in the Middle East. Companies like Sina and Baidu in China, in Mobi in India, Maktoob and Rubicon in Jordan, Supercell and Rovio in Finland, Spotify in Sweden, and Odigeo and 24Symbols in Spain, to name just a few, are all examples of technology-driven start-ups that have emerged in less likely places—thousands of miles from Silicon Valley and without most of the conditions and the factors once believed necessary for a Silicon Valley environment to emerge.

It is against this background that I decided to examine the rise of successful technology start-ups outside Silicon Valley, and in fact, outside the USA or any other Silicon Valley-type regions. Unlike the other previously mentioned books, which focus on emerging trends in specific regions, the units of analysis in this book are individual tech start-ups which have emerged outside of and without the support offered by incubator hubs but which have gone on to achieve exceptional levels of success over many years. They are what I call 'black swan' start-ups, or start-ups which are now established firms with well-established brands which defy conventional expectations and have surprised many by their emergence in the absence of artificial or natural Silicon Valley conditions.

Understanding how they began, evolved and overcame challenges helps us understand the conditions and factors that make success possible outside the supposedly 'model' conditions of Silicon Valley. Moreover, these conditions and factors hold the promise of being more universal than those pertaining to the unique experience of Silicon Valley. This is not a trivial aspiration; if we can understand successful results under the different and potentially difficult-to-change macroconditions that often characterise the world around us, we may be able to develop new models—and new prescriptions—for success under more universal conditions.

The book is written in an accessible business-like style but remains academic at heart. As I have done over the majority of my research career, I researched this book with the aim of applying a pragmatic understanding of theory in order to advance practice. Theories that work only with everything being equal or held constant have little use in the real world. The real world is neither equal nor constant. It is therefore my opinion that a useful theory in the social sciences is not necessarily one that demonstrates a consistent inherent logic under static conditions but one that is pragmatic enough to explain a dynamic reality.

Black Swans

A black swan is a characterisation that typically refers to an atypical occurrence or an anomalous observation. The specific characterisation itself is said to date back to Roman times when such a creature (as distinct from a white swan) was believed to exist only in myth: 'a rare bird in the lands, very much like a black swan,' wrote Juvenal, a first-century poet and satirist (Puhvel 1984). The first actual documented sighting by a European of a black swan was made in January 1696 by the Dutch explorer Willem de Vlamingh, on the west coast of Australia. Upon sighting it he knew instantly that he had arrived in a new world, flourishing with life beyond the parameters of his previously known universe. The essential point of the black swan metaphor is that any well-established system of belief that we may hold about the nature of reality will rapidly unravel if something unexpected occurs to undermine the fundamental premise upon which that system rests.

This book looks at 11 black swans—highly successful tech companies launched in such unlikely places as Amman, Jordan; Tallinn, Estonia; Espoo, Finland; Lahore, Pakistan; and Fuschl-Am-See, Austria, which prove Bas C. Van Fraassen's point that 'a son is not the same as a man, even if all sons are men, and every man is a son' (1980). The same can also be said about technology businesses in that a successful Silicon Valley technology business is not the same as a successful technology business, even if all successful Silicon Valley businesses are technology businesses. The 11 companies studied in this book are black swans because they were not supposed to exist and succeed where they have, just like the black swans of Australia. While some might argue that some of the locations studied in this book are now considered start-up hubs, such as Amsterdam, Berlin, Dubai or Helsinki, they were in fact all considered far from start-up friendly at the time when these 11 black swan firms were founded.

Thus, these 11 firms challenge our assumptions, force us to modify our theories, and urge us to adopt a more pragmatic framework of analysis. In this regard, the cases help us to construct a more cogent theory to explain why these firms succeeded against such apparent odds and why and how you need not be in Silicon Valley to succeed.

A big part of the answer, as this book will show, lies in the particularities of context. All businesses and all company founders in all locations had individual contexts. This does not mean that they did not share common challenges and pressures, because they did. But the various pressures arose from different forces and manifested themselves in different forms, and the ways the entrepreneurs responded were shaped by their local and personal realities. It is perhaps these particularities that often render the general prescriptions of a magic (Silicon Valley) formula irrelevant. If the formula worked, Zafar Khan, the founder of Sofizar Constellation, would not have left Silicon Valley to set up his technology business in Lahore, Pakistan; Janus Friis (a Dane) and Niklas Zennström (a Swede) would not have left Stockholm to set up their company in post-Soviet Tallinn in Estonia. And neither would Rabea Ataya have left Silicon Valley for Dubai, nor would have Alexander Ljung and Eric Wahlforss have left Stockholm, a Nordic start-up hub, for Berlin at a time the city government was bankrupt.

But not all the counter-intuitive examples in this book are about entrepreneurs trading one place for another; a majority of them are about founders who should, or could, have left but chose not to. As various researches have shown, entrepreneurs tend to prefer staying at home (Mueller and Morgan 1962; Reynolds and White 1997; Figueiredo et al. 2002). In Amman, Jordan, despite the many difficulties often facing founders of start-ups, Samih Toukan and Hussam Khoury preferred the advantages of Amman over other potentially superior locations. Likewise, at the height of big business in Helsinki when founders of small technology start-ups in Finland felt disadvantaged in every respect when it came to sharing a space with a global giant like Nokia, the founders of Rovio, the company behind the world-famous videogame Angry Birds—Niklas Hed, Jarno Väkeväinen and Kim Dikert—chose to remain in freezing, expensive and highly taxed Helsinki than move to London or Silicon Valley. A similar situation is observed in the case of TomTom in the Netherlands, a country that is better known for its century-old multinationals than its start-ups, but where a group of three Dutch and one French entrepreneurs–Peter-Frans Pauwels, Pieter Geelen, Harold Goddijn and Corinne Vigreux—managed to beat the odds and create the first new global Dutch corporate brand in living memory.

Sometimes the black swan is a national story with a local context. StormGeo, the world's largest meteorological information systems company, unlike a majority of Norwegian start-ups which tend to gravitate towards the capital city of Oslo, made its home base the western rainy city of Bergen, a city nestled between seven mountains and better known for its isolation than technology ventures. StormGeo's founder, Siri Kalvig, who had in fact left Oslo for Bergen several years previously when she was still a student, concluded it was the perfect niche location for her future endeavour, despite not being from the town herself. The personal preference of the entrepreneur more often than not appears to be a main driver of location choice, as recent research from Catalonia, Spain, has shown (Lafuente et al. 2010), but when we dig deeper, we find that personal preferences often reflect a perceived locational advantage in the minds of a founder. For example, to start a business at home or to move somewhere else appears less important than the established familiarity of an entrepreneur with a place (Dahl and Sorenson 2012). What emerges as critical from all the case studies in this book is what I call the convenience of familiarity with a place. Some places appear highly inconvenient for outsiders, but less so for those familiar with them. This creates a different understanding of the notion of comparative advantage as it manifests itself at the micro rather than the macrolevel. In other words, a place that has little comparative advantage because of various shortcomings would seem to discourage a fledgling start-up from setting up shop there, but it may actually serve as a business shelter for those who know how to navigate the terrain. This is supported by studies that present evidence that place familiarity is positively correlated with start-up survival and performance rates (*ibid.*). The comparative advantage in this respect involves two different and opposing levels of dynamics. At the macrolevel, restricting the entry of new economic actors can slow the dynamism and the competitiveness of a place, yet at the level of the firm, it offers meaningful protection from outside competition.

Nevertheless, while location choice is central to this book, it is neither its real focus nor its main theme. Location choice, which is usually either opportunity or problem driven (Cyert and March 1963), has already been made in our 11 cases; what the book seeks to explain is how these entrepreneurs succeeded despite the less favourable conditions prevailing at their locations of choice at the time. With regard to location, Erik Stam in his work on entrepreneurs' location decisions found that the criteria for choice evolve and grow with the stage of business development. Like caterpillars transforming into butterflies, as they grow, Stam (2007) argues, entrepreneurial firms move to different locations. This is largely due to the evolving and changing position of the firm within its inter-organizational networks of clients and suppliers.

While economic geography focuses on factors external to a firm, pertaining to the overall cost and ease of doing business, as determinants of comparative advantage,[1] scholars in management and business schools have focused on factors internal to the firm pertaining to strategy (e.g. Porter 1996), core competencies (Prahalad 1993), and leadership (Storey et al. 1987). These two streams of research tend to focus on a set of factors that fall into three categories (to be introduced subsequently in the book): cost, calibre and convenience. The extent to which internal and external factors pertaining to cost, calibre and convenience intertwine in a particular location influences both the comparative advantage of a place and the competitive advantage of a firm. I shall return to this point later in this chapter and several times again in the book.

A third growing stream of research which has moved to high prominence in policy circles over the last decade comes from urban and human geography. This stream of research focuses on external and internal factors as they relate to the people behind the firms. These comprise factors such as serendipity, familiarity and the clustering of specific communities of practice. This stream of research explains the success and failure of firms and places in terms of factors that I categorise into two further groups: creativity and community. I shall return to this particular categorisation of factors later in this chapter and again at various points in the book. Thus, the comparative advantage of a place plays itself out at three different levels: the macroeconomic-jurisdictional level, the firm level and the human-community-centred level. The academic literature usually divides these into two streams, business-related and location-related, or, in other words, the firm and the location.

---

[1] See for example Galbraith, Craig S. "High-technology location and development: the case of Orange County." California Management Review (pre-1986) 28.000001 (1985): 98; or Felsenstein, Daniel. "High technology firms and metropolitan locational choice in Israel: a look at the determinants." Geografiska Annaler. Series B. Human Geography (1996): 43–58.

The important point here is that the urban geography stream of research championed by researchers such as Richard Florida (2002, 2004) and made popular by writers like David Brooks (2010) and others[2] has changed the debate around place and location competitiveness, putting a greater emphasis on the so-called softer factors of place attributes. In fact, Richard Florida went on to develop a Bohemian Index—based on a composite index of metrics that pertain to tolerance, talent and technology—to measure and rank different locations around the world in terms of their attractiveness as places to live, work and invest for professionals active in creative/innovation sectors (Florida 2002). According to such an index, a place which is cost-effective and has an excellent physical infrastructure and institutional framework which make it easy to do business there will still be at a disadvantage in a place which lags in this regard but which is superior in terms of cultural openness, convivial lifestyle, talent and technology. In this vein, Toronto and Berlin are better places to launch a technology business than Tokyo and Munich.

Enter the Place Surplus

In this book, I try to reconcile these different levels of analyses, and in fact I draw on inputs from economic geography and human and urban geography. What became obvious to me through field work and an accompanying review of the literature was that the comparative advantage of place cannot be reconciled along a scale, or a zero-sum game, and cannot be measured by an index. Instead, it is more like a basket of goods, where the most competitive place is where a basket of the same set of goods can be acquired most cheaply overall. Entrepreneurs are more like grocery shoppers in that they will invariably head to the places where they know they can find most of the important ingredients they need at the best price and then shop for the few missing items elsewhere. They also typically favour shops with which they are familiar, where they know exactly where to find things, as well as the general quality of goods and services

---

[2] For a good literature review see Lafuente, Esteban, Yancy Vaillant, and Christian Serarols. "Location decisions of knowledge-based entrepreneurs: Why some Catalan KISAs choose to be rural?" Technovation 30.11 (2010): 590–600.

offered. The chances that they will shop somewhere else and go elsewhere depends on the perceived cost, quality and convenience of other competitors. But if a shopper is looking for very specific items not readily found in local shops, then a distant, less convenient and more expensive place might just be their only option.

This observation led me to the work of Roger Bolton and the notion of 'place surplus'. In a book chapter entitled 'Place Surplus, Exit, Voice, and Loyalty,' Bolton (2002) develops the concept of 'place surplus' as an extension of the notion of 'consumer surplus' previously introduced by Albert Hirschman (1970) to refer to the gains that individuals accrue from their membership of an organization. According to Bolton, a 'place surplus' is the extra utility that a particular actor (individual or organisation) derives from being in a particular place at a particular point in time. That is, entrepreneurs assess the cost and benefit of being at a particular location and decide to exit it or stay on accordingly.

I found this phenomenon evident across all cases. In the case of Sofizar (Lahore), SoundCloud (Berlin) and Skype (Tallinn), the founders decided to exit their home regions and move elsewhere in order to derive greater benefit in areas deemed important for their respective enterprises. In the case of Maktoob in Amman, Jordan, and Bayt. Com in Dubai, the founders decided to split their operations between Amman and Dubai in order to tap the different advantages provided by the two locations. In the case of 24Symbols in Madrid, the founder established a delicate balance between staying in Madrid with its strong access to Latin America and moving to London or New York for their strong access to venture capital. Both in the case of Lahore, Pakistan, and Fuschl-Am-See, Austria, the two places appear on paper as hardly desirable for start-up activity, and yet in both cases the founders concluded that they offered a greater place surplus than anywhere else. The assessment made by the entrepreneurs resulted in a positive evaluation of the suitability of the location for their businesses.

Like grocery shoppers, entrepreneurs appear to continually customise their comparative 'sourcing' advantage. They assess local conditions in terms of (a) their needs, (b) how much value can be leveraged locally and (c) how much value can be leveraged globally, and then they seek to compensate for the missing critical factors by reaching out beyond their location, most often overseas. They look for resources within their own personal and professional networks to lessen the disadvantage of the place, especially with regards to risk capital. In all 11 cases, the start-ups opened offices in other countries to access relevant resources that were absent locally. In all cases, the founders used their own personal and social networks and took advantage of national and regional competitions and events to raise funds and develop international contacts.

The personal and professional backgrounds of the entrepreneurs thus emerge as very important for locational decisions in all cases. Individuals enrich their locations with the social capital that they bring with them. The founders of Sofizar, Skype, SoundCloud, StormGeo, Rovio, TomTom and 24Symbols all managed to survive in their home or host locations owing to the social capital and business networks they had developed in previous endeavours. Much of the success is driven by the people behind the ventures rather than the socioeconomic and institutional attributes of place. In our cases, we find entrepreneurs who moved from highly ranked regions, such as Stockholm, Sweden, or the USA to lower ranked places such as Berlin, Tallinn and Lahore.[3] We also see start-ups emerging and scaling up in traditional locations affected by high taxation regimes, with challenging climates and geographies, and highly homogenised societies with very low appetite for risk, such as Rovio in Helsinki, Finland, and StormGeo in Bergen, Norway.

What emerges as the most important criterion that needs to be present for success in a particular location is the ability of the founders to transcend any shortcomings involved in operating there. As Stam has shown in his research on what he calls the spatial organisation of firms, these conditions change and evolve with the growth of the firm and its operations (Stam 2007). The nature of the resource base required for the entrepreneur to succeed changes dramatically at the different phases of growth. The ability of entrepreneurs to adapt to changing conditions emerged as an important factor in almost all 11 start-ups. Maktoob in Jordan could tap into funding sources in Dubai and Egypt, Sofizar in Lahore drew upon its US business networks to scale up globally, and Red

---

[3] For example, when measured using data from WEF Global Competitiveness Index 2013–2014 and the EU Regional Competitiveness Index 2013.

bull was able to reach out to the whole world from its mountain location in Austria. Successful entrepreneurs maximise the use of events and associations that expose and connect them to a variety of resources outside their primary location. 24Symbols, Rovio, SoundCloud and Sofizar all benefitted enormously from organising or participating in networking events, both to raise funds and to gain visibility.

The home-base locations of the start-ups may not have all the recommended factors and conditions required for start-ups to grow and succeed, but they appear to need to have at least a minimum set of conditions to make them attractive enough for entrepreneurs to stay put and persevere. These factors and conditions varied across the cases we studied, but there were always a minimum of 50 % of the identified 'relevant' factors present in each one.

Notes About the Research

I began my research journey standing on the shoulders of giants, equipped with what numerous scholars and researchers have uncovered about how entrepreneurs decide where to locate their businesses and what makes Silicon Valley and other such places around the world apparently so hospitable for technology businesses in general and start-ups in particular. I draw on this wealth of literature in the next chapter and throughout the book. Through 40 in-depth interviews with company founders and expert informants from 11 different locations, I sought to find out how many of the factors identified in the research were indeed relevant to their success, how many of them were present at the time of starting the business in a location, and how many relevant factors were missing. But my intention was not to create a small survey. This would have been too easy to achieve and perhaps would have allowed me to include a few extra black swan firms from around the world. I wanted to document their stories and, in doing that, to relate them to the evolving stories of the places where they were located.

The stories of the entrepreneurs, the firms and the places proved intertwined and are perhaps best understood in relation to one other. By way of example, to understand the firm context, one must also understand the industry it operates in and its stage of evolution at a given point in time. It is only through such triangulation of perspectives that it becomes possible to appreciate and verify the real significance of the different conditions and factors that came to play a role in each success story. And such significance varies across the journey and with it the importance of the location, too.

Selecting the 11 Black Swan Firms

In selecting firms as black swans, I was interested in technology businesses that met the following criteria:

- Operating outside traditional technology hubs,
- Technology-based or knowledge intensive,
- Founded within the past 25 years,
- Scaled up and recognised as brands outside their home countries.

My specific rationale for the 11 cases selected is outlined in Table 1.1.

While internal drivers of success (or failure), such as leadership, strategy and management skills, remain important, they are not the focus of this book. These particular black swan case studies were undertaken to understand the location-related conditions that underpin the success of technology start-ups. It is necessary to mention in this context that while these 11 firms represent exceptional cases of success at their home and host locations, they are not the only cases. Black swan firms exist nearly everywhere. An example that I would have liked to have included is Greece-based Upstream Systems. Founded 15 years ago by two Greeks—Marco Veremis and Alex Vratskides—spanning two locations, London and Athens, as an online commerce company, it has grown into a digital monetising firm that operates in 40 countries with revenues over 200 million euros. The company's surging success and continued growth in Greece, where 75 % of its workforce remains, represents a remarkable example of a black swan technology company that emerged and scaled up under adverse conditions and against the tide of a failing Greek economy.[4]

---

[4] See an interview Marco Veremis in the Financial Times, http://www.ft.com/cms/s/0/440ce 4a6-ef3f-11e4-87dc-00144feab7de.html#axzz3eR2wQNtr

Table 1.1 Rationale for case selection

Case	Reason for selection
Atlassian, Sydney, Australia	Australia's only unicorn start-up, valued above 3 billion USD
Bayt.com (online careers and HR solutions), Dubai, UAE	First major Middle East based Online Job-board
Maktoob (online portal), Amman, Jordan	First major start-up to come out of Jordan in the last 20 years to be acquired a global company (Yahoo). It is also the first and main Arabic email service provider in the Middle East
Red Bull (beverage/marketing), Fuschl Am See, Austria	Main and only global company to emerge out of Austria in the last 40 years
Rovio (gaming), Espoo, Finland	One of only two (the other being Supercell) successful start-ups only to come out of Finland. Due to its highly popular game: angry birds, has the strongest global brand
Skype (VOIP company), Tallinn, Estonia	Main global start-up, one of two (the other being PlayTech), to come out of Estonia since independence from the Soviet Union in 1989. Currently owned by Microsoft
StormGeo (weather company) from Bergen, Norway	One of two only start-ups to come out of Bergen, Norway, to grow internationally
Sofizar (online marketing), Lahore, Pakistan	One of handful companies to emerge out of Lahore, Pakistan and to expand in the US by spinning off sister companies
SoundCloud (music), Berlin, Germany	First and main global start-up to emerge successfully out of Berlin since 1989
24Symbols (online books), Madrid, Spain	One of two global internet based start-ups (other being Odigeo in Barcelona) to come out of Madrid, Spain
TomTom (GPS), Amsterdam, Netherlands	Main company with a global brand coming out of the Netherlands

In this respect, I would have liked to include in the book one or more possible candidates in each of the locations chosen. For example, there was Talabat.com, an online food-ordering company from Kuwait, which is both the largest such company in the Middle East and the biggest foreign acquisition in the region (sold for US$170 million for German e-commerce group Rocket Internet) since Maktoob, an Internet portal, of Jordan was acquired by Yahoo for US$165 million in 2009. Another potential black swan was eDreams Odigeo from Barcelona, Spain, which bills itself as the world's largest online travel company and was formed by the merger of three companies, eDreams, Opodo and Go Voyages, with both the US and European roots and Barcelona as its headquarters. The company is particularly interesting because the founders moved from Silicon Valley to Barcelona to scale up their business, which became the first company to sell online travel out of Spain with revenues totalling around five billion euros. And there are BlaBlaCars, the trip sharing company in France valued at over 1.5 billion euros, SkyScanners in Scotland and MercadoLibre in Argentina—all black swan start-ups because they emerged as pioneers in environments that were not previously known to be supportive of start-up activities.

In this regard, the list of cases in this book should not be considered as representing a definitive or exhaustive survey. They are examples of a breed of start-ups that succeed against the odds. They come to show that place attributes alone are irrelevant if not perceived as an opportunity from the entrepreneur's perspective.

Exploring the Black Swan Start-up's 'Grocery Basket'

The interviews were undertaken with key representatives of start-ups, incubators and academics involved in entrepreneurship and start-up communities in locations related to the 11 black swan firms. Interviews focused on the core factors that drew entrepreneurs to establish operations in their particular locations, as well as the location-based challenges that they encountered. The relative importance of the 15 core supporting conditions identified in the review of Silicon Valley and other hubs for technological entrepreneurship was explored. This included, inter alia, the importance of collaborative networks, entrepreneurial culture, supply of skilled talent, infrastructure requirements, government support, ease of doing business (including in the regulatory and legal context) and the availability of venture capital.[5] Informants' judgements and statements

---

[5] Serendipity was excluded as a condition as it was deemed too amorphous in nature and thus difficult for interviewees to establish whether it was in short or plentiful supply.

(e.g. whether or not a place possessed a certain supporting factor) were crosschecked for accuracy against data and information from sources, where available, such as government and industrial reports.

These field research interviews were further augmented by additional interviews or other information from publications by the founders and senior executives, as well as other parties active within the start-up communities in the regions of the 11 black swan firms. This includes material published in books, business magazines, case studies and videos posted on online platforms. A list of non-bibliographic sources is provided at the end of the book for each chapter. While some such sources are not classical academic sources, they represent a rich and relevant source of secondary data.

In a small population like this one, we are not interested in trends and percentages, but rather in rich insights. It is important to note here that these are all exceptional cases that are not meant to be representative of the norm but rather exceptions.

Finally, I chose to keep as much information about each of the 11 start-up cases as possible without distracting the reader's attention too much from the core theme of the book. This is in order to keep each individual case study as potentially a standalone source for further study and analysis.

References

Bolton, R. 2002. Place surplus, exit, voice, and loyalty. In *Regional policies and comparative advantage*, ed. B. Johansson, C. Karlsson, and R. Stough. Cheltenham: Edward Elgar.

Brooks, David. 2010. *Bobos in paradise: The new upper class and how they got there*. New York: Simon and Schuster.

Cyert, Richard, and James March. 1963. *A behavioral theory of the firm*. Englewood Cliffs: Prentice-Hall.

Dahl, Michael S., and Olav Sorenson. 2012. Home sweet home: Entrepreneurs' location choices and the performance of their ventures. *Management Science* 58(6): 1059–1071.

Figueiredo, O., P. Guimaraes, and D. Woodward. 2002. Home-field advantage: Location decisions of Portuguese entrepreneurs. *Journal of Urban Economics* 52: 341–361.

Florida, Richard. 2002. Bohemia and economic geography. *Journal of Economic Geography* 2(1): 55–71.

Florida, Richard. 2004. *The rise of the creative class and how it's transforming work, leisure, community and everyday life* (Paperback Ed.). New York: Basic Books

Galbraith, Craig S. 1985. High-technology location and development: The case of Orange County. *California Management Review* 28(1): 98 (pre-1986).

Hirschman, A.O. 1970. *Exit, voice, and loyalty: Responses to decline in firms, organizations, and states.* Cambridge: Harvard University Press.

Lafuente, Esteban, Yancy Vaillant, and Christian Serarols. 2010. Location decisions of knowledge-based entrepreneurs: Why some Catalan KISAs choose to be rural? *Technovation* 30(11): 590–600.

Mueller, E., and J.N. Morgan. 1962. Location decisions of manufacturers. *American Economic Review* 52: 204–217.

Porter, Michael E. 1996. *What is strategy?* Boston: Harvard Business School Press.

Prahalad, Coimbatore Krishnarao. 1993. The role of core competencies in the corporation. *Research Technology Management* 36: 40–47.

Puhvel, J. 1984. The origin of Etruscan Tusna ('Swan'). *The American Journal of Philology* 105: 209–212.

Reynolds, P., and S.B. White. 1997. *The entrepreneurial process.* New London: Quorum Books.

Rogers, Everett M., and Judith K. Larsen. 1984. *Silicon valley fever: Growth of high-technology culture.* New York: Basic Books.

Saxenian, Annalee. 1985. Silicon valley and route 128: Regional prototypes or historic exceptions? In *High technology, space and society,* ed. M. Castells. Beverly Hills: Sage.

Saxenian, Annalee. 1983. The genesis of Silicon Valley. *Built Environment* 9: 7–17 (1978-).

Senor, Dan, and Saul Singer. 2011. *Start-up nation: The story of Israel's economic miracle.* New York: Random House LLC.

Schroeder, Christopher. 2013. *Startup rising.* New York: St. Martin's Press.

Stam, E. 2007. Why butterflies don't leave: Locational behavior of entrepreneurial firms. *Economic Geography* 83(1): 27–50.

Storey, David J., et al. 1987. The performance of small firms: Profits, jobs and failures. Urbana-Champaign's academy for entrepreneurial leadership historical research reference in entrepreneurship, University of Illinois.

The Global Competitiveness Index 2013–14, World Economic Forum, Geneva.

Van Fraassen, Bas C. 1980. *The pragmatic theory of explanation.* http://www.fitelson.org/290/vanfraassen_pte.pdf

2

Start-up Success and the Five Types of Place Surplus

Mid-way through the twentieth century, the 30 by 10-mile stretch of land between San Francisco and San Jose in Northern California was known for its rich agricultural soil and bountiful production of apricots and walnuts. Today, however, we know this place as *Silicon Valley*—the most recognised location for high-tech start-up activity in the world. The remarkable transformation from agricultural region into a world leading hub of technology, talent and prosperity is well documented (Adams 2005; Chong et al. 2000; Cohen and Fields 1999; Florida and Kenney 1990; Kenney 2000; Nicholas and Lee 2013; Perry-Piscione 2013; Reinhardt et al. 1997a, b; Saxenian 1991, 1994).

Around the world, researchers and policymakers interested in entrepreneurship in technology sectors recognise the seminal role of Silicon Valley in inspiring a global proliferation in technology clusters and incubator hubs and regions. This is remarkable, not just because of the technological advancements and world-changing discoveries that have resulted, but because of the driving role that such technology hubs have had in kick-starting economic growth in locations in decline (Bresnahan and Gambardella 2004; Delgado et al. 2011; Menzel and Fornahl 2007; Porter 1990, 1998, 2000; Simmie 2003).

© The Editor(s) (if applicable) and The Author(s) 2016
S. Mahroum, *Black Swan Start-ups*,
DOI 10.1057/978-1-137-57727-6_2

While some technology hubs have emerged in the 'organic' unplanned manner that gave rise to Silicon Valley, others have emerged in response to top-down government planning directives—albeit often aimed at emulating various structural characteristics of Silicon Valley. The result has been the study of two broad classes of idealised 'framework condition' models for technology hubs: *bottom-up* grass-roots approaches or top-down initiated and organised models, the latter derived from investigations into the relationship between place and enterprise in Silicon Valley and other prominent locations for technological entrepreneurship.

Organic Models

The Silicon Valley Model

Compared to academic research centres, a standout feature of technology hubs is their unambiguous commercial imperative. Indeed, we can trace the very seeds of Silicon Valley's evolution from an agricultural region into a technological and economic powerhouse to a decision in the 1920s by the local Stanford University campus to recruit more 'entrepreneurially minded' faculty members. One such staff member was Fred Terman, a researcher and lecturer in electronics. Now broadly regarded as an icon in the remarkable Silicon Valley story, Terman actively encouraged his students to commercialise applications of technologies. In the years preceding World War II, he provided both laboratory support and funding to two students, David Hewlett and William Packard, to sell an application of an audio-oscillator to Disney Corporation. The profits which these two entrepreneurs earned were used to develop and sell additional products and to grow a customer base. The resulting Hewlett-Packard corporation is similarly iconic of Silicon Valley as it grew to play a pioneering role in the early development of the region as a hub for high-tech activity (Rogers and Larsen 1984).

It is important to note that the role of government policy in the emergence of Silicon Valley was comparatively more indirect—most notably in the form of broader support for the tertiary academic sector and occasional public procurement contracts. However, none of this activity was undertaken as part of a centrally determined plan to facilitate the region's emergence in the way that we see today. The success of Silicon Valley is mostly attributable to non-government factors.

The academic rather than business backgrounds of individuals in Silicon Valley, such as Terman, Hewlett and Packard, had an important additional consequence for the type of organisational culture that evolved within early technology ventures in the region. The decentralisation of power and an absence of rigid management hierarchies that was a characteristic of these firms remains a hallmark of businesses in the region (Saxenian 1994), with divisions within a company often being given significant autonomy and with employees viewed and treated more like family members than as expendable resources to be exploited, as is more often the case in mainstream American industry.

The decentralisation of power and less rigid organisational structures gave firms in Silicon Valley an advantage. Firstly, camaraderie developed readily among engineers and scientists in the same or even across competing firms. This included both socially and when seeking advice and assistance on technical matters (Wolfe 1983). Firms within the Valley were thus better able to resolve technical challenges with considerable efficiency. Secondly, the growth of these important informal networks also served to facilitate entrepreneurial risk-taking. This was because founders of new start-ups knew they were part of a supportive community from which they could access technical help or venture capital when necessary and, if their project failed, could help them to find another job without too much difficulty. Indeed, movement of personnel from company to company became an accepted part of the business culture of Silicon Valley (Saxenian 1994).

The vast body of research into Silicon Valley as a hub for high-tech entrepreneurship points to a number of factors as critical to its enduring success. These are summarised in Table 2.1.

Table 2.1 Factors identified as contributing to the making of Silicon Valley as a hub for technological entrepreneurship

Factor	Relevance
1. Access to highly skilled talent	Silicon Valley companies have access to a highly skilled workforce, drawing talent not only from universities such as Stanford and Berkeley but globally, with Silicon Valley's attractive lifestyle as a draw for immigrants (EIU 2011; Perry-Piscione 2013)
2. Entrepreneurial university	Stanford University was pivotal in the region's development. It gained government support for basic research and postgraduate study in the post-WII period, especially in the defence industry. Stanford also fostered a local entrepreneurial and start-up culture that has seen its alumni and academics found many high-tech firms and provide employment for a "community of technical scholars" (Adams 2005)
	University–Industry collaboration has been instrumental in the development of Silicon Valley (Mercan and Goktas 2011)
3. Highly skilled entrepreneurial immigrants	Skilled immigrant entrepreneurs have played an important role in the development of Silicon Valley (Micklethwait 1997; Saxenian 2000). Wadha et al. (2007) found Silicon Valley to be the leading centre of immigrant technology entrepreneurship in the USA, with more than half of its science and engineering workforce foreign-born in 2000
4. Flexible specialisation	A willingness to experiment with organisational structures has resulted in industry which is highly diverse, comprising a network of specialist, highly competitive and innovative firms. Saxenian (1991, 1994) terms this a system of "flexible specialisation" that is diverse, adaptable and resilient. Silicon Valley's system of flexible specialisation has meant that the region is well placed to capitalise on technological advances as they occur, including the personal computer and Internet (Cohen and Fields 1999; Kenney 2000; Lee et al. 2000)
5. Culture of risk-taking	Silicon Valley has also developed a vibrant entrepreneurial culture that rapidly turns ideas into new products and services and creates new companies and in which failure is accepted as providing a valuable learning experience (Cohen and Fields 1999; Lee et al. 2000; Nicholas and Lee 2013; Perry-Piscione 2013; Saxenian 1994)

(*continued*)

Table 2.1 (continued)

Factor	Relevance
6. Open and collaborative social and professional networks	Professional and technical networks have developed a tradition of collective learning, horizontal integration and community (Ferrary 2003; Florida 2008; Perry-Piscione 2013; Saxenian 1994; Sorenson 2003)
	The region is characterised by strong social capital, with a sense of community that bestows high levels of 'trust', underpinned by past performance and shared experience (Cohen and Fields 1999; Kenney 2000)
	Wadhwa (2013) likens Silicon Valley's open and collaborative networks to 'a giant, real-world social network' that extends relationships that immigrants have in their home countries and which provides the region with a competitive advantage when expanding into global markets (Perry-Piscione 2013)
7. Venture capital	Silicon Valley's venture capital (VC) industry has been instrumental in supporting entrepreneurial activity. Its VC industry grew rapidly during the 1960s and 1970s, replacing military spending and expanding beyond a group of successful entrepreneurs into a professional industry (Cohen and Fields 1999; Florida and Kenney 1990; Nicholas and Lee 2013; Saxenian 1994)
8. Temperate regulatory environment	The region's success has also been underpinned by its business-friendly regulatory environment and temperate bankruptcy laws (Armour and Cumming 2003; Lee et al. 2000)
9. Serendipity	Serendipity has played an important role in the success of Silicon Valley.[a] For example, in the early years, government spending on defence contracts fuelled technological innovation (Leslie and Kargon 1996)
10. Attractive lifestyle	Silicon Valley's temperate climate, coastal location and wide range of outdoor activities have been an important draw and encouraged immigration (Perry-Piscione 2013)

[a]Porter (1990, 1998) argues that 'chance' in the form of a specific innovation or historic event plays an important role in cluster development, while Brenner and Muhlig (2013) refer to 'triggering events'

Route 128

The geographical region along the 65-mile Route 128 highway around Boston hosts another major North American hub for electronics and communications-related commerce. Route 128 is home to a number of start-ups that are now major global players, including Digital Equipment Corporation (DEC), Raytheon and Lotus Development. In 1990 it was estimated to be home to over 3000 high-technology firms (Rosegrant and Lampe 1993).

While Route 128's growth and expansion features a number of similarities to the Silicon Valley story, such as proximal access to skilled graduates from world-class scientific research universities, such as the Massachusetts Institute of Technology in nearby Cambridge, the culture within and between firms in this particular area, however, markedly differs as a consequence of the significant role that federal funding from agencies such as the Department of Defence and the National Science Foundation have played since its formative years. In contrast to workers and businesses in Silicon Valley that maintain strong inter-organisational networks and where movement from company to company is not atypical, businesses in the Route 128 area operate in a far more reserved and conventional manner. This may be attributed to the premium on secrecy associated with major defence-related projects that fund many firms and the generally more conservative culture of the Boston area itself and long-standing and dominant firms such DEC and Lotus Development. The flip side to the more internal focus is the prevailing perception that firm loyalty and dedication are rewarded by greater job security, promotion prospects and retirement pensions. In this regard, Route 128 businesses also tend to be more vertically integrated, with prominent functions centralised.

The research of Mayer (2009), Mayer and Cortright (2001), Moye (2013) and Stangler (2013) into the development of high-tech sectors across the USA in locations such as Silicon Valley as well as Atlanta, Austin, Boise, Boston, Dallas, Denver, Kansas City, Portland, San Diego and Seattle, highlights not only the diversity in the evolution of high-tech centres but also the importance of factors such as entrepreneurial culture, access to highly skilled talent, level of spin-off activity, role of research universities and institutions, anchor firms and government policy.

Given the pre-eminence of Silicon Valley as a role model for high-tech hubs globally, it is not surprising that we find a number of overlapping similarities in the key factors attributed to the success of technology sectors in emerging economies such as Taiwan (Mathews 1997), Bangalore (Subramanian 2014), Beijing (Greenwald 2013) and Israel (Kalman 2013; Tannert 2013). This includes the availability of VC, collaborative networks and an entrepreneurial culture. No country, however, is more inspired by the success of US models than its northern neighbour, Canada.

Triangle of Ontario

Similar to both Silicon Valley and Boston's Route 128, the triangular area about an hour's drive west of Toronto that is marked out by the towns of Waterloo-Kitchener, Cambridge and Guelph is the high-tech hub known as the *Triangle of Toronto*. Historically, the Kitchener and Guelph metropolitan areas have been home to a highly diversified manufacturing sector. Today its reputation is more due to technology start-ups which have enjoyed international success such as Research In Motion (RIM), the creators of Blackberry.

Strong links between industry and local universities in the Triangle date back to its inception when local industry leaders, such as Ira Needles from the rubber producer BF Goodrich, played an active role in the process of its design. The resulting industry-oriented focus and openness toward private-sector collaboration is evidenced in decisions such as that taken by the University of Waterloo to allow members of its faculty to own patents from their research (Bramwell and Wolfe 2008).

As with its US counterparts, the success of the region has been supported by ready access to skilled workers and technology emanating from local research institutions such as the University of Waterloo, Wilfrid Laurier University, Conestoga College Institute for Technology and Advanced Learning and the University of Guelph. The value of the strong informal networks that characterise Silicon Valley is recognised in the region in the form of non-profit organisations such as Communitech to actively support professional relationship building. At the same time, many high-tech firms in the Triangle also operate like the silos that typify the Route 128 area, with a pattern of international rather than local networks and partnerships.

In Europe, Too, Silicon Valley Has Been a Source of Inspiration

Oxford's Milton Park

Milton Park is a science and business hub in Oxfordshire County in the south-east of England. Oxfordshire has grown to become an important source of high-tech manufacturing and employment in Europe. By the mid-2000s, it already had approximately 3500 high-tech businesses employing 45,000 (representing 14 % of the county's total employment). In fact, Oxfordshire was once considered one of three British counties that collectively had the highest percentage of employment in high-tech knowledge-intensive services in the EU region (Lawton Smith et al. 2007).

Milton Park started in the 1930s as a railway military-supply depot and subsequently became a post-war industrial estate. In 1984, it was acquired by the private Milton Estates Property Company and transformed itself into an integrated hub of offices, industry and science parks. Despite the fact that Milton Park is located 20 miles south of Oxford city, it has more high-tech firms and university spin-offs than other science parks in the region (Lawton Smith and Glasson 2010). At present, Milton Park is home to over 250 high-tech organisations employing up to 7500 people. A key factor behind the success of this innovation hub is its single ownership, which has enabled a strong focused control of how various parts of the park have been leased and developed (Milton Estates Property Company 2015).

Cambridge Science Park

The Cambridge Science Park, founded by Trinity College in 1970, is the UK's oldest science park. It is situated 3 km north of Cambridge City

Centre and has strong links with the University of Cambridge (Massey et al. 2003). In fact, the park itself was established in response to a report by the Cambridge University-sponsored Mott Committee, which called for the expansion of science-based industry and the strengthening of collaboration within the Cambridge scientific community. The growth of this park was slow and cautious in its first 5 years owing to an unfamiliarity on the part of the local business community with the concept of a science park. During the 1980s, however, several VC companies opened offices there, including the UK's leading VC company, 3i. A period of particularly strong growth took place in the mid-1980s following the break-up of the BTG's monopoly on IP originating in UK universities. Not only did academics start to found companies in the park, but the park also began to accommodate spin-offs from regional companies as well as UK subsidiaries of multinational companies. By 1999, there were around 65 companies at the park employing over 4000 people. The year 2005 saw the opening of an innovation centre at the heart of the Cambridge Science Park which provides furnished workspace with flexible lease structures.

This has allowed businesses to steadily expand over time, while only paying for the space and facilities that they currently need. In essence, such flexible and practical renting arrangements have allowed early-stage companies to grow and flourish (Cambridge Science Park 2015). The centre has become a key initiator and a host to several initiatives, such as the EU Relay Centre, all of which has contributed to enhancing the park's place as a crucial node in the region's technology ecosystem (Hodgson 2015).

The models outlined so far can be said to represent a more bottom-up organic type of economic development which is driven by technology companies. While the government in each of the places discussed has played various direct and indirect roles by providing infrastructure or acting as an important procurer, the private sector has been the main agent of change and driver of growth. Furthermore, none of the emerging regions discussed earlier can be said to have resulted from some government master plan. These hubs for technology entrepreneurship can thus be contrasted with others created ostensibly to emulate them by national and local governments around the world.

Top-Down Models

Hsinchu Science and Industrial Park

Like Silicon Valley, the nation of Taiwan has undergone significant transformation from a labour-intensive and light-industry economy to one that
is now characterised by capital-intensive high-tech and heavy industries,
beginning with the creation of what was then a world-leading free-trade
and duty-free zone in 1966 to attract foreign investment and technology
driven primarily by low-cost labour. The government played a leading
role in the creation and nurturance of a small and medium enterprise
(SME) industrial base and the economic miracle that ultimately unfolded
in this nation over the last 30 years. Taking a very top-down approach,
the Taiwanese government undertook a deliberate process to establish a
hub for high-tech enterprises modelled on what they observed in Silicon
Valley, launching Hsinchu Science-based Industrial Park Project (HSIP)
in 1979. A 10-year, US$500 million fund was provisioned to develop a
600-ha site in Hsinchu, already home to two major universities and a
government-funded research centre. The broad objective was to create a
high-quality work environment to attract and retain highly skilled workers
and to capitalise on advanced technology and research and development
(R&D) from other locations. The local skilled workforce was comparatively much cheaper than their counterparts in the USA and Japan. The
government leveraged this comparative advantage to achieve three aims:
kick-start economic growth, establish a base for high-tech industry, and
abate the talent brain drain plaguing Taiwan at that time. Like Silicon
Valley, a professional networking culture eventually and progressively
evolved among the businesses in the HSIP area which permeated its various incubator, R&D and production activities.

By 2010, the 460 companies based in HSIP accounted for 8 %
of the nation's GDP, employing over 130,000 persons. The Global
Competitiveness Report 2010–2011 from the World Economic Forum
ranked Taiwan at an impressive seventh place (among a total of 133
countries) for innovation, and seventh overall for global competitiveness.
The HSIP project offers a classic example of a top-down state-driven

model in which early-stage government intervention drove innovation and stimulated entrepreneurship. This top-down approach is also very much apparent in neighbouring South Korea.

Korea's Daedeok Science Town

Daedeok Science Park (in 2005 renamed Daedeok Innopolis) was created by the Korean government in 1973 to agglomerate high-tech research institutions. Daedeok was built with the investment of over US$3 billion over 40 years. It is located in Daedeok Valley in the northern Daejeon region. The cluster was built around KAIST (formerly the Korea Advanced Institute of Science and Technology), which was established by the Korean government in 1971 as the country's first research-oriented science and technology institution. Besides KAIST, Daedeok Innopolis houses the Chungnam National University, a group of government research institutes, corporate research centres and over 1000 venture companies. In its early days the park housed only government-led organisations. Today, Daedeok hosts 242 public and private research organisations with 24,000 employees, including 6200 Ph.D. holders. This research complex is divided into four sectors: information technology, biotech, nuclear technology and nanotech (Campbell 2012; Oh 2014).

Over the last 40 years of its existence, Daedeok Innopolis has undergone several transformations in order to cater for the nation's changing economic demands. More specifically, Daedeok has undergone a deliberate three-stage development model, beginning as a science park, before evolving into a technopolis and finally a regional innovation cluster. In the initial stage (1973–1989), it was setup to be a science park serving as a national hub for the development of science and technology. Like Taiwan, it too benefitted from a comparative advantage of cheap highly skilled workforce, and compared with other global hubs, its scale of employment is relatively small. Led mainly by public research institutions, the park was a concrete attempt by the central government to create a science city outside the capital region. In the middle stage (1990–2000), it was rejuvenated as a 'technopolis' to promote industrial development and to upgrade technology among local businesses with a particular emphasis on the commercialisation of new technologies in start-up firms. Since 2001, Daedeok has become a regional innovation cluster and a centre for high-tech industry that is now oriented towards wider global markets.

Over the past 20 years, a large number of successful high-tech start-ups and spin-offs have emerged from the Daejeon area. At present, not only is Daedeok home to 10 % of Korea's science/engineering Ph.D. holders, but it is also a stronghold of state-of-the-art technologies at a global level. Daedeok Innopolis has thus served a critical role in raising the country's scientific competitiveness to the highest global standards (Daedeok Innopolis 2013; Oh and Yeom 2012).

Sophia Antipolis

In Europe, France has pioneered the development of state-led innovation hubs. Sophia Antipolis, located north-west of Antibes and south-west of Nice, remains an exemplary model of top-down initiative for a technology park. In 1961, it was the first science park in Europe, named after Sophie Glikman-Toumarkine, the wife of French Senator Pierre Laffitte—the founder of the park who was at the time assistant director of the Ecole Nationale des Mines. Laffitte envisioned 'a city of 20,000 researchers' living by the sun and the sea in a climate and environment similar to that in Silicon Valley. The local and regional governments, in addition to the local chamber of commerce, were driven by a desire to attract high value-adding activities to the French Riviera region, whose economy has historically been driven by tourism. Unlike, Cambridge, Oxford and Silicon Valley, Sophia Antipolis did not have the advantage of being co-located with a world-class university or near global technology firms. In fact, in his study of Sophia Antipolis, Christian Longhi observed that 'Sophia Antipolis has developed in vacant space, in a region without industrial or university tradition [but] nevertheless today among the best known centres of high technology activity in Europe' (Longhi 1999). Longhi ascribes the success of the park to the active role of the top-down public sector as well large corporate players, including DATAR, the Delegation for Spatial Planning and Regional Action of the Ministry of Rural Affairs and Regional Planning; INRIA, the French Institute for Research in Computer Science and Automation; Ecole des Mines de Paris, and other French public research centres. In addition, large French corporations such as Air France and France Telecom played leading roles as anchor tenants inducing new economic activity through start-ups and spin-offs and, hence, sparking a wave of domestic high-tech entrepreneurship (ibid.). The government also played an active role in managing and marketing the project to prospective American investors, in addition to its role in providing the telecommunication and transport infrastructure which was instrumental to attracting large firms from outside the region (including IBM and Texas Instruments) which acted as anchor firms for other tenants. At present, the park houses 1400 companies—mainly belonging to the fields of computing, electronics, pharmacology and biotechnology. Most of the start-ups born inside Sophia Antipolis work with government and higher education entities in addition to incubators and venture capitalists (Strategic Management Institute 2002).

The Top-Down Place Imperatives

Both in South Korea and Taiwan (Koh et al. 2005; Malerbaand Malerba and Nelson 2011), but also in France, the government has played a bigger role in inducing high-tech entrepreneurship than in places such as Silicon Valley, Oxford or Ontario. This came at the realisation that without government intervention, this type of risky activity would not be undertaken by the private sector alone. Therefore, in such places where bottom-up activities had no genesis for evolution, strategic government intervention has been seen as effective in driving technological entrepreneur-led growth through a combination of supply-side and demand-side incentives. This conviction was particularly strong in emerging markets and laggard regions, where success has been associated with a strong government role in managing business costs, access to and quality of infrastructure, access to global networks and level of technological diffusion and in providing framework conditions conducive to start-up activity. In this regard, the top-down models point to six additional enabling factors. Table 2.2 outlines these with reference to technology hubs around the world.

Table 2.2 Factors and conditions associated with successful high-tech entrepreneurship in regions outside the USA

Supporting factor	Relevance
1. Access to global networks	The importance of firms having access to global networks, such as Taiwan's Hsinchu connection to Silicon Valley and the USA in general (Koh et al. 2005), and likewise Israel's Silicon Wadi's connection—from which emerged the Israel/Silicon Valley *super cluster of innovation* with one of the largest pools of VC outside of North America (Engel and Del-Palacio 2009a)
2. Anchor firms	Anchor firms have also played a pivotal role through spin-off entrepreneurial activities (e.g. spinoffs from Amazon and Microsoft in Seattle, Washington);anchor firms have also compensated for the absence of world-class research universities in some regional locations (e.g. IBM in Boulder, Colorado; Hewlett-Packard in Boise, Idaho; Tektronix and Intel in Portland, Oregon) (Mayer 2009; Strangler 2013)
3. Low production cost	Access to lower production costs contributed to the development of some regional clusters, such as Boise, Idaho, a short drive from Silicon Valley, due to its relatively cheap labour and land costs (Mayer 2009)
4. Infrastructure	The availability, quality and cost of infrastructure such as roads, airports, seaports and housing afford important advantages to locally based businesses. Kansas City's high-tech cluster, for example, has benefited from Google Fibre's high-speed Internet (Stangler 2013)
5. Knowledgebase	An ability to leverage existing technologies is important where products and services must be tailored to the needs of local markets. For example, companies based in Beijing's Zhongguancun technology hub are said to have successfully leveraged their language skills and understanding of Chinese user behaviour to tailor technologies to meet the unique demands of the local market (Greenwald 2013)
6. Government	The government-sponsored model has been especially important for cluster development in places such as Israel's Silicon Wadi (Kalman 2013), South Korea's Taedok Science Town (Leslie and Kargon 1996; Malerba and Nelson, 2011), Taiwan's Hsinchu Science-based Industrial Park (Mathews 1997), and China's Zhongguancun cluster in Beijing (Greenwald 2013)

The Pre-conditions for Success Between Bottom-Up and Top-Down Propellers

In this book, I discuss both the attributes that make a place supportive or not for start-up success and start-ups' own coping and leveraging strategies. It is important for the reader to keep this distinction in mind because without an appropriate coping and leveraging strategy by a start-up, place attributes become less relevant. Thus, the discussion in Chaps. 2 and 3 focus primarily on the attributes of place, while the case studies focus on the strategies and actions of the entrepreneurs behind the different start-ups.

The study of bottom-up versus top-down approaches has underpinned a growing realisation that many of the insights into the success of technology hubs can be observed at the intersection between place and enterprise (Aula and Harmaakorpi 2008; Bianchi 1998; Bresnahan and Gambardella 2004; Capello 1999; Cook and Morgan 1994; Engel and del-Palacio 2009a; Ku et al. 2005; Piergiovanni 2010; Tiits and Kalvet 2012; Walcott 2007). In the work of scholars of innovative places, such as David Keeble and Helene Lawton-Smith, it was found that for a place to support high-tech activities certain social and institutional pre-conditions need to exist to manage that interface (e.g. Keeble et al. 1998). These can be in the form of business associations, banks, colleges, universities and other private and public institutions that collectively create a nurturing environment for high-tech businesses. Such institutional and social actors facilitate what Longhi called a continuous learning process (Longhi 1999).

While these location-related factors influence the chances of success for entrepreneurs located in particular countries, cities and regions, it is not clear what effect these factors have or when and how they have their effect. In this context, I introduce an analytic framework that allows us to employ the conclusions from the literature to create a better understanding of place comparative competitiveness. I draw upon Roger Bolton's notion of 'place surplus' as presented in 'Place Surplus, Exit, Voice, and Loyalty' (Bolton 2002), and with Hans Westlund (2003, 2006), in which **'place surplus' represents the extra benefits that an individual or an**

organisation derives from being in a particular place. I develop this place surplus idea further by collapsing the 15 factors (I chose to exclude the serendipity factor from the original list of 16 since by definition it cannot be controlled for or observed in advance) identified in the different analyses of high-tech business development into five key categories: **Cost, Caliber, Convenience, Creativity and Community** (see Table 2.3 below). These **five Cs** provide us with a parsimonious framework for understanding the advantages (or risk factors) which a business has by virtue of its location—in terms of the place surplus afforded. In other words, businesses are likely to be successful in locations where they enjoy a combined cost, caliber, convenience, creativity, or specific community advantage. In this regard, different types of businesses will value different types of surpluses. These could include, for example, access to cheap labour, advanced infrastructure, or being amidst a creative community. It is important to note that the five Cs should not be seen as mutually exclusive characteristics. Indeed, it is often the case that any one factor or indicator can fall under more than one category, as shown in Table 2.3, where I have grouped the 15 place-making conditions identified in the literature into five key categories.

Table 2.3   Classifying the 15 core factors by the five Cs

Cost	Calibre	Convenience	Creative destruction	Community
Low cost production Government support	Infrastructure Access to highly skilled talent Flexible specialisation Knowledgebase	Access to global networks Business-friendly regulatory environment Highlyskilled entrepreneurial immigrants Risk capital Attractive lifestyle	Entrepreneurial university Culture of risk-taking	Open and collaborative social and professional networks Anchor firms

- *Cost* includes such factors as business and living costs which add to the total cost of production. It also includes the cost of government, reflected in fees and taxes. The extent of government support impacts positively or negatively total production costs.
- *Calibre* includes the quality of inputs required for conducting business, such as workforce, business services quality and infrastructure.
- *Convenience* includes ease of doing business, regulatory and legal environment, proximity to key markets and technological readiness, as well as the availability of risk capital.
- *Creativity* the resourcefulness and ingenuity of the local community, which among the 15 conditions can be reflected in access to an entrepreneurial university, a strong knowledge base, and being in a place that tolerates risk.
- *Community* includes being at a place where peer networks exist, as well as important and critical professional and industrial stakeholders, such as key potential clients or key suppliers.

The assignment of each of these conditions to one of the five categories is informed by an analysis of the literature and field research undertaken for this book. While others may disagree or have a different opinion on whether a particular condition belongs in one category or another, the truth is that these conditions are not exclusive and can in fact be understood as belonging to more than one category. The usefulness of this categorisation is that it provides a more parsimonious, higher-level explanation of the dynamic impact of the 15 conditions. In essence, according to Bolton: 'People who get the greatest place surplus, relative to the place they would move to if they exited, will lose the most if they exit quickly.' It thus follows that companies are likely to be successful in locations where the types of cost-, convenience-, calibre-, creativity-, or community-related surpluses which are most important to them are in relative abundance. The layer of analysis offered by the five Cs model thus provides an answer to the 'so what?' question. For example, while the lack of risk capital in a particular location may not be detrimental if it can be tapped into elsewhere, this creates a problem of inconvenience. Convenience becomes a policy issue, a problem that can be discussed and addressed as such. Without the concept of convenience, the presence or absence of access to risk capital cannot be seen so easily in context. It is only when risk capital is explained in terms of convenience that its absence in a particular locality becomes a problem; a problem of inconvenience. Start-ups are therefore more likely to succeed if they are able to overcome the inconvenience, or the 'place deficit', of what might otherwise advantageous locations by tapping into the place surpluses of other locations. If they are not able to do that, they will invariably die or 'exit' the location.

Thus, the collective utility of the *five Cs* in a particular place determines that place's relative comparative advantage over other locales. This proposition is consistent with other recent analyses of entrepreneurship and location, for example, by Kronenberg (2013), who reported that regional characteristics profoundly affect the decisions made by firms when choosing where to locate or relocate. It is therefore important that start-ups be able to effectively match the opportunities and challenges of a location with their capabilities and needs (Pe'er and Keil 2013). Places compete, knowingly or otherwise, on the basis of how these *five Cs* collectively generate a perceived 'surplus' among different economic players and industries. Based on the five Cs framework, start-ups are most likely to succeed where the type of surpluses they need to acquire a competitive advantage are in plentiful supply. This assumes that the persons behind the start-ups adopt the right coping and leveraging strategies vis-à-vis their locations. Theoretically, this creates a link between the notions of comparative advantage and competitive advantage. A firm whose business strategy is based on cost competitiveness will derive more surpluses from a place whose comparative advantage lies in lower costs, whereas a firm whose business strategy is based on specialised skill sets will derive more surplus from a place that has a surplus of these skill sets. The comparative advantage of a location remains a potential outcome until it is leveraged by economic agents who are able to take advantage of it. A place that enjoys an abundance of cost, convenience, caliber, creativity or the presence of a supportive community does not automatically gain a comparative advantage until certain entrepreneurs design and enact business plans that derive a competitive edge from one or more of the *five Cs* which are present in that place. As such, a surplus of any type becomes a source of competitive advantage to economic actors in a place if—and only if—those actors can successfully leverage that surplus to their advantage. In the absence of the latter, the surplus risks can become a source for economic deficit (or latent potential) such as unemployment and underemployment. This is an observation that merits further investigation because of its potentially significant implications for policymaking in investment locations.

Can We Talk of 'Domesticating' Start-ups?

In his book, *Guns, Germs and Steel* (1997), Jared Diamond identifies six groups of reasons for failed attempts to domesticate various animals. These include diet, growth rate, nasty disposition, problem of captive breeding, tendency to panic and social structure. The presence of a deficiency in any of these six groups of factors meant that a particular animal could not be domesticated. Factors relating to geography and the literature on entrepreneurship yield a much longer set of conditions which bear upon the success of high-tech start-ups. In this book we will examine closely the experience of the 11 black swan start-ups in order to, like Jared Diamond, identify the conditions that are most critical for a high-tech start-up to domesticate—that is, the conditions that they must have under control in order to achieve success.

In the next 11 chapters, I examine 11 high-tech start-ups that have succeeded to 'domesticate' within their locations without the availability of needed conditions for domestication. Being exceptions to the rule, the black swan firms comprise too small and too diverse a sample to allow us to propose a theory or statistical power to make normative predictions. However, our 11 black swan firms are rich with information and insights and offer useful instructive learning material. While not being able to prescribe a formula that guarantees a happy start-up, we will instead be able to understand how each of the black swans managed to escape the unhappy fate of their neighbours.

References

Adams, S.B. 2005. Stanford and Silicon Valley: Lessons on becoming a high-tech region. *California Management Review* 48(1): 29–51.

Armour, J. and D. Cumming. 2003. The legal road to replicating Silicon Valley. Retrieved from AltAssets, http://www.altassets.net/pdfs/replicating_silicon_valley.pdf

Aula, P., and V. Harmaakorpi. 2008. An innovative milieu—a view on regional reputation building: Case study of the Lahti Urban. *Region Regional Studies* 42(4): 523–538.

Bianchi, G. 1998. Requiem for the third Italy? Rise and fall of a too successful concept. *Entrepreneurship and Regional Development* 10: 93–116.

Bolton, R. 2002. Place surplus, exit, voice, and loyalty. In *Regional policies and comparative advantage*, ed. B. Johansson, C. Karlsson, and R. Stough. Northampton: Edward Elgar.

Bramwell, A., and D. Wolfe. 2008. Universities and regional economic development: The entrepreneurial University of Waterloo. *Research Policy* 37: 1175–1187.

Brenner, T., and A. Muhlig. 2013. Factors and mechanisms causing the emergence of local industrial clusters: A summary of 159 cases. *Regional Studies* 47(4): 480–507.

Bresnahan, T., and A. Gambardella (eds.). 2004. *Building high-tech clusters: Silicon Valley and beyond*. Cambridge: Cambridge University Press.

Campbell, J. R. 2012. Building an IT economy: South Korean science and technology policy. Brookings' Issues in Technology Innovation, no. 19, Sept 2012.

Cambridge Science Park. 2015. About the park. http://www.cambridge sciencepark.co.uk/about/history/

Capello, R. 1999. SME clustering and factor productivity: A milieu production function model. *European Planning Studies* 7(6): 719–735.

Chong, M.L., W.F. Miller, M.G. Hancock, and H.S. Rowen (eds.). 2000. *The Silicon Valley edge: A habitat for innovation and entrepreneurship*. Stanford: Stanford University Press.

Cohen, S.S., and G. Fields. 1999. Social capital and capital gains in Silicon Valley. *California Management Review* 41(2): 108–130.

Cook, P., and K. Morgan. 1994. The creative milieu: A regional perspective on innovation. In *The handbook of industrial innovation*, ed. R. Rothwell and M. Dodgson. Northampton: Edwards Elgar.

Daedeok Innopolis. 2013. Hub for global technology commercialisation. https://www.innopolis.or.kr/attach/brochure/c8b9603c60bafeb583f 9978a12d65ce8.pdf

Delgado, M., M. Porter, and S. Stern. 2011. Clusters, convergence, and economic performance. Retrieved from http://www.isc.hbs.edu/pdf/DPS_ Clusters_Performance_2011-0311.pdf

Diamond, Jared. 1997. *Guns, germs and steel*. New York: W.W. Norton.

EIU. 2011. Fostering innovation-led clusters: A review of leading global practices. Retrieved from http://www.managementthinking.eiu.com/sites/default/files/downloads/EIU-ATIC_Report2_Web_Revised.pdf

Engel, J., and I. del-Palacio. 2009a. Global networks of clusters of innovation: The case of Israel and Silicon Valley. *Business Horizons* 52(5): 493–503.

Engel, J., and I. del-Palacio. 2009b. Global networks of clusters of innovation: Accelerating the innovation process. *Business Horizons* 765: 493. doi:10.1016/j.bushor.2009.06.001.

Ferrary, M. 2003. The gift exchange in the social networks of Silicon Valley. *California Management Review* 45(4): 120–138.

Florida, R., and M. Kenney. 1990. Silicon Valley and route 128 won't save us. *California Management Review* 33(1): 68–142.

Florida, R. 2008. Megaregions: The importance of place. *Harvard Business Review*. Retrieved from http://hbr.org/2008/03/megaregions-the-importance-of-place/ar/1

Greenwald, T. 2013. Beijing's great leap forward. In *Business report: The next Silicon Valley*, ed. MIT Technology Review, 4–5. Cambridge: Massachusetts Institute of Technology.

Hodgson, R. 2015. High-tech technology entrepreneurship in a university town. In *The entrepreneurial university*, ed. L. Foss and D. Gibson. London: Routledge.

Kalman, M. 2013. Israel's military-entrepreneurship complex owns big data. In *Business report: The next Silicon Valley*, ed. MIT Technology Review, 7. Cambridge: Massachusetts Institute of Technology.

Keeble, D., C. Lawson, H. Lawton Smith, B. Moore, and F. Wilkinson. 1998. Collective learning processes and internal networking in innovative high-technology regions. Working paper 86, ESRC Centre for Business Research, University of Cambridge.

Kenney, M. (ed.). 2000. *Understanding Silicon Valley: The anatomy of an entrepreneurial region*. Stanford: Stanford Business Books.

Koh, F.C.C., W.T.H. Koh, and F.T. Tschang. 2005. An analytical framework for Science Parks and technology districts with an application to Singapore. *Journal of Business Venturing* 20: 217–239.

Kronenberg, K. 2013. Firm relocations in the Netherlands: Why do firms move, and where do they go? *Regional Science* 92: 691–713.

Lawton Smith, H., and J. Glasson. 2010. Milton park: Developing a successful high-tech business park. In *Local knowledge: Case studies of four innovative places*. London: NESTA.

Lawton Smith, H., et al. 2013. Entrepreneurial regions: Evidence from Oxfordshire and Cambridgeshire. *Social Science Information* 52(4): 653–673.

Lee, C., W.F. Miller, M.G. Hancock, and H.S. Rowen (eds.). 2000. *The Silicon Valley edge: A habitat for innovation and entrepreneurship.* Stanford: Stanford University Press.

Lawton Smith, H., J. Glasson, and A. Chadwick. 2007. *Enterprising Oxford: The Oxfordshire model.* Oxford: Oxfordshire Economic Observatory.

Leslie, S.W., and R.H. Kargon. 1996. Selling Silicon Valley: Federick Terman's model for regional advantage. *Business History Review* 70: 435–472.

Longhi, C. 1999. Networks, collaborative learning and technology development in innovative high-tech regions. *Regional Studies* 4: 333–342.

Malerba, F., and R.R. Nelson. 2011. Learning and catching up in different sectoral systems: Evidence from six industries. *Industrial and Corporate Change* 20(6): 1645–1675.

Massey, D., P. Quintas, and D. Wield. 2003. *High-tech fantasies: Science parks in society, science and space.* London: Routledge.

Mathews, J.A. 1997. A Silicon Valley of the east: Creating Taiwan's semiconductor industry. *California Management Review* 30(4): 26–54.

Mayer, H., and J. Cortright. 2001. High tech specialisation: A comparison of high technology centers. *Survey series.* Washington: The Brookings Institution. Retrieved from http://www.brookings.edu/~/media/research/files/reports/2001/1/01%20high%20tech%20regions%20cortright/specialization.pdf

Mayer, H. 2009. *Bootstrapping high-tech: Evidence from three emerging high technology metropolitan areas,* Metro Economies Series for the Metropolitan Policy Program. Washington, DC: The Brookings Institutions. Retrieved from http://www.brookings.edu/research/reports/2009/06/metro-hightech-mayer.

Mercan, B., and D. Goktas. 2011. Components of innovation ecosystems: A cross-country study. *International Research Journal of Finance and Economics* 76: 102–112.

Menzel, M., and D. Fornahl. 2007, October 30. Cluster life cycles: Dimensions and rationales of cluster development. *JENA Economic Research Papers,* 76. Jena: Friedrich-Schiller University & Max Planck Institute of Economics. Retrieved from http://papers.ssrn.com/sol3/papers.cfm?abstract_id=1025970

Micklethwait, J. 1997, March 27. The valley of money's delight: Special report: Silicon Valley. *The Economist.* Retrieved from http://www.economist.com/node/366753

Moye, J. 2013. Why Austin Sits atop the next wave of U.S. start-up locations. Retrieved from http://www.coca-colacompany.com/stories/why-austin-sits-atop-the-next-wave-of-us-start-up-locations

Nicholas, T., and J. Lee. 2013, January 30. The origins and development of Silicon Valley. Case 813-098. Cambridge: Harvard Business School.

Oh, D.-S. 2014. Business incubation strategy of high-tech venture firms. In *Technopolis: Best practices for science and technology cities*, ed. D.-S. Oh and F. Phillips. London: Springer.

Oh, D.-S., and I. Yeom. 2012. Daedeok Innopolis in Korea: From science park to innovation cluster. *Best Practice of Science/Technology Park* 1: 141–154.

Park, C.-B. 2012. Issues and impacts of Daedeok Innopolis on regional development policy in Korea. http://www.hkip.org.hk/ci/powerpoint/Prof.%20Park.pdf

Pe'er, A., and T. Keil. 2013. Are all start-ups affected similarly by clusters? Agglomeration, competition, firm heterogeneity, and survival. *Journal of Business Venturing* 28: 354–372.

Perry-Piscione, D. 2013. *Secrets of Silicon Valley: What everyone else can learn from the innovation capital of the world*. New York: Palgrave Macmillan.

Piergiovanni, R. 2010. Gibrat's Law in the "Third Italy": Firm growth in the Veneto region. *Growth and Change* 41(1): 28–58.

Porter, M.E. 1990. *The competitive advantage of nations*. New York: The Free Press.

Porter, M.E. 1998. Clusters and the new economics of competition. *Harvard Business Review* 76(6): 77–90.

Porter, M.E. 2000. Location, competition, and economic development: Local clusters in a global economy. *Economic Development Quarterly* 14(1): 15–34.

Reinhardt, A., J. O'C. Hamilton, and L. Himelstein. 1997a, August. Silicon Valley special report: How it really works: What transformed a patch of prune orchards into the Epicenter of Global Technology? *Business Week*. Retrieved from http://www.businessweek.com/1997/34/b35414.htm

Reinhardt, A., J. O'C. Hamilton, and L. Himelstein. 1997b, August. Silicon Valley special report: What matters is how smart you are. *Business Week*. Retrieved from http://www.businessweek.com/1997/34/b35414.htm

Rosegrant, S., and D. Lampe. 1993. *Route 128: Lessons from Boston's high-tech community*. New York: Basic Books.

Saxenian, A. 1991. Silicon Valley and route 128 won't save us: Response to Richard Florida and Martin Kenney. *California Management Review* 33(3): 136.

Saxenian, A. 1994. *Regional advantage: Culture and competition in Silicon Valley and route 128*. Cambridge: Harvard University Press.

Saxenian, A. 2000. Networks of immigrant entrepreneurs. In *The Silicon Valley edge: A habitat for innovation and entrepreneurship*, ed. C. Lee, W.F. Miller, M.G. Hancock, and H.S. Rowen. Stanford: Stanford University Press.

Simmie, J. (ed.). 2003. *Regional and policy development 18: Innovation networks and learning regions?* London: Regional Studies Association.

Sorenson, O. 2003. Social networks and industrial geography. *Journal of Evolutionary Economics* 13: 513–527.

Stangler, D. 2013, September. *Path-dependent start-up locations: Comparing metropolitan performance: High-tech and ICT start-up density.* Kansas City: Ewing Marion Kauffman Foundation. Retrieved from http://www.kauffman.org/uploadedFiles/DownLoadableResources/path-dependent-start-up-locations-comparing-metropolitan-performance-high-tech-and-ict-start-up-density.pdf

Subramanian, L. S. 2014, January 9. Is Bangalore the technology start-up capital of the world? *Information Week.* Retrieved from http://www.information-week.in/informationweek/news-analysis/287037/bangalore-technology-start-capital-world

Tannert, C. 2013. Great tech start-up cities: Tel Aviv. Retrieved from http://www.coca-colacompany.com/stories/great-tech-start-up-cities-tel-aviv

Tiits, M., and T. Kalvet. 2012, February. Working paper: Nordic small countries in the global hi-tech value chains: The case of telecommunication systems production in Estonia. *Technology Governance and Economic Dynamics,* 38. Retrieved from https://www.etis.ee/portaal/ITpublikatsioonidVaata.aspx?VID=387247&TextBoxName=kalvet&PersonVID=37557&lang=en&FromUrl0=isikud.aspx&FromUrl1=isikuPublikatsioonid.aspx

The Guardian. 2012, June 12. Which is the World's Most Expensive City? Cost of Living Survey 2012. Retrieved from http://www.theguardian.com/news/datablog/2012/jun/12/city-cost-of-living-2012-tokyo

Wadha, V., A. Saxenian, B. Rissing, and G. Gereffi. 2007, January 4. America's new immigrant entrepreneurs: Part 1. *Duke Science, Technology and Innovation Paper No. 23.* Durham, NC: Duke University and Berkeley: University of California.

Wadhwa, V. 2013. Silicon Valley can't be copied. In *MIT technology review, business report: The next Silicon Valley* (pp. 3–4). Cambridge: Massachusetts Institute of Technology.

Walcott, S.M. 2007. Wenshou and the Third Italy: Entrepreneurial model regions. *Journal of Asia-Pacific Business* 8(3): 23–36.

Westlund, Hans, and Roger Bolton. 2003. Local social capital and entrepreneurship. *Small Business Economics* 21(2): 77–113.

Westlund, Hans. 2006. *Social capital in the knowledge economy: Theory and empirics.* New York: Springer.

Wolfe, Tom. 1983. The tinkerings of Robert Noyce: How the sun rose on the Silicon Valley. *Esquire Magazine* (pp. 346–374). http://www.brightboys.org/PDF/Wolfe_Noyce.pdf

3

Skype in Tallinn, Optimizing the 'e' in Estonia

Soviet authorities did not choose Estonia as the location of particular technical universities for political reasons but rather because of the country's long-standing involvement in information and communication technologies. This dates back to the early 1900s when Ericsson, at the time an emerging Swedish telecommunication company, set up manufacturing facilities in the country after having to relocate them from St Petersburg owing to the Bolshevik Revolution (Tiit and Kalvet 2010, 2012).

The technical universities established by the Soviets in the Mustamae area of Tallinn, where Skype would 1 day be based, have over time become a melting pot for 'liberated Estonian IT junkies' (Løcke and Bjerge 2013). Education and information technology have increasingly come to be seen as vehicles to future prosperity. Estonia was among the first of the Soviet communist-bloc states to be allowed limited autonomy to experiment with setting up small-scale enterprises (Kilvits 2002). In fact, Ahti Heinla, an Estonian techie who was one of the original forces behind Skype, was the son of two Soviet-era programmers working at the institute who were able to provide him with privileged access to computers and who taught him to write source code at an early age' (Løcke and Bjerge 2013).

© The Editor(s) (if applicable) and The Author(s) 2016
S. Mahroum, *Black Swan Start-ups*,
DOI 10.1057/978-1-137-57727-6_3

These combined capabilities afforded Estonia what in this book I call a place surplus–the utility arising from a country's mix of highly skilled information technology (IT)-related engineers, expertise in production and manufacturing, and proximity to the major industrial powerhouses of northern Europe such as Norway and Sweden. It is therefore perhaps not surprising to find that the technology required to exploit the Internet through platforms such as KaZaa and Skype came from the city of Tallinn, along with other successful online companies such as Playtech, TransferWise and GrabCAD.

Following Estonia's emancipation from Soviet rule in 1991, the legacy of the Soviet-era Institute of Cybernetics—engineers and scientists dedicated to IT—provided Estonia with its place surplus and proved to be an essential ingredient in the resurrection of the Estonian economy' (Løcke and Bjerge 2013).

Adversity Drives Development

But the road to economic transformation was not an easy one. After gaining independence from the Soviet Union, the Estonian economy fell into crisis because of the cessation of various Soviet-bloc subsidies and credits. Its exports collapsed, domestic demand fell, and many companies went bankrupt. From 1990 to 1994 the Estonian economy contracted by an estimated 36 % (Parvatham 2013). Left with few natural resources and poor infrastructure, the country soon took steps to move from a centrally planned communist economy to a market-driven capitalist economy. Their economic reforms included the rapid liberalisation of prices; tariff-free open-market trade policies; privatisation of state-owned firms; a simple tax system, including zero tax on reinvested profits; a balanced budget in the central government; unrestricted and free movement of capital; and a stable and fully convertible national currency (Sölvell and Porter 2006). Estonia's economic openness offered a very favourable commercial and regulatory framework that attracted foreign investors and entrepreneurs.

Professor Rainer Kattel, head of the Ragnar School of Innovation and Governance at Tallinn University of Technology, explained the government's openness strategy (Kattel 2010):

It is a strategy focusing on attracting as much foreign investments, foreign money, foreign knowledge, foreign managers, and foreign specialists as possible—all that from wealthier, more developed, and more innovative countries than ours. If these have been attracted here thanks to the openness, there should be a so-called spill-over effect—the know-how and information brought by them will also spread in Estonia. Local entrepreneurs will see how things are organised elsewhere and try and copy.

As part of its modernisation efforts, the government decided to focus on upgrading the country's large but dilapidated telecommunications networks and to pioneer the concepts of e-government and a digital society. Unable to afford large and costly IT systems from the West, Estonia's new government instead focused on the Internet as an 'inexpensive, open and yet robust platform for building new IT systems', creating an online platform to connect people, businesses and government (Løcke and Bjerge 2013). This proved to be a very successful strategy. Compared to its Nordic and EU neighbours, Estonia had no place surplus to speak of. It could not compete against Finland and Sweden in terms of infrastructure, skilled workforce, venture capital (VC) or technology. But with the nascent Internet technology, Estonia was at least able to be a peer with its neigbhours, fast-tracking its development and leveraging its small size and the abundance of IT workers. By 2000, Estonia became the first country to adopt a system of e-governance, and in 2002, a digital national ID was also introduced (EUbusiness 2014).

The country's parliament even passed a law declaring Internet access to be a fundamental human right, with Estonians being provided access to free wifi (Pena 2011). The Estonian government's focus on rebuilding its telecommunications network and establishing e-government thus proved beneficial to businesses located in the country, particularly those involved in IT (Estonian Ministry of Economic Affairs and Communication 2004).

I would not consider it an exaggeration to say that "e" has put Estonia back on the world map. Living in a small country with limited resources, the pressure to make public administration as efficient as possible forced our Government to look for opportunities to take advantage of modern technology and turn Estonia into eEstonia.

MeelisAtonen, Minister of Economic Affairs and Communications

Elsewhere in the World...

An important backdrop to these developments in Estonia was the con-current deregulation and privatisation of the European telecommunications industry (Plunkett Research, accessed 8 October 2015). During the 1990s, many European telecommunications monopolies were being privatised, including Sweden's Televerket (Telia AB), Norway's Telenor and Finland's Telecom Finlan. Significant developments were also occurring in the emerging area of mobile telephony in Nordic countries to which the nearby Baltic states, such as Estonia, are closely linked. This included the launch in 1981 of the first fully automatic mobile phone system by a team of Nordic telecommunications engineers. Likewise, the GSM digital standard for second-generation mobile telephony was subsequently launched in 1991 and became the de facto global standard for some 80 % of the world's mobile communications (Högselius 2002).

Högselius (2002) contends that these developments fostered the innovation capability in Estonia's newly liberalised telecommunications sector because of the country's collaborative links with its Nordic neighbours and aided the expansion and modernisation of Estonia's telecommunications network, including its mobile telephony system in the early 1990s. These collaborations saw Estonia gain significant physical infrastructure, technology and administrative know-how in the areas of network operations and service provision. The resultant knowledge transfer proved particularly important in the late 1990s as mobile telephony and the Internet started to grow. This provided Estonia's telecommunications and Internet companies with considerable place surplus in newly emerging telecommunications markets, depending on the availability of both physical infrastructure and the corresponding skills among workers in telecommunications. Moreover, Högselius (2002) contends that Estonians were quick to adopt and develop this acquired knowledge further, which, combined with their country's urgent need for modernisation, made Estonia a perfect place for testing new technologies and services.

And yet one might reasonably still question whether the rise and success of Skype can be attributed to Estonia's suggested place surplus alone? After all, one could argue that some of the other former East Bloc European countries, such as the Czech Republic, Poland and Hungary, were not behind Estonia in IT or in terms of possessing an abundance of cheap, skilled labour. In fact, by East Bloc standards, these countries were more advanced industrially. Estonia had some comparative advantage for IT entrepreneurs for sure, and this is what I refer to as its place surplus, but such a place surplus manifests itself not on the national macro level, but at the micro level. In other words, at the macrolevel, it is more accurate to speak of a comparative and a competitive advantage; a place surplus, however, can only be identified at the microlevel, the level of the firm and the entrepreneur. A place surplus is therefore in the eyes of the beholder. So what kind of place surplus did the founders of Skype identify in Estonia? Why did they choose Estonia over anywhere else? Was it just a matter of serendipity?

The Founders

As Estonia was transforming itself into an e-capital in the newly liberalized Baltic region in the 1990s, two young men who would become Skype's founders were looking for engineers. Niklas Zennström, from Sweden, and Janus Friis, from Denmark (both employees of the Swedish telecom company Tele2 Corporation) were experienced with P2P technology and were tasked with developing the company's online Internet portal everyday.com (Løcke and Bjerge 2013).

Unlike many Swedish companies, Tele2 had an entrepreneurial culture and was organised into small decentralised units that operated autonomously. In 1999, unable to find Swedish programmers within their budget, Zennström turned to the city of Tallinn in neighbouring Estonia to recruit talented yet cheap programmers. This resulted in the hiring of Jaan Tallinn, Ahti Heinla and Priit Kasesalu, known as the Blue Moon team. Each had strong capabilities in the newest developments in programming, computers and technology (Løcke and Bjerge 2013).

Linnar Viik, from Estonian IT College, contends that the Blue Moon team was 'driven by a hacker culture that runs very deep in Estonia' (Løcke and Bjerge 2013). The team started to produce computer games—including the first Estonian computer game to be sold abroad—but was low on funds and therefore seeking new opportunities. They were joined by fellow Estonian Toivo Annus, an engineering manager who coordinated technical development.

Tele2 had found the Estonians to be highly skilled and was pleased with their work. Nevertheless, having completed the project, the Estonian programming team was once again looking for new opportunities. It was at this time that Zennström and Friis–having left Tele2 and looking for new business ideas themselves to develop—approached them to develop KaZaa, a file-sharing program that leveraged P2P networks across the Internet (IBS CDC 2004). For Zennström and Friis, turning to Estonia made lots of sense as it was a place they were familiar with, knew people in, and already had professional ties with. In other words, they had the so-called insider's advantage which afforded them an additional and unique place surplus in Estonia. Friis and Zennström realised that the Estonian programmers could create a better and more decentralised P2P technology that could share not only music but also videos, documents and other files (Løcke and Bjerge 2013). In its first year, KaZaa software was downloaded over a million times.

Thus, inspired by Napster, the US-based file-sharing music system which enabled people to download music for free on the Internet, KaZaa rapidly became another dot-com success story. Yet, like Napster, troubles followed. In late 2002, a US judge ruled that Napster must stop illegal music-sharing, effectively shutting down the service. The Estonian programmers attempted to side-step this risk by creating FastTrack software that ensured KaZaa did not retain information concerning what files were being swapped and, therefore, any evidence that it was directly involved in illegal activity. In some respects, the legal leniency afforded Estonia another place surplus for potential P2P developers. And while the KaZaa program quickly became the most downloaded of its type in the world, a lawsuit filed against KaZaa by the US music industry in late 2002 caused Zennström and Friis to sell the global licensing rights to KaZaa in late 2002 while setting up a software company called Joltid, to which they transferred KaZaa's source code (IBS CDC 2004). Joltid developed and marketed P2P solutions and P2P traffic optimisation technologies to enterprises (Langley et al. 2006). Zennström and Friis, together with the Estonian development team, thus converted KaZaa into Skype, enabling voice calls and sharing data on the technology platform in much the same fashion as KaZaa did with music files, and Skype was launched the following year.

In coming up with the original idea for Skype, according to Friis, 'we looked at areas where we could use our experience and where P2P technology could have a major disruptive impact. The telephony market is characterised both by what we think is rip-off pricing and a reliance on heavily centralised infrastructure. We just couldn't resist the opportunity to help shake this up a bit' (CNET 2008).

The Dark Side…

But while the technical side went smoothly, there were other difficulties to contend with in Estonia, despite its place surplus. Estonia also had some significant so-called place deficits, which without the insider's advantage of Zennström and Friis made the country less attractive. A lack of transport connections and social infrastructure, a relatively obscure language, an under-developed financial sector (Kuokstis 2011) and little collaboration between universities and companies weakened the local business landscape (Technopolis Group 2013). While Tallinn's small size meant an informal sharing of networking and collaboration across the tech sector, it also made the company's growth dependent solely on a domestic labour force and consumer base. These deficits would later force Skype management to turn to other countries to compensate for them. But perhaps the main early challenge for Estonia and the city of Tallinn was the absence of a history of successful tech start-ups to champion would-be 'technopreneurs' and a local VC community and other financial backers to support their early growth and expansion.

The country lacked a developed VC and private equity market to support new free-market start-ups. Zennström also claims that in the case of Skype, European VCs were unfamiliar with Skype's business model and sceptical of the P2P technology with which they were aiming to change the telecommunications industry. Zennström and Friis travelled around

Europe looking for seed funding to finance the early-stage development of Skype, but they met with little success. They consequently bootstrapped the start-up using their own savings and through loans from family and friends and with the support of staff members who also went without salaries for a period (Løcke and Bjerge 2013).

But by mid-2003, the company was still not making money, and management remained undecided about the charging of user fees. In the wake of the dot-com bubble burst and tainted by the legal issues faced by KaZaa and Napster, investors were also weary of putting their money into Skype (Tänavsuu 2013). As a result, development work at Skype came to a halt until American venture capitalist William Draper and several other angel investors who were familiar with the international reputation of Zennström and Friis established through KaZaa decided to invest in the fledgling company.

The programmers set about transforming KaZaa's technological plat-form into Skype by placing a communications platform on top of the P2P technology (Low 2013). They also purchased a license to use Voice Codec, which translates speech into something that can be sent over the Internet, so instead of exchanging pictures, songs and videos, Skype was designed to exchange voices (Løcke and Bjerge 2013). And while Voice over Internet Protocol (VoIP) had been in existence since 1996, by the early 2000s there was enough bandwidth on networks and computers were sufficiently developed to enable the launch of Skype on 28 August 2003 (Friis 2008). Steve Jurvetson, one of Skype's original angel inves-tors, in speaking of Skype's talented team of Estonian programmers com-mented (Tänavsuu 2013):

> *I remember wondering: how can they be so good? How can such a small group do so much so quickly, compared to typical development efforts in, for example, Microsoft? I had the impression that maybe coming out of a time of Soviet occupation, when computers were underpowered, you had to know how to really program, effectively, parsimoniously, being very elegant in sculpting the programming code to be tight, effective, and fast. [That's] not like in Microsoft, which has a very lazy programming environment, where programs are created that have memory leaks and all sorts of problems, that crash all the time and no one really cares—because it's Microsoft!*

Riding the VoIP Wave

The company's location in Europe—with main offices in London and Stockholm—was an advantage since most European telecommunications companies were no longer state-owned (due to sweeping deregulation) and could not control telecommunications rights for the sake of their own profits. European regulators wanted more competition and encouraged Skype to push forward. Additionally, European telecommunications companies (despite deregulation, or perhaps because of it) were charging customers for making local calls; hence, when Skype launched free computer-to-computer voice calls, the service was an immediate success and managed to attract a million registered users in only a few months (WEF 2011). And—important in the eyes of investors—as copyright laws did not apply to private phone calls, Skype was also not subject to the same legal challenges that had confronted KaZaa and Napster (Friis 2008).

In analysing Skype's success, Estonian IT and innovation journalist Toivo Tänavsuu claimed that while competition in the VoIP market increased, a major advantage of Skype's technology was that it 'slipped easily through firewalls. The program left no footprints on the Internet, the sound was improved dramatically, and the service worked like a charm' (Tänavsuu 2013).

Subsequently, services such as SkypeOut and SkypeIn calls to and from regular phone lines (land and mobile) and video calls were added, although these services incurred a charge. This so-called *freemium* revenue model, which offers basic services for free but charges a fee for additional premium features, trumped traditional telephony revenue models (IBS CDC 2004) because, as Zennström explained to Talking to Business Week in 2004: 'We have zero costs of getting new users and zero costs of running traffic. Our costs are only business development and software development' (Business Week 2004). Skype's success attracted the attention of other venture capitalists, and in 2004, the company successfully raised two rounds of international funding from new and existing investors. This enabled further software development, which led to the release in 2004 and 2005 of additional services such as SkypeOut and SkypeIn calls to and from standard phone lines (Langley 2006).

Recognising opportunities presented by smartphones, it was not long before the team also released Skype for iOS, Android and Windows RT, making Skype a viable alternative to satellite phone services. The new services helped the company address increasing competition from companies such as AT&T, Microsoft, Google and Time Warner which by 2005 were entering the VoIP market (Business Week 2004; Goswami 2009).

Growing Pains

By early 2005, the company was reported to be growing so quickly that it was estimated to be taking on five to ten new employees a week in Tallinn. But as Skype began to grow, the deficits of operating in Estonia and Tallinn were exacerbated. Tallinn's small population of around 400,000 people, with a national population of less than 1.3 million inhabitants (CIA 2015), limited the size of the local workforce and consumer markets. Importantly, while the local labour supply is highly skilled, the supply is limited in the face of growing demand.

Labour taxes are also high—21 % of salaries in some cases. Companies began relocating abroad to avoid the tax burden and to seek greater opportunities than those on offer in the small domestic market, as well as to source later-stage VC and new business partners to expand (Kattel 2014). These factors collectively drove Skype to set up new business units in other locations (notably London and Stockholm) to access necessary surpluses that were not available locally. At the same time, in the face of mounting competition from the likes of Yahoo, Microsoft and Google and regular offers to buy the company, the temptation to sell Skype grew (Tänavsuu 2013).

In September 2005, the online auction site eBay acquired Skype for US$2.6 billion in up-front cash and eBay stock, in what appeared to be a bid to purchase a new revenue stream to offset slowing growth in its core auction business (eBay 2005). As well as generating revenue in its own right, eBay hoped to integrate Skype into the auction Website by providing, for example, sellers with the opportunity to buy a so-called click-to-call option that would allow prospective buyers to call them directly via Skype. Nevertheless, market analysts questioned the synergies that this deal offered either company, and eBay's share price fell (Goswami 2009).

Cultural differences between the Estonia-based programmers and the growing number of Anglo-Saxon brand managers in other offices such as London also plagued development work at Skype (Tänavsuu 2013). In 2008, a legal dispute occurred between Skype and its original founders over the rights to Skype's underlying P2P communications technology. And while Skype's share of the international call market continued to rise from 2.9 % in 2005 (TeleGeography 2006) to 12 % in 2009 (Malik 2010), by November 2009, eBay decided to sell a 65 % stake in Skype to a consortium that included the original Scandinavian founders. It received US$1.9 billion in cash and a note from the buyer in the principal amount of US$125 million in a deal that saw Skype valued at US$2.75 billion (Wauters 2009). Meanwhile, in 2007, the company released its own mobile phone, while the release of video calling on iPhones in January 2011 marked a new milestone for Skype that saw its customer base grow rapidly (Savov 2011).

Enter Microsoft

Not long after, in May 2011, Microsoft purchased Skype for US$8.5 billion in a deal that resulted in Skype being introduced as a new business division within Microsoft. Microsoft estimated that approximately 300 million min of Skype video were being made each day, representing over 40 % of Skype-to-Skype total minutes. Colin Gillis, an analyst at BGC Financial, suggested that Microsoft purchased Skype because it was 'a strategic asset and a defensive move', and that if it could put Skype on Windows 8 (subsequently released) it would represent a significant advantage in the tablet market. Other analysts also indicated that Microsoft's aim was to improve its video-conferencing services (BBC 2011).

Following Microsoft's purchase of Skype, the company withdrew licensing for a number of third parties producing software and hardware compatible with Skype. Microsoft also phased out its Windows Live Messenger instant messaging service in favour of Skype. Skype also continued to release new services, including supporting conference calls for up to 25 people, group video calling for up to 10 people[1] and the introduction of free video messaging services that could be

---

[1] http://www.skype.com/en/features/

operated from all its major platforms, including Windows and MacOS, Android and BlackBerry (Smith 2013). Shortly before Microsoft's purchase of Skype, it was estimated that Skype had approximately 30 million concurrent online users (March 2011) (Skype 2011). This rose to an estimated 36 million by March 2012 (Skype 2012) and 50 million by January 2013 (Mercier 2013).

By 2013 major decisions were no longer being made in Tallinn or London but at Microsoft's headquarters in Redmond, Washington. Most of the original employees were also reported to have now left, and the future of the Tallinn office was in question (Tänavsuu 2013). The utility of the so-called Tallinn Surplus in terms of the advantages that it once afforded in cost, convenience to the founders and calibre seemed to have diminished in the face of the growth in surpluses in other areas of value to what was now a global company and, more importantly, with the departure of the original owners. Skype's proximity to Scandinavia had become insignificant.

How Did Skype Do It?

Jaan Tallinn, one of Skype's founders, reportedly has said, 'Because we started anew, we got new laws, new leaders, and new technology. The big winners were the start-ups' (du Pommereau 2011). The choice of Skype's Swedish and Danish founders to establish the development team and core of Skype's operations in Tallinn, the capital of a small, relatively isolated and poor Baltic nation, can be inferred to have been based on the following perceived place surplus:

- Cost: A low-cost environment in terms of rents and living costs, especially compared to the other Nordic countries.
- Convenience: Familiarity with and proximity to the founders' home countries made Tallinn seem more convenient than other possible locations, for example, in Asia or the USA. Likewise, the Estonia had a business-friendly environment facilitated by the open and liberal policies of the Estonian government, its support of IT and Internet businesses and the establishment of e-government, reflecting its policies to develop Estonia as a digital economy.

- Calibre: A ready supply of high-calibre skilled cheap programming graduates and IT professionals with a strong work ethic (Salumaa 2012).
- Creative destruction: The spirit of the times engendered a population which through necessity needed to innovate and adopt an entrepreneurial approach to drive economic growth following withdrawal from the Soviet Union in 1991. Also, the simultaneous liberalisation of various telephony markets across Europe and the development of Internet technology allowed Skype to offer international communication under a model that radically undercut the pricing regimes of existing telecom providers.
- Community: Estonia had more or less a homogenous community which gave the country both strengths and weaknesses. The close-knit community of engineers, government officials and business leaders engendered a sense of loyalty to the place and the urge to make things happen for shared collective benefit. However, as the firm grew and took on international workers based elsewhere, this was progressively eroded.

Despite the place surplus offered by Tallinn in the early 2000s, start-ups operating there also faced a number of challenges. A lack of transport connections and social infrastructure, a relatively obscure language, an under-developed financial sector (Kuokstis 2011) and little collaboration between universities and companies weakened the local business landscape (Technopolis Group 2013).

These factors constrained growth, especially as more countries began to compete with Estonia on the basis of its place surplus. Perhaps the main early challenge for Estonia and Tallinn has been the absence of a history of successful tech start-ups to champion would-be so-called technopreneurs and a local VC community and other financial backers to support their early growth and expansion. Moreover, Tallinn's small population of around 400,000 people, with a national population of less than 1.3 million inhabitants, limited the size of the local workforce and consumer markets. These factors collectively drove Skype to set up new business units in other locations as a coping strategy to access necessary surpluses that were not available locally. The decreasing utility of its home base was further compromised by diminishing loyalty among workers as they were recruited and based in different countries and cultures. Over time, Estonia has played a much smaller role in the fortunes and fate of Skype, which is now more entrenched in the ecosystem of its US-based parent company.

References

BBC. 2011. Microsoft confirms takeover of Skype. *BBC*, 10 May. http://www.bbc.com/news/business-13343600

Business Week. 2004. Phone service the "Zero Cost" way? *Business Week*, 5 Jan. http://www.businessweek.com/printer/articles/242264-phone-service-the-zero-cost-way?type=old_article

CIA. 2015. The world Factbook: Estonia. CIA. https://www.cia.gov/library/publications/the-world-factbook/geos/en.html. Accessed 8 Oct 2015

CNET. 2008. http://news.cnet.com/2008-1082_3-5074558.html

du Pommereau, I. 2011. Why Estonia may be Europe's model country. *The Christian Science Monitor*, 18 May. http://www.csmonitor.com/World/Europe/2011/0518/Why-Estonia-may-be-Europe-s-model-country

eBay. 2005. eBay to acquire Skype. eBay, 12 Sept 2005. https://investors.ebayinc.com/ReleaseDetail.cfm?releaseid=172666

Estonian Ministry of Economic Affairs & Communication. 2004. Estonian IT policy: Towards a more service-centred and citizen-friendly state. *Principles of the Estonian Information Policy 2004–2006*, May. http://unpan1.un.org/intradoc/groups/public/documents/other/unpan032398.pdf

EUbusiness. 2014. Linnar Viik – Estonia's Mr. Internet, 20 Apr 2014. http://www.eubusiness.com/europe/estonia/040420021538.qhs3vusx

Friis, J. 2008. Conversation with Janus Friis, MidemNet. http://www.youtube.com/watch?v=cbmLMmBaGQE

Goswami, R. 2009. VoIP, Skype and the disruptive telecom revolution. IBS Research Centre, Case study: 306-145-1.

Högselius, P. 2002. Telecommunications in Estonia: The making of a sectoral innovation system, in a paper prepared for the DRUID winter conference, Aalborg, 17–19 Jan 2002, Sweden. http://citeseerx.ist.psu.edu/viewdoc/download?doi=10.1.1.134.2233&rep=rep1&type=pdf

IBS CDC. 2004. *From KaZaA to Skype*. Hyderabad: IBS Case Development Centre.

Kattel, R. 2010. Estonian innovation: From enclave to openness. *Eesti Päevaleht*, 13 Apr.

Kattel, R. 2014. From interview conducted by INSEAD with Professor Rainer Kattel, Head of Ragnar School of Innovation and Governance at Tallinn University of Technology.

Kilvits, K. 2002. Convergence of small open industry in Estonia. IES Proceedings 1.1, November 2002, pp. 1–23.

Kuokstis, V. 2011. What type of capitalism do the Baltic countries belong to?. Employment and Economy in Central and Eastern Europe, emecon.eu, Jan. http://www.emecon.eu/fileadmin/articles/1_2011/emecon%201_2011%20 Kuokstis.pdf

Langley, T. E. 2006. Skype technologies, S.A. Stanford Graduate School of Business, Case EC-37, 24 Aug 2006.

Langley, T. E., H. Mendelson, and H. Hartenbaum. 2006. Skype technologies, S.A. Stanford Graduate School of Business, Case: EC-37, 24 Aug 2006.

Løcke, L. O., and P. Bjerge. 2013. Billionaire on skype: How Janus Friis made billions selling skype. Twice!, Scribilis, 17 Oct 2013.

Low, J. 2013. Skype turns ten: The long strange trip. The LowDown Blog, 8 Sept 2013. http://www.thelowdownblog.com/2013/09/skype-turns-ten-long-strange-trip.html

Malik, O. 2010. Skype by the numbers: It's really big. Giga.com, 20 Apr 2010. https://gigaom.com/2010/04/20/skype-q4-2009-number/

Mercier, J. 2013. 50 million concurrent users online! Skype Numerology. http://skypenumerology.blogspot.se/2013/01/50-million-concurrent-users-online.html

Parvatham, N. 2013. e-Estonia: An inspiration to the world. Bangalore: Amity Research Centers Headquarters (Case Study reference no. 213-001-1).

Pena, A. V. 2011. Free wi-fi: Estonia. https://www.youtube.com/watch?v=a2EF0ysSeOc

Plunkett Research. 2015. Telecommunications industry market Research. http://www.plunkettresearch.com/telecommunications-market-research/industry-and-business-data. Accessed 8 Oct 2015.

Salumaa, P. 2012. Estonian mafia: The insider view. University of Tartu Blog, 19 Jan 2012. http://blog.ut.ee/estonian-mafia-the-insider-view/

Savov, V. 2011. Skype hits new record of 27 million simultaneous users in wake of iOS video chat release. *Engadget*, 11 Jan. http://www.engadget.com/2011/01/11/skype-hits-new-record-of-27-million-simultaneous-users-in-wake-o/

Skype. 2011. Skype blog, 28 Mar 2011. http://blogs.skype.com/2011/03/28/30-million-people-online/

Skype. 2012. Skype blog, 5 Mar 2011. http://blogs.skype.com/2012/03/05/35-million-people-concurrently/

Smith, M. 2013. Skype video messaging officially launchers on Windows, Max, iOS, Android—But not windows phone. *Gadget, Engadget*, 17 June. http://www. engadget.com/2013/06/17/skype-video-messaging-launches-free-unlimited/

SÖlvell, Ö., and M. Porter. 2006. *Estonia in transition*. Boston: Harvard Business School (9-702-436).

Tänavsuu, T. 2013. "How can they be so good?": The strange story of Skype. Ars Technica, 3 Sept 2013. http://arstechnica.com/business/2013/09/ skypes-secrets/

Technopolis Group. 2013. Technopolis report sourced from: http://www. technopolis-group.com/resources/downloads/reports/Technopolis_ loppraport_25062013_KOKKUVOTE_EN.pdf

TeleGeography. 2006. TeleGeography update: International carriers. Traffic grows despite Skype popularity. TeleGeography, 1 Dec 2006. https://www. telegeography.com/products/commsupdate/articles/2006/12/01/ telegeography-update-international-carriers-traffic-grows-despite-skype-popularity/

Tiits, M., and T. Kalvet. 2010. *Estonia; ICT RTD technological audit: Detailed report*. Tartu: Institute of Baltic Studies.

Tiits, M., and T. Kalvet. 2012. Nordic small countries in the global hi-tech value chains: The case of telecommunication systems production in Estonia. Working papers in technology governance and economic dynamics no. 38, Feb.

Wauters, R. 2009. Confirmed: eBay sells Skype in deal valuing it at $2.75 billion. TechCrunch, 1 Sept 2009. http://techcrunch.com/2009/09/01/ confirmed-ebay-sells-skype/

WEF. 2011. WEF entrepreneurship report 2011, p. 239. http://www3.weforum. org/docs/WEF_Entrepreneurship_Report_2011.pdf

4

SoundCloud in Berlin, Sharing the Vibe

SoundCloud is an audio platform that enables sound creators to upload, record, promote and share their original creations. It was the brainchild of two Swedish-born music enthusiasts, Eric Wahlforss and Alexander Ljung, who suspected that there was a large enough community of potential music makers and users to justify the creation of an interactive online audio platform on which to launch and host new music. Their efforts to fill this niche market resulted in SoundCloud (Wahlforss 2012). The company has grown rapidly following its launch in October 2008, attracting over 250 million listeners per month around the globe by the end of 2013 (Dillet 2013). While originally based in Sweden, the company quickly relocated to the more musically inclined Berlin. It now has satellite offices in San Francisco, New York City, London and Sofia(Bulgaria) (Taylor 2013) and can count Paul McCartney and 50 Cent among the many artists to have released singles on the platform (WEF 2013).

© The Editor(s) (if applicable) and The Author(s) 2016
S. Mahroum, *Black Swan Start-ups*,
DOI 10.1057/978-1-137-57727-6_4

Berlin's Somber History

'With Depression, war, fascism, the wall, and the mass migration of talent out of Berlin, it's quite clear that the city was set back by historical circumstances. Looking at the experience of other cities that remade themselves, like Pittsburgh, shifting to an open technology-savvy creative economy takes at minimum a generation.' These observations about Berlin were made by Richard Florida, Director and Professor of Business and Creativity at the Rotman School of Management, University of Toronto, who has studied creativity across the world (Kulish 2011).

The Berlin Wall—which had divided the city into East/communist and West/capitalist for more than a quarter-century—fell in November 1989. At the time, in the rush of wild enthusiasm that followed this astonishing event, many expected that the unification of the city's two political systems, economies and cultures would be facilitated by the strength of West Germany's economy. But while the reunification process ran high on emotions, the immediate economic consequences were dire (Leventhal 2010; Maier 2009). The city declined for the next 20 years, having been abandoned by many larger businesses. Although the centre of the city—Potsdamer Platz—was the site of Europe's largest private urban development in the 1990s, from 2005 early investors, such as German automaker Daimler and Japanese electronics giant Sony, pulled out as the district failed to develop into a thriving commercial hub (DW. com 2008; Spiegel 2007). Despite being the centre of government, Berlin could count no DAX-30 companies among its inhabitants (The Economist 2010).

On the human front, statistics showed that an estimated 2.5 million Berliners lost their jobs during the early years of reunification. In a labour market reminiscent of the Great Depression, unemployment rose to 15 % in the early 1990s. A third of the population was unemployed, retired (around 800,000 were forced to retire at 55), employed in state-created jobs or in job retraining. Between 1989 and 1993, the agriculture and forestry sectors contracted to a quarter of their former size and industrial employment to a third, a decline only partially offset by increases in employment in the construction and service sectors (Maier 2009).

With the steep rise in unemployment and competition, many former East Germans found the transition to an open-market system difficult. Far-reaching changes were announced by the government after the wall came down, but their implementation was slow and disjointed at best; East Germans found themselves having to adjust to a society that they had not participated in shaping and being forced to assimilate at the cost of their own sociocultural identity (Leventhal 2010). Many emigrated in search of work, and the birth rate declined sharply (Kulish 2009). The population of Berlin fell from 4.5 million to 3.4 million in the two decades following reunification (The Economist 2010). With East Berlin largely ungoverned for almost a year after the fall of the wall, squatters moved into the abandoned buildings (Rosenthal 2010). Many apartments stand empty to this day.

What's more, post-World War II Germany was traditionally home to large multinationals, with small and medium enterprises (SMEs) largely concentrated along their supply chain—an environment not conducive to a culture of entrepreneurship and risk-taking. Not surprisingly, German investors and financial institutions were reluctant to invest in early-stage technology start-ups or to back high-tech innovation (Scott 2013; The Economist 2013).

So the choice of Berlin by SoundCloud's Swedish entrepreneurs may seem counter-intuitive; indeed the Swedish capital Stockholm (ancestral city of SoundCloud's two founders) is better known for the competitiveness of its business environment. The European Commission's *Regional Competitiveness Index 2013* ranked the Stockholm region fourth, while the Berlin region ranked 42nd in terms of 'the ability to offer an attractive and sustainable environment for firms and residents to live and work' (Annoni and Dijkstra 2013).

Hatched from a Hunch

Alexander Ljung, a British-born Swede and graduate of Stockholm University, was a music lover whose career began as a sound designer for ALC Ljuddesign (European CEO, 2012). In 2005, in a computer lab at Stockholm's Royal Institute of Technology, he met fellow Stockholm University graduate and music enthusiast Eric Wahlforss. As sound designers who composed their own music, they were conscious of the gap between artists' musical talent and their business acumen—for example, negotiating with the music industry and its complex network of producers, publishers, distributors and retailers. This, they believed, hindered the success of many aspiring artists.

According to Wahlforss, 'Things around at the time—cheap file-sending services and MySpace—were just horrible.' With SoundCloud, 'We were scratching our own itch' (Mac 2013). After 3 months visiting Silicon Valley in 2006, Ljung and Wahlforss returned to Europe full of ideas. They were particularly inspired by a meeting with Catarina Fake, one of the founders of the photo-sharing Website Flickr (Wahlforss 2012). Instinctively they felt they could create something similar through which people could share music and sounds with others via a cloud computing arrangement involving a large number of computers connected through a real-time communication network—the Internet. In short, SoundCloud would be for sound what Flickr was to photos and Vimeo to videos.

In the early days of SoundCloud, the founders simply gathered talent they had known previously and started working to develop a company. With little knowledge of how to run a business, let alone set up an office, create a team or raise funds, they began by calling on their contacts in Stockholm and were put in touch with a prominent Scandinavian venture capitalist. With no prior experience of how to pitch ideas to investors, Wahlforss and Ljung tried to explain their idea for SoundCloud. Although the investor lacked an understanding of the Internet or the analogy with Flickr and other social media sites, he was won over by their enthusiasm and offered them the leftovers of a failed start-up sitting in his garage. This helped the duo establish a basic office and survive the early days while incurring only minimal costs (Wahlforss 2010).

But while Stockholm's technology cluster was rich with start-ups, such as the commercial music streaming service Spotify and Mojang, creator of the hit online game Minecraft, the generally reserved nature of Swedes (or the *Jante* phenomenon, which roughly translates as 'don't stand out') made hype or self-promotion by new businesses culturally distasteful (Wood 2013). So in 2007 the duo decided to relocate elsewhere, hoping to expand their network of contacts beyond Sweden and to leverage this to fund the development of the platform.

The Move to Berlin

Talking at Slush 2012, a start-up conference held in northern Europe, Wahlforss explained why they settled on Berlin. He had previously worked in the city, releasing a record there in 2001, and was familiar with the local music scene (Wahlforss 2012). Berlin's vibrant underground music scene and nightlife meant they were close to their main target group of users (DJs, music producers and artists).

Ljung described how in the early days they went clubbing most weekends, increasing their network by asking people to use SoundCloud when they were on the dance floor. Berlin was also more affordable than most other cities for starting a company, especially compared to Stockholm (Weigert 2010; Wood 2013). It had a surplus of advantages that could help develop their new venture (Wahlforss 2012).

'Berlin is the best start-up city in the world. It is full of creative, crazy people and a lot of art. And it also has strong technology traditions. Having both of these things in one place is really cool', said Alexander Ljung (Le Meur 2011). With its thriving start-up scene, there was palpable excitement in the entrepreneur community in Berlin. Graduates of Berlin's many universities and research institutions provided a pool of relatively low-cost employees for the high-tech sector. Moreover, the city had seen an increase in skilled labour arriving from elsewhere, including a large number of designers and engineers attracted by the cheap rent, underground music and art scenes, and lively nightlife (Scott 2013). Collectively, this pool of skilled and talented people contributed to the calibre of potential recruits for companies based in Berlin.

Berlin offered the benefit of being a major centre of German culture and creativity, which attracted talented young people from around the globe, which in turn enriched the city's creative potential (Berlin.de 2008).

According to Ingrid Walther of Berlin's Senate Department for Economics, Technology and Research, the merging of the two sectors was a logical consequence of the structural advantages of the city: *'Berlin is bursting with creativity and entrepreneurial spirit, has an excellent research and university landscape, and continuously attracts new international talent. No wonder that music and technology have entered into a new symbiosis here'* (Muller 2013).

Launching the Platform

SoundCloud was launched in October 2008 and initially functioned as a semi-professional service and was in private beta for around 18 months within the networked community prior to launch. The company grew organically, beginning as a small network of electronic music producers—many parts of Wahlforss' musical colleagues—forming a grassroots following in Berlin's underground music scene, with artists debuting tracks on the platform (Mac 2013). Berlin's music scene and nightlife offered close proximity to a community of early adopters for testing prototype services prior to release on the platform. The Berlin connection was there from the beginning in terms of early adopters.

SoundCloud featured a freemium revenue model: it charged users for premium services but offered basic services for free (Whiteboard 2013). Unlike competing sites, the original focus was to allow people to upload sound files with their own URL, making it an effective distribution platform for artists. With its simple-to-use platform for sharing music files online, SoundCloud differentiated itself by focusing on the creative process, allowing users not only to record and upload sounds but also to share their creations, thereby facilitating online artistic collaboration on a global scale (WEF 2013).

Located in Berlin's hip Mitte district, the StormCloud office building featured a rooftop terrace, which was also home to St. Oberholz Café, a hotspot on the start-up scene (The Economist 2012). The founders used the popular venue to kick-start broader promotion for the company, inviting local and other artists from around Europe to perform and try out SoundCloud for themselves. By flying in some 30 artists and giving each a 30-min set, they had enough musicians for an attention-grabbing

2-day event. Since the artists themselves invited others, they ended up with 200 people partying on the rooftop.

By drawing attention to SoundCloud in this way, they started getting e-mails and requests from other people in the industry. The event proved to be an effective means of bootstrapping the SoundCloud venture, and the platform started gaining traction (Wahlforss 2010).

Building Applications for Growth

One big obstacle to growth was the need to build applications on the SoundCloud platform to make it viable for businesses to use for recording and producing audio files. But before they could develop applications, they had to find people to use them—very much a 'chicken-and-egg' situation (Wahlforss 2010). An answer to the dilemma came through a friend in London who suggested that they organise music hack days, a term used by the programming community to describe a gathering of programmers, graphic designers and others involved in creating software who would spend 24 h working on creating something new. The music hack days were based on the same concept, but with a focus on creating music.

The first of a series of hack days around the globe was held in London in 2009. Wahlforss claimed that SoundCloud achieved more in the course of this event than in the previous 18 months, at minimal cost. Hack-day events also allowed the company's sales team to demonstrate the ease with which projects could be built on the SoundCloud platform (Wahlforss 2010). The SoundCloud Website was based on user profiles personalised according to musical genre and type of audio content. In the 2 years following public launch, SoundCloud focused on electronic music. Other musical genres were subsequently introduced. The platform was developed to allow artists to share their creations on other social networks and to leave comments on any part of an audio track.

In 2010, SoundCloud also launched a 'record' button which facilitated the introduction of all sound types to the platform. This allowed the Website to host music, DJ tracks, audio books, Webshows and podcasts, sound effects and other audio files, differentiating it from competing sites such as MySpace (Wahlforss 2012). Like other social media Websites, a list of updates was shown on a users' SoundCloud homepages based on their preferences.

Funding Expansion

Despite the success of their marketing events and the growing interest in SoundCloud, Wahlforss and Ljung struggled to attract venture capital (VC) for the first 18 months of operation. They contacted more than 200 companies but received few responses (Mac 2013; Wahlforss 2010).

To scale up, they needed funds to upgrade servers. Even with a small team of people, salaries had to be deferred, as a result of which the viability of the venture was put in jeopardy (Mac 2013; Wahlforss 2010). Moreover, German investors and banks were reluctant to invest in unproven early-stage tech start-ups or to back innovation in digital products and services, particularly after losing money in the fallout of the dot-com bust (Scott 2013).

In a bid to grab the attention of the VC community, Ljung had the SoundCloud logo laser-cut onto his leather jacket and wore it every day, even to conferences, standing out in a sea of suited investors. The jacket became a conversation starter and a 'peacocking' strategy that created tremendous publicity for the start-up, including with investors. In 2009, the company managed to attract 2.5 million euros in Series A VC funding from the London-based Doughty Hanson Technology Ventures, which enabled SoundCloud to expand its service to a million subscribers by May 2010.[1] It subsequently raised a further US$10 million in Series B funding from Union

---

[1] According to Investopedia (http://www.investopedia.com), seed capital is the initial capital used to start a business, often coming from the founders and their friends and family. Series A funding is the first round of financing undergone for a new business venture after seed capital. Generally, this is the first time that company ownership is offered to external investors. Series B funding is the second round of financing for a business by private equity investors or venture capitalists. Successive rounds of funding a business are termed Series A, Series B (and so on) financing. The Series B round will generally take place when the company has accomplished certain milestones in developing its business.

Square Ventures and Index Ventures in early 2011, which was used to scaleup more quickly and to develop a presence in the USA. All the VC funding, it should be noted, came from outside Germany. By June 2011, SoundCloud had opened an office in San Francisco and reached five million users.

The Beat Goes On

The Berlin Music Commission, a network representing the interests of mid-size music businesses in Berlin, estimated that by 2012 the city's music industry comprised approximately 1400 companies, employing around 14,000 people, and that companies in the information and communications technology (ICT), media and creative industries were able to recruit around three-quarters of their staff from the Berlin–Brandenburg region, bearing testimony to the city's calibre and convenience surpluses. It is estimated to be home to around 250 live music locations, over 90 recording studios and more than 150 music publishers.[2]

However, unlike the typical international music company, Berlin's creative industries were typically small and mid-sized (often one-person companies) with limited equity capital to cushion against business risks (Puchta 2008). This made the sector vulnerable to economic shocks and presents a challenge for policymakers seeking to promote economic development through local industry.

SoundCloud stands out as an example of a successful high-tech start-up that has flourished by identifying and seeking out the type of place surplus required to succeed in its line of business. However, Forbes magazine reported that by April 2013, SoundCloud had 38 million registered users in around 200 countries and was expanding by approximately 70,000 users per day. However, with only 5 % of users estimated to be paying customers, the company was yet to realise a profit and was reportedly seeking partnerships to source additional revenues (Mac 2013; WEF 2013).

---

[2] http://www.berlin-music-commission.de/en/about/music-industry-facts.html

How Did SoundCloud Do It?

A closer analysis of the two main areas of comparative advantage SoundCloud has been able to leverage—cost and community surpluses—is provided in what follows. Comparing Berlin to other tech start-up hubs in Europe such as London, Ljung cites Berlin's relatively low-cost base (especially rents) as a key advantage of locating in the city, particularly for early-stage start-ups. According to Mercer's 2012 Cost of Living Survey, which provides a worldwide ranking of 214 cities, Berlin is ranked 106 because its living costs are significantly cheaper than those of many other European cities such as London (25), Stockholm (46), Amsterdam (57), and Helsinki (65).[3] High-tech entrepreneurs also benefit from incentives available in the city which help reduce their direct operating costs. Technische Universität Berlin is an example of a local technology university which, in addition to graduating students to meet the needs of the high-tech sector, also offers small amounts of seed funding to assist entrepreneurs and start-ups (Dieterich 2011).

Being next to a community of leading users of SoundCloud services was very important for the founders. The Berlin art scene began growing around a decade ago, followed by a music scene, and more recently tech start-ups have been showing interest in the city. The decision of SoundCloud's founders to establish the start-up in Berlin in fact reflected their familiarity with the local music scene, with Wahlforss having lived in Berlin and produced a record there in 2001. Wahlforss pointed out that SoundCloud grew organically from a small community of Berlin-based music producers, of which he was a part, and that provided important place surplus which the start-up leveraged in its early days. He explains that the music sharing platform initially started as a semi-professional service which was in private beta for around 18 months within this networked community prior to its public launch (Wahlforss 2012).

Berlin's music scene and nightlife have also enabled the company to derive important place surplus by being within close proximity to a community of early adopters for testing SoundCloud's prototype services

---

[3] http://www.romandie.com/news/pdf/PDF_Etude_Mercer__Gen_5_ville_la_plus_ch_au_monde_ROM_120620120906.pdf

prior to release on the platform. The importance of the place surplus which tech start-ups are able to take advantage of by leveraging Berlin's community of creative talent is also exemplified by the start-up incubator and accelerator hub:raum, which claims to have been established by Deutsche Telekom in Berlin because 'next to relatively cheap living costs, Berlin has a tremendous scene of creative people that thrive [on] innovative ideas. This attracts talent from all over the world and all areas to Berlin. Therefore, Berlin is the perfect place to look for new, disruptive ideas and this is why hub:raum choose [*sic*] Berlin as its location-to-be in Germany.'[4]

In Conclusion

Post-war Germany has traditionally been home to large multinational companies, with SMEs largely concentrated along their supply chain. In this environment, a culture of entrepreneurship and risk-taking has not emerged. German investors and financial institutions have been reluctant to invest in early-stage technology start-ups or to back high-tech innovation, and thus Berlin's particular place surplus has not benefitted from the broader traditional German surplus.

Despite these challenges, today the city is emerging as one of Europe's leading start-up hubs in the creative sector. A confluence of creativity, technology and counterculture has created an ideal environment that has led to the flourishing of a thriving tech start-up scene in the historic German capital. Home to art galleries, a strong underground music scene, stylish bars and nightclubs, and an exciting counterculture, Berlin has developed a very creative atmosphere which is conducive to the formation of new and disruptive ideas (Winter 2012).[5] In a discussion with Francesco Baschieri, CEO of Spreaker, a social radio platform that relocated to Berlin from San Francisco and Italy, Baschieri claimed that Berlin was the 'next big thing after San Francisco', but nevertheless pointed out that, apart from SoundCloud, there remains a lack of big success stories such as Google and Facebook.[6]

---

[4] https://www.hubraum.com/locations/berlin

[5] https://www.hubraum.com/locations/berlin

[6] According to a recent discussion by Baschieri on Friday at Six, a monthly talk show about start-ups in Berlin which broadcasts interviews with entrepreneurs and company founders: http://fridayatsix.com/

SoundCloud stands out as an example of a successful high-tech start-up that has flourished by identifying and seeking out the type of place surplus required to succeed in its line of business. The Berlin business landscape seemed best suited to the company's needs, notwithstanding the lack of VC support in its early stages. SoundCloud's story highlights the importance of managing a place surplus to one's advantage. The company was able to leverage Berlin's vibrant music scene and the potential benefits of government policies and industry initiatives aimed at developing the city's creative sector. In this regard, SoundCloud has effectively identified and derived the place surplus it has required to successfully launch and grow from the ecosystem offered in Berlin.

References

Annoni, P., and L. Dijkstra. 2013. EU regional competitiveness index. JRC scientific and policy reports. Brussels: European Commission, 2013; Sourced from: http://ec.europa.cu/regional_policy/sources/docgener/studies/pdf/6th_report/rci_2013_report_final.pdf

Berlin Music Commission. 2012. Facts & figures of the music industry in the capital region. Berlin Music Commission. http://www.berlin-music-commission.de/ueber-uns/fakten-musikwirtschaft.html

Berlin.de. 2008. Creative industries in Berlin: Development and potential. ProjectZukunft Berlin, Senate Department of Economics, Technology and Research. http://www.berlin.de/projektzukunft/fileadmin/user_upload/pdf/magazine/Report_Creative_Industries_Berlin_2008.pdf

Creative City Berlin. Music: Creative City Berlin. Creative City Berlin.http://www.creative-city-berlin.de/en/creative-sector/music/

Dieterich, H. 2011. Berlin startup tour – Kreuzberg 61. Berlin Startup Tour, 15 Oct 2011. http://www.youtube.com/watch?v=BQfNXb-0hGM

Dillet, R. 2013. SoundCloud now reaches 250 million listeners in its quest to become the audio platform of the web *TechCrunch*, 29 Oct. http://techcrunch.com/2013/10/29/soundcloud-now-reaches-250-million-listeners-in-its-quest-to-become-the-audio-platform-of-the-web/

DW.com. 2008. Berlin's Sony center sells for Bargain price DW.com, 28 Feb 2008. http://www.dw.com/en/berlins-sony-center-sells-for-bargain-price/a-3157354-1

European CEO. 2012. Alex Ljung. EuropeanCEO: Profiles, 30 Apr 2012. http://www.europeanceo.com/profiles/alexander-ljung/

Kulish, N. 2009. In East Germany, a decline as stark as a wall. *New York Times*, 18 June. http://www.nytimes.com/2009/06/19/world/europe/19germany.html?_r=0

Kulish, N. 2011. Berlin hopes growing tech community will lift city's economy. *New York Times*, 16 Sept. http://www.nytimes.com/2011/09/17/world/europe/berlins-tech-scene-offers-hope-to-economy.html?_r=0&pagewanted=print

Le Meur, L. 2011. Meet alexander Ljung explain how he made SoundCloud a success. 11 Nov 2011. https://www.youtube.com/watch?v=JKsldoAiqT8

Leventhal, C. R. 2010. Berlin after the wall: Decades after its fall, history still haunts. *Student Pulse* 2(4). http://www.studentpulse.com/articles/232/3/berlin-after-the-wall-decades-after-its-fall-history-still-haunts

Mac, R. 2013. Breaking the sound barrier. *Forbes* 191(6): 78.

Maier, C. S. 2009. Twenty years after the fall of the Berlin Wall: The travails of east Germany's economic transition. United Nations University, World Institute for Development Economics Research Newsletter, November. http://www.wider.unu.edu/publications/newsletter/articles/en_GB/Maier-article-1109/

Muller, V. K. 2013. Berlin music week 2013: Startups music, startups corner. deutsche-startups.de, 15 Aug 2013. http://www.berlin.de/projektzukunft/fileadmin/user_upload/pdf/magazine/Report_Creative_Industries_Berlin_2008.pdf

Puchta, D. 2008 An engine for creative industries. *The German Times*, June. http://www.german-times.com/index.php?option=com_content&task=view&id=6188&amp

Rosenthal, J. 2010. Being There: Berlin. *The Economist: Intelligent Life, Autumn*. http://moreintelligentlife.com/print/content/places/jonathan-rosenthal/being-there-berlin

Scott, M. 2013. Technology startups take root in Berlin. *Deal Book, New York Times*, 29 Apr. http://dealbook.nytimes.com/2013/04/29/technology-start-ups-take-root-in-berlin/?_r=2

Spiegel. 2007. Berlin landmark changes hands: Daimler sells potsdamer platz to Swedish Bank. *Spiegel Online*, 14 Dec. http://www.spiegel.de/international/germany/berlin-landmark-changes-hands-daimler-sells-potsdamer-platz-to-swedish-bank-a-523434.html

Taylor, C. 2013. TC cribbs: Inside SoundCloud, The Berlin-based startup fueled by music (and club-mate). *TechCrunch*, 26 Nov. http://techcrunch.com/2013/11/26/tc-cribs-inside-soundcloud-berlin/

The Economist. 2010. Berlin's economy: The hole in the middle. *The Economist*, 11 Nov. http://www.economist.com/node/17472852

The Economist. 2012. Les Miserables. *The Economist*, 26 July. http://www.economist.com/node/21559618

The Economist. 2013. Business creation in Germany: A slow climb. *The Economist*, 3 Oct. http://www.economist.com/news/business/21587209-vigorous-start-up-scene-has-yet-produce-its-first-big-breakthrough-slow-climb

Wahlforss, W. 2010. The story of SoundCloud – From a Boot-Strapper's perspective. SUD2010. https://vimeo.com/11420397

Wahlforss, E. 2012. Fireside chat with Eric Wahlforss (SoundCloud) at Slush 2012. StartupSauna, 24 Nov 2012. https://www.youtube.com/watch?v=ZpxUtJ6AMmo

WEF. 2013. Technology pioneers 2013: Pushing new frontiers. World Economic Forum report. http://reports.weforum.org/technology-pioneers-2013/

Weigert, M. 2010. From Stockholm to Berlin: Interview with SoundCloud CEO Alexander Ljung. twingly.com, 18 May 2010. http://blog.twingly.com/2010/05/18/from-stockholm-to-berlin-interview-with-soundcloud-ceo-alexander-ljung/

Whiteboard. 2013. SoundCloud co-founder Eric Wahlforss: "How we built SoundCloud". Whiteboard, 24 Apr 2013. http://www.berlin.de/projektzukunft/fileadmin/user_upload/pdf/magazine/Report_Creative_Industries_Berlin_2008.pdf

Winter, C. 2012. Berlin cracks the startup code. Bloomberg Business, 12 Apr 2012. http://www.bloomberg.com/bw/articles/2012-04-12/berlin-cracks-the-startup-code

Wood, A. 2013. Forget Berlin, Stockholms' startup scene comes of age. *Tech City News*, 30 Aug. http://techcitynews.com/2013/08/30/stockholms-start-up-scene-comes-of-age/

5

Sofizar in Lahore, Turning the Competitiveness Index Upside Down

Sofizar-ConstellationCK is an online Search Engine Optimization (SEO) and Internet marketing company specialising in online ticket sales and educational services. Sofizar itself was founded in 2004 in Lahore, Pakistan, by Zafar Khan, of the Pakistani-American diaspora. With the support of global networks, in early 2009, Khan partnered with US-based serial entrepreneur Carlos Cashman to launch Sofizar's sister company, ConstellationCK. The two companies merged soon thereafter, operating out of a shared facility in Lahore, with front offices in the USA, and have developed a strong presence in the global industry for Internet marketing, especially in the highly competitive US market. By 2014, the combined operations of Sofizar-ConstellationCK, together with a more recent spin-off company, OrionCKB, generated some US$30 million in annual revenue and employed approximately 170 people, the majority of whom were located in Lahore. During his freshman year of college, Khan declared to friends that he was going to be a millionaire. He did it.

© The Editor(s) (if applicable) and The Author(s) 2016

S. Mahroum, *Black Swan Start-ups*,

DOI 10.1057/978-1-137-57727-6_5

Why Lahore?

Whenever I talk about Sofizar, I start off by showing a couple of international benchmarking indices on place competitiveness, mostly from the World Economic Forum (WEF) and the International Institute for Management Development (IMD), a business school in Lausanne, Switzerland. The indices show the USA ranked among the top 10 in the world, sometimes at number 1, whereas Pakistan ranks among the bottom 10, sometimes at the very bottom. WEF's Global Competitiveness Index (GCI) 2013–2014 ranked Pakistan a low 105 out of 148 countries for its capacity to retain talent and in the 111th position for its capacity to attract talent. Further, a quality-of-life survey conducted by Mercer in 2012 ranked Lahore 188th out of 221 cities, indicating that lifestyle considerations are likely to detract from the attractiveness of Lahore and encourage 'brain drain'.

I then ask my audience which location they would choose to set up their business, Silicon Valley or Lahore? As one would expect, the answer is almost always unanimously the USA. This is exactly what makes the story of Sofizar so intriguing and counter-intuitive. Pakistan was ranked a relatively low 116 out of 121 countries in terms of entrepreneurial attitudes, aspirations and activity according to the 2014 Global Entrepreneurship and Development Institute Index. Similarly, the Global Entrepreneurship Monitor 2011 found that a third of the country's working age population believed that the fear of failure would prevent them from starting a business.

The list of bad news goes on. According to the World Bank (2013a, b) Pakistan performs poorly in terms of ease of doing business, on which it ranked 110th out of 189 countries. Particular weaknesses included access to electricity (175th), paying taxes (166th) and enforcing contracts (158th). The cost of real estate in Pakistan is higher than in neighbouring India and China, and companies must contend with Pakistan's unreliable utilities, whose costs must be offset against other cost savings.

Corruption and rent-seeking behaviour within Pakistan's government and business community also present major challenges for start-ups and constrain innovation and entrepreneurial activity (Haque 2007). Arif and Sonobe (2012) claim that 'the entire system of law enforcement is inefficient and corrupt' and contracts are notoriously difficult to enforce. It is estimated to take on average 976 days to enforce a contract, and doing so involves a total of 134 procedures (Bilbao-Osorio et al. 2014). This reflects the country's poor performance in a number of areas, including irregular payments and bribes (123rd), favouritism in decisions of government officials (130th), the efficiency of the legal framework for settling disputes (112th), organised crime (141st) and the ethical behaviour of firms (112th) (WEF 2013). This provides Pakistan's information technology (IT) start-ups with further impetus to develop export markets for their products and services as a way of bypassing the challenges of operating in the local market.

Nevertheless, Lahore in Pakistan had something that gave it an edge over Silicon Valley

A number of factors within the entrepreneurial ecosystem in Lahore, Pakistan, were instrumental to the success of high-tech start-ups launched to service international markets in the fields of Internet marketing and e-commerce. As Internet companies, being based in Lahore did not matter so long as they maintained a physical, front-office presence in the USA. Indeed, Sofizar founder Zafar Khan considered that the cost, calibre and convenience benefits of the ecosystem in Lahore provided its sister companies with a strong competitive advantage over foreign rivals. The US-based front-office operations were seen as important not only because they provided more immediate access to the company's key market segment, but also because the company's US presence helped it to avoid image problems associated with Pakistan.

Pakistan is the second largest economy in South Asia after India and the seventh most populated country in the world. Its population of just over 196 million (est. July 2014) has a young age profile, with over half of the population aged under 25 years. Lahore is Pakistan's second largest city, with a population of just over seven million. It is also the capital of the Punjab province, the largest province in Pakistan by both population and national income. Punjab is estimated to account for more than 50 % of Pakistan's national income and is widely considered Pakistan's engine of growth. Agriculture has been the backbone of the Punjab economy since the British administration invested heavily in agricultural infrastructure (i.e., irrigation, road networks and railways). However, after gaining independence in 1947, Pakistan's policymakers focused on developing Punjab's urban economy and in doing so failed to adequately maintain infrastructure critical to the agricultural industry.

Zafar Khan sums up his personal difficulties as follows: 'Overseas markets offered infinite potential, while operating successfully in Pakistan required strong political connections and a disregard for ethics, something that did not sit well with me.' However, he contends that, fortunately, as an Internet company—with few tangible assets, in an industry still relatively unknown to the government—he was left alone. Graft did not become an operating issue, nor was he burdened by time-wasting demands for special permits and other red tape hurdles which companies operating in more traditional sectors typically encounter in Pakistan.

Many of Pakistan's IT start-ups have adopted an export focus and commenced operations by building their businesses and reputations abroad rather than at home. Underlying reasons have included the low level of Internet usage and computer literacy across much of Pakistan, with the World Bank estimating an Internet penetration rate of 10 % in 2012; although higher than a decade earlier (2.6 %), this was still well below the average in OECD countries of 73.3 %.

The Story of Zafar Khan

After graduating from the California Institute of Technology in 1992 with a degree in electrical engineering, Zafar Khan worked in several technology jobs for companies, including indirect material management company Nexiant and media company Gemstar in China, Hong Kong and the USA (Ara 2009). During his 7 years at Gemstar, Khan worked in the field of interactive television technology, travelled the world, successfully registered several patents and, as one of Gemstar's first employees, profited greatly from his stock options. By the late 1990s, Gemstar was employing approximately 3500 staff (Khan had been the company's 16th employee) and had a market capitalisation of around US$35 billion. Khan claims that by his late 20s he had achieved his dream of being a millionaire many times over, and his future was looking rosy.

Early 2002 saw Khan, now cash rich, leave Gemstar to launch his own company in the new area of digital television. He established a company which was licensed to provide digital technology services to Shanghai Broadcasting, a company which in the end proved an unreliable partner. Following an initial payment of 20 % of the cost of providing converter boxes to the broadcaster, Khan claims that they failed to meet further payment obligations. This ultimately led to the collapse of his company. Khan contends that this experience left him with an enduring fear of payment collection, a lesson he took with him in his new entrepreneurial ventures.

In what would stand out as a particularly eventful period in his life, no sooner had Khan's business venture unravelled than he was involved in a serious car accident. In the same month, he was diagnosed with cancer.

Not to be deterred by this turn of events, Khan announced that he was also to be married. While the USA appeared to be an attractive location for the couple to settle, and despite the fact that Khan held the US citizenship, the lengthy wait for his Pakistani wife's green card caused the couple to select the Pakistani city of Lahore as their new home. Khan explains that they had also considered Islamabad and Karachi but settled on Lahore partly because the security situation was better. Khan was also familiar with Lahore, having studied there when he was young; additionally, good friends from the USA had recently relocated there.

Thus, after having lived abroad for most of his adult life, in 2004 Khan found himself back in his home country. He brought with him a strong desire to regain his lost wealth and create a company that would generate sustainable value (MIT 2011). His next challenge was to identify new business opportunities. With little capital to his name, of paramount importance was the need to effectively leverage the advantages offered by Lahore.

Assessing opportunities in the technology space, Khan decided to establish an outsourcing company offering services in the growing area of search engine marketing (SEM). Not only did this allow him the opportunity to utilise his technical skills, but the required capital investment was within his means. Moreover, establishing a start-up in

Lahore provided opportunities to take advantage of Pakistan's relatively lower cost of doing business vis-à-vis business costs in foreign markets, especially in the USA. Of particular importance was the opportunity to leverage the low-cost yet talented pool of IT graduates and technology professionals available in Lahore.

Describing himself as a relatively inexperienced entrepreneur at the time, Zafar claims that Pakistan's relatively low cost of living and cheap labour also afforded him the time he needed to learn the ropes as the head of a start-up. 'It took some of the pressure off. I could afford to make some mistakes in the early days as I gained experience and slowly grew the business.'

Despite a relatively plentiful supply of quality ICT talent in Lahore, Khan claimed that as a start-up operation bootstrapped out of his house, Sofizar encountered difficulties attracting good talent. A common problem for entrepreneurs worldwide, Khan asserted, was that quality talent preferred to work for large and well-established organisations in what he termed a 'MNC' (multinational corporation) culture. In the early days this preference for working for multinational companies with offices in Pakistan, such as Google and Facebook, presented a considerable competitive challenge for Sofizar. Nevertheless, Khan managed to hire several talented people who believed in his vision and left established firms to work for the fledgling start-up. As an incentive he also offered them equity options in the company.

After launching Sofizar in 2004 Khan raised a first round of finance which was subsequently withdrawn in early 2005 owing to investor reluctance to invest in a Pakistani company. Feeling responsible for his employees—now numbering around a dozen—Khan invested his personal savings as well as proceeds generated by Sofizar's consulting contracts to develop analytics software. He hoped to sell the software online for a license fee of US$100, which represented a significant discount to an existing product sold by competitor Urchin Software. Unfortunately, shortly prior to launch, Google announced the purchase of Urchin and offered their software free of charge as part of Google's wider suite of products.

Adding to Khan's troubles, he discovered that two employees were engaging in what is known as click fraud, a process whereby false 'clicks' are generated on a customer's Website to boost the number of visitors, thereby deriving extra revenue. Khan sacked the employees and began investigating this form of fraud. Discovering the prevalence of this unethical practice, and recognizing a new niche, he set about developing software to detect click fraud. At the same time, and to maintain cash flow, Sofizar continued to take on outsourcing work.

Google required that Sofizar use a Website with real advertisements and selling actual products to test the effectiveness of Khan's click-fraud-detection software. This turned out to be the silver lining and led to the development of a lucrative sideline business. The company registered a domain name and, in what Khan describes as a 'quite random choice', decided to develop an online ticket sales Website to test the software.

Sofizar worked with ticket consolidators in the USA to develop the site and establish a legitimate business vehicle on which to test the ability of his software to detect any fraudulent clicks Google might have missed. At the same time, the company received a percentage of all ticket sales generated by the site. Primarily serving buyers in the US market, a bemused Khan soon realised that because of time differences, 'we were making money in our sleep' from ticket sales. He responded to this new-found source of revenue by applying Sofizar's skills in SEO and Internet marketing to improve the effectiveness of the Website and generate more sales.

A Game Changer

In what proved to be an important turning point for Khan, he entered Sofizar in a competition run by the Massachusetts Institute of Technology Enterprise Forum Pakistan (MITEFP). Known as the Business Acceleration Programme (BAP), the programme assists IT companies operating in Pakistan to accelerate their businesses and improve start-up success. Sofizar won the competition in November 2007 on the basis of its track record, innovative business plan and growth prospects. As a result, Khan received mentoring and coaching support from the MIT Entrepreneurship Center and enrolled in several executive development programmes. In turn, three members of the MIT faculty joined Sofizar's board of advisors. Khan was also provided with networking opportunities that gave him valuable access to people in the USA who could help him grow his business. The support he received from the Pakistani diaspora as a result of winning the competition and the increased profile it afforded Sofizar were instrumental to the company's future growth.

Khan estimated that between 2007 and 2010, Sofizar grew by 593 %. Over the same period it was ranked as one of Pakistan's fastest growing companies (6th), according to the All World Network, which ranks fast-growth entrepreneurial companies in the emerging world. By 2009–2010, Khan says that Sofizar was scaling up quickly and generating some US$17 million per annum, with growth expected to double the following year.

Encouraged by this success, Khan felt that he could benefit by finding a suitable business partner to scale the business further. 'I was looking for a person who could not only bring new business and new ideas, but also challenge me by asking the right questions and provide me with a sounding board when I was making decisions', he explained. On a daily operational level, with the ticket sales business growing quickly in the USA, Khan was finding it increasingly difficult to manage the US business, including important relationships with US vendors. Hence, finding a suitable partner in the USA became an important part of the company's growth strategy.

As part of the networking opportunities, the MITEFP provided to entrepreneurs, Khan was introduced to successful businessmen, including serial entrepreneur and MIT graduate Carlos Cashman. Cashman had worked with numerous successful start-ups as an executive, founder and adviser. His first company, Opus360, had been publicly listed on NASDAQ in 2000 and then sold a year later. In 2005, Cashman co-founded the SEM company CourseAdvisor, which generated online leads for the tertiary education sector, which was sold to the *Washington Post* for over US$100 million in 2007.

Collaboration Leads to Success

The introduction to the Silicon Valley-based Cashman was a game changer for Khan. Partnering with Cashman gave him the scaling up opportunity he had been looking for. Khan explains: 'What I was doing in the free part of Google, Carlos was doing in the paid part of Google.' The synergies were obvious. In 2009, after exploring different options, and with Khan reluctant to dilute his ownership in the now highly profitable Sofizar, they decided to establish a new company, ConstellationCK, which would specialise in online marketing, including SEO, SEM and digital advertising.

In the early days of ConstellationCK, in what represented an important strategic decision, they recruited Boston-based Scott Briggs. Briggs, who had worked with Cashman at CourseAdvisor and co-founded a successful SEM business in 2006, was a valuable addition and was soon made a junior partner.

While the business was initially slow to grow, after signing a deal to lease the Excite.com Website in 2010, the company grew quickly. ConstellationCK leveraged the capacity provided by the Excite.com Website—originally designed as a search engine—to expand beyond online ticket sales into new verticals, including online lead generation for the tertiary education sector, student loans and insurance. Among other things, the company also started running the education vertical for the US-based company McGraw-Hill (MIT 2011).

As ConstellationCK grew, it developed a strong capability in the emerging area of social media marketing. It first ran Facebook advertising when the social networking platform released its advertising interface, API, in 2011. Recognising the power of Facebook advertising, ConstellationCK made the decision to spin off the business as an entirely new sister company named OrionCKB in late 2013. According to Khan, the new company grew quickly and received 10 % of all advertising expenditures made by clients. By January 2014, OrionCKB was reported to have increased its client base fivefold and its client-managed advertising spent on Facebook by 600 %; in January 2014 alone it doubled its Facebook advertising under management.

Like its sister companies, OrionCKB was self-funded by the company's co-founders. In establishing OrionCKB, an additional co-founder, Sanaz Limouee, was also added to the partnership team. Limouee was an expert in marketing optimisation and had extensive experience working with technology companies in the USA. OrionCKB's development team and back-office operations were also based out of the Sofizar-ConstellationCK offices in Lahore to enable the Facebook advertising company to leverage its high-calibre talent and low-cost base.

Importantly, in growing the business, Khan claimed that he was able to develop a world-class SEM force out of Lahore by leveraging the cost advantages of the location that enabled him to effectively compete with US companies, such as StablerArena.com (acquired in 2007 by eBay for US$307 million) and TicketsNow.com (acquired by Ticketmaster for US$265 million).

Finding the Funding

Recognising the limited opportunities for Pakistani tech start-ups to raise seed or venture capital (VC)—either through local investors (who were both reluctant to invest in IT start-ups and handed large equity shares in return for investments in start-up operations) or through international investors (who were deterred by Pakistan's international image problems)—Khan elected to instead focus on execution rather than fundraising activities. He was also deterred by the US-based venture capitalists who typically demanded strong execution and linear results.

From his experience, Carlos Cashman estimates that the costs of doing business in Pakistan are as much as 80 % lower than in the USA. Also contributing to Pakistan's low-cost environment is its top marginal personal income tax rate of 20 % which is among the lowest in world. As a result, Cashman says, 'In Pakistan, you can make a lot of small investments by US standards and you only need one in every 8–10 to work to get a great return. There are huge opportunities for investors here. You do not need to invest a lot in them [businesses] to get them going due to the low cost of doing business in Pakistan' (Iiahi 2012).

Nawab (2013) suggests that start-ups can recruit new graduates from Pakistan's technical colleges for salaries as low as US$250 per month. Sabir et al. (2010) argue that Pakistan's talent pool is also cheaper than in neighbouring India and China, with labour costs estimated to be 30–40 % lower. As a result, Pakistani entrepreneurs are able to leverage the country's 'talented, cost-effective workforce' to derive comparative advantage. Self-funding for much of the growth process afforded Khan the opportunity to learn and experiment with different strategies as he grew Sofizar in what he indicates was 'a nonlinear growth path', the road less travelled by.

How Did Sofizar Do It?

In launching Sofizar in 2004, followed by sister company ConstellationCK in 2009, and then OrionCKB, the founders were able to clearly identify a market opportunity and effectively leverage the unique resources and characteristics of the Punjab capital of Lahore in order to compete effectively in the global Internet marketing industry. Khan posits that by leveraging the surpluses of Lahore, the companies were able to derive competitive advantage in three key areas: cost, calibre and convenience.

Cost

Of paramount importance was the low-cost business environment and cost arbitrage opportunities associated with being located in Lahore, both as small start-ups and as the companies grew. By way of example, Khan explains that providing 'lead generation' services entail very labour-intensive processes, including extensive research using the Internet, Websites and search engines to generate leads for clients. As a result, the ability to access relatively low-cost yet technically skilled labour in Lahore provided the companies with an important competitive advantage in international markets, especially in the USA. The tax exemption provided to Pakistan's IT companies also added to the cost-related place surplus of Lahore.

Lahore's low-cost environment allows companies to have the proverbial nine lives, posits Khan: 'You can make mistakes and retry things, and so long as you keep innovating in this fast moving space, you can win.' He indicated that the low cost of doing business in Lahore effectively subsidised the companies' product and service development activities (MIT 2011), and, like many start-up operations, the companies were able to reduce costs further by offering staff stock options in lieu of higher salaries.

Calibre

Khan was also pleased with the calibre of talent the companies were able to attract in the local market, especially as the companies grew. Moreover, he considered his staff to be very loyal. While Sofizar had initially encountered some difficulties attracting people who were prepared to work for his IT start-up, as the company grew and established a good reputation in the IT industry—aided by winning the MIT Enterprise Forum's competition and gaining the support of the community of the Pakistani diaspora—it became easier to recruit the talent he needed. Khan explained that he could only attract less experienced, albeit talented, people initially, as those with more experience typically gravitated towards more established companies in what he termed a 'MNC' culture. Khan offered employees stock options and encouraged a healthy work–life balance in order to provide an attractive work environment and retain quality employees. To attract talented women, a large and underutilised resource in Pakistan, he also introduced a 'Mums with Laptops' initiative.

Cashman, Khan's partner in ConstellationCK and OrionCKB, commended Pakistan for the quality of its IT talent pool. He claimed that the country's schools were producing a good calibre of graduates and considered the technical resources available in Pakistan to be 'top notch'. Added to this, Cashman claimed that the English language skills of educated Pakistanis combined with the country's low labour costs made Lahore an attractive investment proposition for Internet marketing firms (Iiahi 2012).

Convenience

Despite the challenging business environment many start-ups encounter in Pakistan, Khan stated that he found it relatively easy to establish a company in Lahore since he was operating in the ICT space. He contended that because his was an Internet company, the government left him alone. Graft was not an issue, and he was not burdened by time-wasting demands for special permits and other red tape hurdles companies operating in other sectors typically encountered in Pakistan. Khan also noted that geographic boundaries are not important to Internet companies, especially in terms of back-office operations. However, to overcome the negative perceptions associated with Pakistan in the West, all three companies established front-office operations in the USA.

Sofizar and her sister companies were also able to avoid several of the key factors behind Pakistan's poor ranking by the World Bank for ease of doing business. As IT companies, they were exempt from taxation; by focusing on export markets, they avoided many of the difficulties associated with enforcing contracts in Pakistan, and by installing generators, they were able to largely overcome problems caused by the country's power outages.

And while IT start-ups also encounter difficulties accessing VC in Pakistan, Khan argued that the country's low-cost environment meant that IT companies such as theirs with relatively low-capital requirements could often afford to self-fund growth. Moreover, by avoiding the requirements often imposed by venture capitalists, including strong linear growth, Khan claims he was afforded the opportunity to make mistakes and learn important lessons along the way, which ultimately led to greater success. Diaspora networks, such as OPEN, and Programme such as BAP also provided Pakistani entrepreneurs like Khan with valuable mentoring support and international networking opportunities which are of high significance to companies wishing to operate on a global scale.

In Conclusion

The success of high-tech companies like Sofizar, ConstellationCK and OrionCKB in Lahore is largely a function of a good match between place surplus and a firm's competitive advantage. In the case of these sister companies, the combined cost, calibre and convenience surpluses which their Lahore location provided enabled the companies to leverage the types of competitive advantages they required most to succeed. Thus a firm whose business strategy requires cost competitiveness will achieve greater surplus from a place which provides a relatively lower-cost base, whereas a firm whose business strategy requires, for example, convenience factors to derive competitiveness will derive more utility from a place whose comparative advantage lies in providing convenient access to factors that matter most to the firm. Nevertheless, a surplus only becomes a source of comparative advantage if companies leverage it. If not, it may be a potential source of unemployment or underemployment. The Sofizer–ConstellationCK story carries important lessons for Lahore and other locations around the world. Cost, convenience, calibre, creative destruction and community provide a number of possible configurations for regions to develop a unique competitive advantage. Places with strong social capital and a sense of community tend to be more resilient in the face of disadvantages, and economic actors stick around in such places much longer before they decide to exit.

References

Ara, J. 2009. Zafar Khan, CEO of Sofizar, tells his story on ITLoW. Blog, 29 June 2009. https://jehanara.wordpress.com/2009/06/29/zafar-khan-ceo-of-sofizar-tells-his-story-on-itlow/

Aril, B.W., and T. Sonobe. 2012. Virtual incubation in industrial clusters: A case study in Pakistan. *Journal of Development Studies* 48(3): 377–392.

Bilbao-Osorio, B., S. Dutta, and B. Lanvin (eds.). 2014. *The global information technology report 2014*. Geneva: World Economic Forum and INSEAD. http://www3.weforum.org/docs/WEF_GlobalInformationTechnology_Report_2014.pdf

Haque, N. 2007. Entrepreneurship in Pakistan. Pakistan Institute of Development Economics, Working paper 2007:29, Islamabad. http://www.pide.org.pk/pdf/Working%20Paper/WorkingPaper-29.pdf

Iiahi, J. 2012. Aaj Aaap key sath—business—episode 9—entrepreneurship and investment in Pakistan, 7 Dec 2012. http://www.youtube.com/watch?v=dr5ropITVIU. Accessed 6 May 2014.

MIT. 2011. High tech in low income: Zafar Khan, MIT video, Legatum Center for Development and Entrepreneurship. http://video.mit.edu/watch/high-tech-in-low-income-zafar-khan-10580/

Nawab, A. 2013. Accelerating entrepreneurship in Pakistan. *Teach In Asia*, 24 June 2013. http://www.techinasia.com/how-to-accelerate-entrepreneurship-in-pakistan/

Sabir, S., T. Aidrus, and S. Bird. 2010. Pakistan: A story of technology, entrepreneurs and global networks. MIT Sloan Management, case no. 10-082, 17 Feb 2010.

WEF. 2013. The global competitiveness report 2013–2014. *World Economic Forum.* http://www.weforum.org/reports/global-competitiveness-report-2013-2014

World Bank. 2013a. Pakistan: Finding the path to job-enhancing growth. World Bank report no. 75521-PK, Islamabad. http://www-wds.worldbank.org/external/default/WDSContentServer/WDSP/IB/2013/08/20/000356161_20130820124333/Rendered/PDF/755210REVISED00EM0Final0Book0080513.pdf

World Bank. 2013b. *Doing business 2014.* Washington: World Bank. http://www.doingbusiness.org/reports/global-reports/doing-business-2014.

6

Rovio in Espoo: Epitomizing the Rise of "Palo Espoo"

Almost every time I ask someone whether they have heard of a company called Rovio, they say no. But when I ask again if they had heard of a game called Angry Birds, they almost always say, 'Of course'. Rovio Entertainment is the maker of Angry Birds, released in 2009. It was the Finnish company's 52nd game. And yet very few know about its Finnish identity. By late 2013 Angry Birds had been downloaded 1.7 billion times, making it the most downloaded paid mobile game application in the world of all time—a notable example of entrepreneurship in the electronic entertainment industry. Before we delve into the intricacies of this company, we must first take a look at the gaming industry to put the story in its industrial context.

The Gaming Industry

The global gaming industry can be divided into (1) game software developers and (2) hardware producers that manufacture devices, with the software market accounting for the larger share of revenues. The industry is dominated by Nintendo, Sony and Microsoft, followed by companies

© The Editor(s) (if applicable) and The Author(s) 2016
S. Mahroum, *Black Swan Start-ups*,
DOI 10.1057/978-1-137-57727-6_6

such as Apple, EA Sports and Disney Entertainment. According to Transparency Market Research (TMR), the global gaming market was worth US$70.5 billion in 2011 and will be worth US$118 billion by 2015, assuming a compound average growth rate of 13.7 %. Much of that growth will be driven by the expanding range of advanced gaming features and an increase in the number of Internet users.

TMR claims that growth in the global gaming industry has been buoyed by the increased use of and support for gaming software on mobile devices such as laptops, tablets and mobile phones, high-speed Internet connectivity, more sophisticated gaming techniques, increased disposable income and more compatible hardware. Potential threats to its future growth include the repercussions of fraudulent gaming, the obsolescence of current technology, and competing innovations in other entertainment industries.

The traditional business model in the global gaming industry was one whereby publishing companies financed game developers and production costs in exchange for the intellectual property (IP) rights to the resulting software. Seven out of 10 games were estimated to lose money. Game publishers traditionally worked with developers to prepare games for market, identify the audience and assist in developing revenue models for monetisation (e.g., through freemium models, where basic games are free of charge but extra features incur a charge). But with the emergence of efficient digital distribution channels, the structure of the industry changed considerably. Developers were able to sidestep the publishing companies and distribute games directly through online digital channels such as Apple's iOS app store and Google Play for Android. This transformed the revenue model, with game developers now receiving around 70 % of the revenue stream, while distribution channels and intermediaries garnered the remaining 30 %—in stark contrast to the traditional model where developers received only 8–15 % of revenues generated (Härmä, 2013).

Gaming in Finland: A Brief History

It was the success of Espoo-based game developer Remedy, dating from 1995, which paved the way for the gaming industry take-off in Finland. Its initial success with Death Rally enabled Remedy to develop Max Payne, an international blockbuster which sold over seven million copies. Another contributor to its success, according to gaming company Supercell CEO Ilkka Paananen, was the fact that most developers aimed to make great games rather than just money: 'While an initial push in games development came from the Finnish government and numerous venture capitalists, the growing local scene has maintained its trajectory because of a focus on quality projects in the face of losing money.'[1] According to Paananen 'Helsinki is the centre of gravity for the future of games', as is evident from the presence of gaming companies such as Rovio and Supercell.

The technical know-how in the Finnish gaming industry, including its ability to develop games for multiple platforms, is considered world class. It is difficult to outsource its work to lower-cost countries, which typically lack the high level of technical expertise required. According to Neogames, a non-profit organisation representing the Finnish gaming industry, the industry has grown quickly over the past 3 years, with an estimated turnover of 800 million euros in 2013 and 2200 employees. Compound average growth between 2004 and 2013 was an estimated 39.5 %, significantly higher than the global gaming market as a whole. Drawn by the success of companies such as Rovio, Remedy and Supercell, the total number of Finnish gaming businesses rose from around 20 a decade ago to over 180 by late 2013, many of them small to medium-sized companies, over 40 % of which were established in the past 2 years (Härmä, 2013; The Gaming Industry of Finland 2013).

Nestled Between Sweden and Russia, Finland's Climate and Geography Do Not Play to Its Strength

Bordering Norway, Russia and Sweden, in an extremely cold corner of northern Europe that endures several dark months each year, and a population of five million people, Finland's ability to attract and retain talent from abroad was more of a challenge than somewhere like Silicon Valley (Raunio, 2003). And being a more homogeneous society (approximately 93 % of

[1] http://www.polygon.com/2013/12/4/5174688/finnish-games-renaissance-is-the-result-of-a-lack-of-interest-in

the population is Finnish) than North America, immigrants struggled to learn the language and to integrate socially and to enter the labour market. Being a sparsely populated and relatively remote country meant that most technological innovation and economic activity was concentrated around the capital, adding to the cost of doing business and making it less competitive vis-à-vis emerging regions, particularly in the Baltic countries and Asia. The government has tried to remedy this situation by encouraging economic activities in the regions both through targeted programmes and by upgrading infrastructure. Its location on the northern periphery of Europe made travel to and from the country comparatively expensive.

Finland's reputation for innovation centred on one company, Nokia, the global telecommunications giant best known for its mobile telephones. While not denying the existence of other innovators—both Linux and MySQL technologies were made in Finland—all the indicators pointed to its larger established firms whenever the country's strengths were analysed. For example, on the World Economic Forum's (WEF) 'innovation pillar', Finland ranked first in terms of availability of scientists and engineers, second in terms of university–industry collaboration in research and development (R&D) and capacity for innovation and third in terms of company spending on R&D and patents—all indicators with particular relevance for large-scale technology and engineering companies.

The lack of so-called angel investors in early start-ups in the Espoo/ Helsinki region was detrimental to the emergence of a local start-up scene, making the region less competitive in terms of accessing high-calibre investors. Moreover, most government funding was directed towards research and innovation that focused upon the early stages of the R&D cycle and had spin-off benefits for other companies, in line with national development priorities. Consequently, government contracts restricted the funding available to R&D activity which solely benefitted a single entity. The combined effect was to make access to funding difficult for smaller companies. Even government initiatives aimed at leveraging private-sector capital through co-funding arrangements required private equity contributions to match government loans (provided at favourable rates), again skewing the advantage in favour of larger firms that could afford to participate.

The Finnish model bore little resemblance to the better-known high-tech incubator Silicon Valley. Historically, Finland's start-ups had to overcome significant barriers in the form of high tax rates and restrictive labour and other regulations and comparatively scarce early-stage funding, none of which were typically an issue in North America. For decades, Finland had copied the Swedish model of innovation that revolved around supporting the competitiveness of large firms such as Nokia and Kone, particularly in global markets. As in Sweden, a handful of multinationals dominated private R&D spending, the hiring of talent and the relationship with the broader national innovation system. This ostensibly Nordic approach reflected a wider socioeconomic ethos which underpinned the social contract between unions, business associations and government. Wages, subsidies and taxes were agreed upon through collective bargaining and consensus.

While this provided a cushion against uncertainty and a sense of security against profiteers and free-riders, there was little if any support for start-up entrepreneurs. The Nordic system of collective bargaining failed to recognise their importance as a 'fourth' economic force or to acknowledge their growth needs. It was fundamentally non-conducive to start-ups. Not surprisingly, Finnish companies had a strong track record for generating knowledge capital and IP but often struggled to commercialise their innovations.

A number of other factors emerged as problematic. First, the welfare system, including the provision of free education all the way to the tertiary level, necessitated high levels of taxation. Government subsidies were largely designed to ensure regional equity rather than competition. Rules and regulations governing welfare services (e.g. unemployment benefit) were designed with workers rather than entrepreneurs in mind; there was more incentive to be a worker than an entrepreneur. This was particularly apparent during periods of economic growth, when large firms like Nokia and Siemens were doing very well and providing safe and interesting careers for Finland's graduates.

How Did Rovio Do It?

Rovio was initially called Relude when it was founded in 2003 in Finland by students Niklas Hed, Jarno Väkeväinen and Kim Dikert from the Helsinki University of Technology (now Aalto University School of Science), after winning a competition sponsored by Hewlett-Packard and Nokia for designing multiplayer mobile games (Ratna 2012). As a result of this, Hewlett-Packard executive Peter Vesterbacka—later to become Rovio's CMO—suggested the trio start a company focused on mobile game development.

The company thus began developing a range of electronic games targeting mobile phone holders. The ubiquity of mobile telephony in Finland at the time—with Nokia having the largest share (almost 40 %) of the global mobile phone market and Finland one of the highest rates of mobile phone penetration—likely influenced the founders' decision to enter the market for mobile game applications. The company changed its name in 2005 from Relude to Rovio (Finnish for bonfire).

Over the first 6 years of operation, the Rovio team developed a portfolio of 51 game titles but struggled to remain financially viable. Mikael Hed, current CEO and cousin of co-founder Niklas Hed, explained that the mid-2000s was a difficult time for small to medium-sized game developers. Mobile operators controlled the market. Each had only one or two people in charge of content, typically looking for developers with a proven track record and a line of games under development. Developers had to build games that were compatible with a number of different platforms and handsets. Without the centralised app stores of today, they had to employ sales teams to meet with operators around the globe. And it was the operators that took the lion's share of revenues generated. In these tough conditions and struggling for the attention of operators, Rovio resorted to taking on subcontracting work to survive while producing games of its own.

During this period, one of Rovio's senior game designers, Jaakko Iisalo, was working on a number of ideas for iPhone games, one of which featured artwork for bird characters with large eyebrows but no wings or legs. A musician and graphic artist from Helsinki, Iisalo had worked composing music in the demo scene before moving into game development. He was also a keen gamer and had been a Nintendo fan as a child, which he claimed influenced the relaxed, happy game play experience he tried to create when developing Angry Birds. The team at Rovio loved the humorous birds and, after researching the types of games people enjoyed playing at the time, decided to combine the characters with a simple physics-based puzzle game that Iisalo had been working on to form the basis of the game which was to become Angry Birds.

'When Angry Birds came out, we noticed that we got ranked highly in some countries and then rather rapidly started dropping off the top lists. But when we updated the apps with free content and levels, and we shot back to the top of the list in some countries almost immediately, we knew that that's what we needed to gradually repeat in other countries,' said Petri Järvilehto, head of Rovio's gaming division. On the basis of reactions to the early prototypes, the team knew there was something unique about the game. Being based on the laws of physics and gravity which impact daily life, it was intuitive and easy to learn.

Before long, everyone at Rovio was playing it. Following the release of Angry Birds in December 2009, the game grew in popularity. Initially it became the number one ranked game in the small Finnish market, then in Sweden, and from then on its popularity exploded to achieve number one ranking in the UK and the USA in 2010. Unlike most other successful mobile games, it held on to its number one position for 300 days.

Staying Afloat

With most of the company's resources directed to the design and fine-tuning of Angry Birds, Rovio needed additional sources of funding to complete development work on the project.[2] As might have been expected from the mainstream Nordic innovation system model (skewed in favour of large firms), its application to the Finnish government for funding was rejected. Instead, a Silicon Valley-style solution was found: KajHed, the CEO's father and Rovio's chairman and majority shareholder, mortgaged his parents' home to keep the company afloat. Because success was not guaranteed, this was risky—particularly given Rovio's limited previous success and the modest profits earned by developers of successful iPhone games at the time. There was clearly a lot at stake.

Had it not been for the CEO's father re-mortgaging his house, it might not have completed the R&D needed to produce the working prototypes which were used to attract VC firms. Accessing venture capi-

---

[2] http://www.youtube.com/watch?v=f0Lx4-3LPgw

tal (VC) at the later 'scaling-up' stage of growth did not seem to be a problem for Rovio once it had shown that it had a tangible product with serious growth potential.

At this point, the company managed to attract the interest of several VC firms from within the Nordic region and beyond because, by the end of 2010, Angry Birds had been downloaded 42 million times on mobile phones, of which 25 % were paid versions. With this success, the company started a round of investment with the assistance of Accel Partners and Atomico Ventures, raising US$42 million to expand Rovio's operations. Both venture capital companies were involved in technological entrepreneurship: Accel Partners were investors in companies such as Facebook, Groupon and AdMob, while the CEO and founder of Atomico Ventures was Niklas Zennström, founder of Skype. 'This investment will give Rovio wings', said Zennström at the time.[3]

Thus, an oft-cited barrier to innovation—lack of VC—was suddenly no longer an issue. Rovio's creativity and the calibre of the product were attracting the attention of venture capitalists from elsewhere. By 2011 it was receiving a steady stream of proposals and offers of funding from a range of potential partners. What was important was picking the right partners who it could work with collaboratively without losing its creative control.

Expanding the Brand

The company continued to grow with additional game titles and by leveraging the IP in the Angry Birds game. It released new versions of the game and expanded the Angry Birds brand to capture additional revenues from product merchandising, animated movies and entertainment parks. For the decade following its founding, Rovio succeeded against the odds, which were against them owing primarily to the remoteness of its headquarters in Finland—with its harsh climate and geography—and the dominance of Finnish telecommunications giant Nokia, whose demand for talent and resources had a negative impact on the start-up environment for years (Kerr et al., 2013). The company's success stands

---

[3] http://www.rovio.com/en/news/press-releases/63/42m-series-a-investment-in-rovio/

as a testament to how its founders were able to effectively match the locational advantages derived from their Finnish headquarters with the types of competitive advantage it needed most to succeed. At the same time, Rovio was able to develop strategies to overcome the challenges it encountered on the path to success in the global gaming and entertainment industries.

In what would later prove another pivotal and far-reaching decision, Rovio decided to 'create IP that could be the foundation of a big brand, an entertainment franchise', according to Petri Järvilehto, head of Rovio's gaming division. For Mikael Hed, who joined the company in early 2009, the decision was made to develop game IP in this way so that if and when the company had a hit game, it could be readily turned into something more lucrative. The plan was to build games on a successful smartphone application, then quickly expand to other platforms and devices, and enter licensing deals with manufacturers for physical goods and merchandise using that game brand. The aim was to establish a pipeline and distribution channel that could be reused for future games. As the company grew, it relocated from its original premises to the nearby city of Espoo in the greater Helsinki area, a short distance from Nokia's offices, where it could lure some of the talent fleeing the sinking ship.

Implementing earlier plans to use the IP for the Angry Birds iPhone game to launch other services and products, Rovio subsequently launched additional versions of the game which were compatible with other touch-screen smartphones, including those with Android operating systems. Versions for PC, Mac and Facebook were released. Rovio also collaborated with Hollywood studios to develop new versions, including Angry Birds Star Wars with Lucasfilm Ltd. and Angry Birds Rio with twentieth Century Fox.

The popularity of the out-to-kill cute birds provided great material to develop merchandising activities and allowed Rovio to franchise the universally recognised characters for a range of items, including toys, cups, keychains, clothing, books, soft drinks, candies and other collectables. 'With Angry Birds, we have successfully launched not only a strong new brand, but also a whole new entertainment franchise', claimed co-founder Niklas Hed. By 2011, sales of Angry Birds plush toys had exceeded two million units, while the game's virtual goods were also generating strong sales, with 40 % of new customers reported to have purchased extra downloadable content. At the time, Hed estimated that the total Angry Birds worldwide franchise had grown to around US$1 billion. In contrast to other companies that were mainly focused on 'going digital', he predicted that within a few years, Rovio's physical merchandising would represent around half of its total business.

Over-Expanding the Brand?

The company was also planning to expand into areas such as education and activity parks. In 2012, Rovio opened entertainment parks across Finland, Russia, the UK and the USA, with additional plans to expand into China, Malaysia and Spain. An Angry Birds Space Encounter at the Kennedy Space Center in Houston (USA) was designed to offer both entertainment and learning experiences in the STEM (science, technology, engineering and mathematics) fields, while Angry Birds activity parks and play parks (the latter free and open to the public) focused on family entertainment offering games and rides to visitors. Unable to take on giants such as Disney, Rovio's business model was to develop smaller-scale parks in city locations catering to local populations.

By 2013, Rovio had also released an animated Angry Birds cartoon series and was reported to be working on a movie. It was also developing the Angry Birds Playground learning concept in collaboration with several scientific and educational institutions, such as NASA, CERN, National Geographic and the University of Helsinki. Designed for both local and export markets, the concept was based on the highly respected Finnish National Curriculum for Kindergarten, with subject matter and skills presented in a playful and exciting way.

Going forward, Ville Heijari, Rovio's Senior Vice President of Brand Marketing, suggested that the biggest challenge facing Rovio was its ability to maintain its current momentum and levels of creativity while continuing to build the Angry Bird brand.

Speaking at an industry conference in 2012, Vesterbacka affirmed that the game had 'tens of millions' of active users and the company hoped to grow this to one billion, making Angry Birds a permanent part of popular culture. Not only was Rovio listening to customer feedback to improve its offerings, but it was also looking to established brands, such as Nintendo and Super Mario, to learn how to replicate their long-term success. With over 400 licensees worldwide generating around 50 % of the company's revenue, it could be argued that Rovio had successfully achieved its goal of turning a mobile game app into a successful merchandise franchise.

But questions remained as to whether the company was spreading itself too thin, whether it could continue to draw the talent needed to continue its extraordinary growth around the globe, and whether the public's fascination with the cute little birds might start to wane, especially if new characters were released to the market by competitors trying to rise up in the sector's pecking order.

These concerns turned out to have some weight behind them: soon after the company doubled its workforce in 2012 to meet its needs of expansion, profits fell dramatically, and by the end of 2014, Rovio announced job cuts and reorganisation, while still confirming the release of an Angry Birds animated movie as scheduled in 2016.

In January of 2015, the company announced plans to release a new brand: Storm Sisters, beginning with a book and then expanding into movies, games and other marketing.

Three Major Developments Aided Rovio's Early Years

1. **The creative destruction that followed the decline of Nokia, head-quartered in Espoo.** This resulted in an increased supply of experienced and high-calibre talent looking for work as a result of Nokia's retrenchment who Rovio was able to employ to accelerate its product development.

2. **Espoo's high-tech cluster and the strong support structure provided by Aalto University.** Aalto University's Espoo campus is home to its technology department, which, together with the university infrastructure, promotes R&D, innovation and entrepreneurship in the region. This afforded Rovio competitive advantages in cost, convenience, calibre and community.

3. **The advent of the iPhone and its digitised online platform for selling software applications directly to consumers.** This altered the

global landscape for high-tech gaming software companies. Given Finland's remote location, this innovation offered Rovio a means of overcoming the disadvantage of relying on physical distribution channels to access suppliers and consumer markets. The arrival of a stable, user-friendly global technology platform through the iPhone and the virtual AppStore overcame this otherwise significant geographical disadvantage. The destruction of the old system of selling game software through publishing companies significantly reduced the costs of distribution for Rovio and other mobile application developing firms, who could henceforth compete on an equal footing with the rest of the world. The ubiquitous nature of the creative sector, where goods and services can be developed and distributed around the world without a central physical point, allowed the Finnish mobile gaming industry to overcome the challenges of cost and convenience while leveraging the calibre and creativity of the local workforce.

How Did Rovio Do It?

The presence of Nokia in Espoo also shaped the landscape for tech start-ups. In the 1990s, for example, the advertising slogan 'Nokia: Connecting People' was re-worked in Finland to 'Nokia: Collecting People' with reference to its massive hiring drive in the country. It was Nokia's success that promoted mobile phone penetration among Finland's tech-savvy population, which mobile gaming companies such as Rovio then leveraged. While initially having a negative influence on the development of an entrepreneurial culture, Nokia's subsequent decline was responsible for the release of a supply of skilled talent onto the local labour market. A number of former employees started their own companies. While the company was infamous for paying modest salaries, many former staff cashed in their stockoptions, creating a considerable number of so-called Nokia millionaires, who subsequently became serial entrepreneurs and mentors in the start-up community in Espoo and Finland more generally. A high standard of education continues to be the backbone of the Finnish knowledge economy. The vast majority of Finnish start-ups have been spin-offs of Aalto University. Established on 1 January 2010, with the merger of Helsinki University of Technology, the Helsinki School of Economics, and the University of Art and Design Helsinki, Aalto University was designed to create a new type of higher education institution to promote R&D, innovation and entrepreneurship—a better fit for a newly emerging model of innovation.

Calibre

Like Silicon Valley's Palo Alto, Espoo has developed into the largest high-tech cluster in the Nordic countries and is home not only to Aalto University's technology departments, which offer world-class game development education programmes and research, but also research organisations, such as VTT Technical Research Centre, and a community of other high-tech companies, including Nokia, KONE and Tekla (The Gaming Industry of Finland 2013). The area consequently boasts a large population of technology students and professionals and a skilled talent pool for high-tech start-ups to draw upon. Espoo actively seeks to promote the development of its technology hub through economic and social policies. I therefore chose to nickname it 'Palo Espoo', with Aalto University at its heart. While the country's cost of living is relatively high, Finland's free education system indirectly fuelled the start-up boom since many students chose to combine study with work, with the advantage of cheap on-campus accommodation and free workspace in university-based incubators.

Nevertheless, the number of graduates with qualifications in game development is estimated to be in the vicinity of 150 students each year, well below the 400 additional workers required annually. This represents a potential threat to growth and highlights the need for an expansion of game development programmes in order to offset any future losses in place surplus associated with workforce calibre, cost and convenience. More recently, at the national level, economic development, education and innovation strategies have enabled a unique environment for high-tech start-ups to develop, whose key features include strong government investment in science and technology research, development and innovation, policies that support science-based entrepreneurship and growth and a legal and regulatory framework favourable to the establishment of companies.

Culture and Community

In an interview in mid-2013, Peter Vesterbacka said Finland's open culture and lack of hierarchy promoted networking, and collaboration had benefited Rovio and other start-ups, including newcomers to Helsinki. He claimed that it was relatively easy to reach out and contact people—even the Finnish Prime Minister and governor of the central bank were considered approachable and supportive. This sense of community solidarity is a direct result of the traditional Nordic model of consensus achieved through collective bargaining between business unions, workers and the government. Attributes of Nordic society—trust, transparency, openness and collaboration, which promote information sharing, knowledge exchange and boldness in shared visioning and action—contributed to a high-calibre workforce, institutions and the overall quality of life, and to the place surplus derived from the social capital and sense of community in this isolated location.

References

Härmä, A. 2013. The success factors of the Finnish mobile gaming industry: A strategic overview: Cases Rovio & Supercell. Bachelor's Thesis, International Business Degree programme, Turku University of Applied Sciences.

Kerr, R., R. Nanda, and A. Brownell. 2013. Entrepreneurial finance in Finland?, *Harvard Business School*, Case Study 9-813-068, Mar 2013.

Ratna, G. 2012. *'Angry Birds' Flying to China*. Bangalore, India: Amity Research Centers Headquarters. Case Study Reference no. 312-258-1.

Raunio, M. 2003. Should I stay or should I go? The images and realities of the foreign professionals in Finnish working and living environments, June 2003, http://www.uta.fi/jkk/sente/netlibrary/T_6_2003_Should_I_Stay.pdf

The Gaming Industry of Finland. 2013. Neogames, Nov 2013. http://www.neogames.fi/en/neogames-info/

7

Red Bull in Fuschl am See: A Special Place for Special People

Red Bull GmbH was founded in 1984 by Dietrich Mateschitz, who located the company's headquarters in the Austrian village of Fuschl am See just outside of Salzburg. Before launching the drink in Austria in 1987, Mateschitz spent a year developing the drink's formula to better suit the tastes of western consumers, including carbonating the drink; despite these changes, Red Bull remained an acquired taste.

Red Bull has five user categories: clubbers (an early adopter group who often used Red Bull as a mixer), students, truck drivers, business people and sports people. Essentially, the target market was people who were mentally or physically fatigued. Red Bull's official international advertising agency describes Red Bull's target market as being a 'state of mind' rather than a demographic per se, while the 'Red Bull Gives You Wings' slogan was designed to reflect the brand's personality as being 'cheeky, witty, self-ironic, unpredictable and unique'.

The company's success has also been accompanied by controversy. In the early days, rumours circulated that Red Bull was bad for your health, especially after several deaths following consumption of the drink leading to

© The Editor(s) (if applicable) and The Author(s) 2016
S. Mahroum, *Black Swan Start-ups*,
DOI 10.1057/978-1-137-57727-6_7

calls for the drink to be banned in several countries. Other rumours claimed that a key ingredient in Red Bull was derived from bull testicles. While the company commissioned scientific tests establishing the safety of the drink, Mateschitz believed the controversies generated interest in the drink and even established a page on its Website where people could discuss their concerns.

Red Bull has also faced criticism regarding its promotion of extreme sports with questions arising as to the ethics of the company, which many have claimed encourages young people to partake in thrill-seeking and dangerous sports. At least six fatalities are reported to have occurred during extreme sporting events designed to promote Red Bull and while filming footage for Red Bull videos and movies. Red Bull's emphasis on dangerous sports has thus worked as a double-edged strategy which has generated both considerable attention for the brand but also significant concerns regarding the ethics of the company and has in turn resulted in negative backlash. Nevertheless, Red Bull is one of the five most important companies operating in the region, along with Porsche Holding GmbH, SPAR Österreichische Warenhandels-AG, dm-drogerie markt GmbH and Alpine Bau GmbH.

By 2013, the company estimated it had sold over five billion cans across the globe in a single year. This represented growth of 3.1 % over the previous year, while sales revenue grew by 2.2 % over the same period to 5 billion euros (US$6.9 billion). By 2014, Red Bull was ranked the most valuable brand in Austria, one of only two Austrian brands to be included in the top 500 global brands, and was ranked 203rd globally, with an estimated brand value of US$6.2 billion. It remained in first position in the global energy drink market in 2012 with an estimated 21.4 %market share. In terms of the overall soft drink market, Red Bull ranked 7th with 1.6 % of the global market.

What Is So Special About Austria?

A central European country with a population of around 8.2 million people, Austria is blessed by the quality of its natural assets, such as its pristine alpine regions, picturesque lakes and an abundant supply of fresh spring water. In 2013, the World Economic Forum's (WEF) Travel & Tourism

Competitiveness Report ranked Austria a global leader in terms of the quality of its natural environment. Red Bull has leveraged these natural assets over the years by claiming the quality of the fresh alpine water sourced from springs near its production sites in Austria and Switzerland is critical to ensuring the quality of the Red Bull product.

Red Bull is headquartered in the Salzburg region, which accounts for an estimated 7.3 % of Austrian GDP. The regional economy, concentrated in urbanised areas, is known for its automobile companies, transport and logistics, tourism, and arts and culture. However, the region's southern area has a strong rural and alpine character. The region's population of 531,898 (January 2013) enjoys a per capita income above both the Austrian and EU-27 averages, and unemployment is relatively low. Over recent decades the Austrian economy has transitioned from one dominated by the manufacturing, mining and utilities sectors to one based largely on the services sector. Most of the regional labour force is employed in the services sector (71 %).

The attractiveness of Austria's group taxation laws has improved for companies headquartered in Austria, with new group taxation provisions allowing the consolidation of the taxable business results of all financially affiliated companies within a tax group without requiring an economic or organisational integration of group companies. This allows companies headquartered in Austria to benefit from group taxation that offsets the profits and losses of domestic group members and the losses of foreign subsidiaries within the tax group, thereby reducing the corporate income tax rate (ABA-Invest in Austria 2011). Austria has been ranked second in the world for its quality of life, while the capital of Vienna was ranked the most liveable city in the world by the Mercer Quality of Living Survey 2012. The Salzburg region also boasts a relatively high per capita income.

Beautiful But Not Entrepreneurial

However, Austria is not well known for entrepreneurship (despite being the home country of Joseph Schumpeter).[1] This reflects the Austrian

---

[1] An Austrian economist who coined the term *creative destruction*.

culture and stigma associated with business failure. Austria has also suffered from the lack of a 'circle' or lead community of successful entrepreneurs who could pay it forward by coaching and mentoring a new generation of entrepreneurs. It is perhaps not surprising, therefore, that available data do not rank Austria highly in terms of entrepreneurial activity. In 2013, Austria was ranked a relatively low 84th out of 142 countries for new business formation by the WEF, while the World Bank's Doing Business data (2012) ranked Austria 107th out of 132 countries for new business entry density (defined as the number of newly registered corporations per 1000 working-age people). The WEF Global Competitiveness Report 2013–2014 indicated that Austria ranked only 55th out of 148 countries for the availability of venture capital (VC), 97th for the number of days needed to start a business, 122nd in terms of its total tax rate, 115th for hiring and firing practices and 147th for the flexibility of wage determination (WEF 2013a). Meanwhile, the WEF Travel & Tourism Competitiveness Report 2013 ranked Austria 131rd out of 140 countries for price competitiveness and 58th for visa requirements (WEF 2013b).

Austria's stable employment and low unemployment rates, combined with the high levels of collaboration that emerged in post-war Austria and consequent formation of social partnerships, especially between the respective representatives of capital and labour (Schibany 1998), are also likely to have constrained the development of the entrepreneurial ecosystem in Austria. These relationships contributed to a culture of long-term time horizons in economic policymaking and in turn have led to more predictable economic policies, stabilised demand, prices and profit shares and in doing so contributed to reduced future risks and uncertainty for businesses operating in Austria (Aiginger 1994). This, in turn, reduces incentives for entrepreneurial risk-taking in a climate where job stability is high and people are not driven by necessity into start-up activity.

How Did *Red Bull* Do It?

From the beginning, Mateschitz identified extreme sports as providing a good fit with the energy drink that vitalises the body and mind, providing the company with a target audience that was seeking a clear and focused mind, improved physical performance and a fun and active lifestyle. At the same time this market was seen as being 'countercultural', which also fit the image the company was trying to promote. 'Our roots are firmly planted in outdoor, extreme, adventure and motor sports. By becoming a global brand you have to adapt your marketing and media strategy accordingly. This is why we now also play soccer in New York and race cars in NASCAR with our own teams and take full responsibility for the sport, results and performance. After 20 years the brand may have become a little more mainstream, but we still keep our individuality by staying true to our roots', said Mateschitz.

Mateschitz successfully capitalised on Austria's love of the outdoors and adrenaline-fuelled adventure sports such as skiing, snowboarding, mountain biking, paragliding and rock-climbing to market the Red Bull product. Most of the national Austrian sports champions were his personal friends with whom he spent much of his leisure time participating in adventure sports. In this way, Mateschitz was able to connect the concept for the Red Bull energy drink, promoted as a product which stimulates your mind and body and promotes athletic performance, with the active and healthy outdoor lifestyle he enjoyed within his community of friends in his home country of Austria. Mateschitz's close ties within the Austrian community therefore appear to have been instrumental in the early success of Red Bull and are likely to have contributed to his decision to headquarter the company in Austria rather than elsewhere. Mateschitz established an office at Red Bull's Hangar-7 building at Salzburg's airport, home to Red Bull's collection of historic airplanes and helicopters. This provided the founder, a trained pilot, with opportunities to indulge his passion for flying. Mateschitz made the decision to build the Red Bull brand by developing an anti-brand ideology that used extreme sports and counterculture as a driver of its business model and enabled it to reach a broad audience of consumers.

Having embedded the Red Bull brand in extreme sports, the company then began to target mainstream sporting events, including sponsoring F1 teams, football clubs (e.g. SV Austria Salzburg and the US MetroStars), and even a German hockey team. The space jump (or so-called stratos jump) in October 2012, gave the company enormous global exposure. Establishing Red Bull as a new category of drink was a deliberate decision by Mateschitz. In doing so he avoided competing directly with regular soft drinks. Packaging Red Bull in a small and streamlined can ensured the energy drink would stand out on the shelf as a different beverage category. Moreover, the decision to charge a significant premium for Red Bull, several times the price of a can of Coke, made a clear statement that this was not a soft drink. In an interview with Bloomberg, Mateschitz explained to journalists: 'If we'd only had a 15 % price premium, we'd merely be a premium brand among soft drinks, and not a different category altogether.'

But local laws classified the energy drink as a 'traditional food' and restricted the company from saying that the drink produced performance-enhancing benefits. Mateschitz responded by claiming that Red Bull contained characteristics of all three Austrian food and drug categories (i.e., traditional, dietary and pharmaceutical) and successfully lobbied the government to create a new category—'functional' foods. While this process required extensive documentation to support claims of Red Bull's health benefits, it also presented a significant barrier to entry that reportedly kept its competitors out of the market for 5 years.

Speaking with Forbes Magazine in 2005, Mateschitz indicated that Red Bull also required the approval of the ministries of health in the majority of European countries because some of its ingredients had not been previously used in existing products. In 1987, the Austrian health ministry was the first to give Red Bull the green light, and it was rolled out across Austria. Since approval was granted in other locations, Red Bull was launched in other European markets, starting with Hungary, Slovenia and the UK., Denmark, Norway and France, however, claimed that Red Bull violated their food regulations owing to concerns with the drink's high levels of caffeine and taurine and consequently blocked its release for a number of years (Lobo 2013; Patnaik 2006). Mateschitz responded to negative health claims by building the Red Bull brand around stamina and linking it to the mental and physical resilience of extreme sports. In line with this, Mateschitz asserts Red Bull was never only a drink but always a lifestyle brand.

Marketing Miracles

Much of Red Bull's success can be attributed to the company's innovative marketing strategy. Mateschitz has been described as a 'sports entrepreneur' who has successfully exploited available opportunities by utilising innovative marketing strategies. When first launched in 1987, the Red Bull company (Red Bull GmbH) was responsible for creating the market for energy drinks, a new product category in the global beverage market. Despite encountering some initial hurdles, the company grew rapidly, and by 2013, it estimated that around 40 billion cans of Red Bull had been consumed globally. By 2013 the company was in 166 countries and achieved global revenues of around 5 billion euros. By 2013, Forbes Magazine claimed the company's Austrian co-founder and CEO, Deitrich Mateschitz, was the richest person in Austria, while his Thai co-founder, and silent partner, Chaleo Yoovidhya was listed as the third richest person in Thailand before his death in 2012 (Dolan 2012; Pangarkar and Agarwal 2013).

In avoiding mainstream advertising and adopting non-traditional marketing strategies, thereby avoiding expensive mass-market advertising campaigns, Red Bull has targeted specific groups of consumers, mostly young sports enthusiasts, through the creation and staging of promotional events where talented athletes demonstrate their skills. Examples include the Red Bull X-Fighters and Red Bull Air Race. In this connection, Red Bull has focused on hosting local sporting events, which are relatively inexpensive to run but still make a big impact and create media interest. This type of sports sponsorship has helped the company to both define the brand and develop brand loyalty. Since its early days the company has also hosted 'Flugtags' (Flying Days)—where people compete in home-made flying machines to fly the furthest over water—a series of events that aligns with the brand's humorous and light-hearted side.

The company has also relied heavily on 'word-of-mouth' marketing, based on the notion that people who experience the drink and appreciate its qualities then become advocates of the brand, introduce it to new consumers and create a ripple effect. Hence, product placement and giving away samples at local sporting events, trendy bars and clubs, and parties have been an important part of the Red Bull marketing strategy. In entering new markets the company has also restricted the supply of Red Bull and employed teams of 'consumer educators' to roam streets in Red Bull cars and give out free samples.

To appeal to a wide audience, Markus Obrist, marketing director with Red Bull, says that the company has also developed 'cultural links and sponsors recording studios, music festivals and even break dancing competitions. The brand has also broadened its appeal by targeting adult consumers who need an energy boost during the day—drivers, workers, sportspeople, etc'.[2] Running counter to Red Bull's typical marketing strategy, this has included a series of television advertisements using cartoons. And as Red Bull's first generation of consumers has grown older, the company has also diversified its product range in a bid to remain engaged with its aging customer base. This has included the launching of new drinks, such as Carpe Diem—based on fermented tea—and a 'functional' soft drink but released under a different banner from Red Bull.[3] In the face of increasing competition from rival brands, in 2013 Red Bull also released three new flavours of the energy drink.

Aggressive marketing fuelled sales of one million cans of Red Bull in the first year of operation but resulted in an overall operating loss of US$1 million. To meet the fledgling company's funding requirements, 90 %of this initial loss was financed from the partners' initial capital and the remaining 10 % through a bank loan guaranteed by a friend. Red Bull is reported to have self-funded most of its expansion through internal profits rather than by issuing shares or raising debt, with little profit reported to have been taken out of the company during its first 15 years of operations. This funding strategy has reportedly enabled Red Bull to preserve its unique marketing strategies and resist external pressures to change.

---

[2] http://www.thedrinksbusiness.com/2013/04/red-bull-energy-to-spare/
[3] http://www.carpediem.com/de/produkte

Powering the Globe

It took several years for the company to obtain approval from local authorities to distribute the drink elsewhere, and Red Bull used this time to establish the product and build brand identity in the Austrian market while also developing strategies for launching Red Bull across Europe. Starting in 1992, Red Bull was rolled out across Europe, first in Hungary, followed by, inter alia, the Netherlands, Switzerland, Germany and the UK in 1994, Eastern Europe in 1995, and then further abroad in countries including Australia, Brazil and China (Indira 2005). In 1997, Red Bull was released in what would become its most important market, the USA, with an initial focus on the western states of California, Oregon, Texas and Colorado.

When launching Red Bull into new markets Red Bull adopted a bottom-up approach to sales and marketing, whereby local representatives were given responsibility for product distribution and sales based on the assumption that local representatives were more in touch with the market and better positioned to spread the Red Bull name and image (Gorse et al. 2010). Demonstrating Red Bull's freewheeling culture, the company allowed individual country operations considerable freedom to pursue strategies they believed were most appropriate for their local markets. For example, Red Bull Canada placed a greater emphasis on the company's involvement in music and non-traditional arts than other countries, including running an exhibition gallery space.

Hence, Red Bull sought advantage by tapping into local knowledge and networks and in doing so has been able to capitalise on the unique characteristics and strengths of each location. But in entering the British market Red Bull was forced to use the term *stimulation drink*, because the term *energy drink* was owned by a pharmaceutical company. Red Bull UK launched new products such as Simply Cola and the herbal drink Carpe Diem. Moreover, early attempts to break into the local market targeted English pubs, a strategy that proved unsuccessful. After 2 years of losses, Mateschitz sacked the local marketing team, appointed an Austrian marketing director and re-launched its British campaign by adopting the tried and tested formula of selling the energy drink through night clubs and the student market.

Red Bull also sought market entry points in communities most closely aligned with its brand image. For example, David Rohdy, vice-president of marketing for Red Bull North America Inc., claimed that the company launched its US operations in Santa Monica, California, because of the openness of West Coast consumers to new consumer trends and its outdoor lifestyle.

Because the energy drink was launched internationally, the company experienced enormous growth and created a global market for energy drinks. And while a growing number of new competitors emerged on the market, including Monster Beverage Co. (e.g., Monster Energy), The Coca-Cola Co. (e.g., Burn) and PepsiCo (e.g., Sting), Red Bull continued to be the dominant player (Euromonitor 2013). However, despite its leading market position, Red Bull's international expansion has not always been easy.

The company encountered difficulties gaining traction in the Asia-Pacific market—its weakest region in terms of market share—owing to its premium price, a negative perception of extreme sports in some of the more conservative markets and competition from local energy drinks. TC Pharmaceutical, founded by the late Chaleo Yoovidhya, produces a non-carbonated version of Red Bull and is the market leader in this region. Red Bull's premium pricing and competition from other brands of energy drink also presented challenges as Red Bull tried to gain market share in other emerging markets, such as Latin America. While its production facilities continued to be maintained in Austria and Switzerland to provide access to supplies of natural spring water, in 2010 Red Bull was granted approval to build a production facility in Brazil, its first outside of Austria and Switzerland.

The company also looked for other similar locations around the world to tap into adventure sports and sell the performance-enhancing benefits of the energy drink to potential consumers attracted to an active, healthy and adrenaline-filled lifestyle. For example, in 1989, the company tapped AustriFormula One driver Gerhard Berger, who became the first motor sports athlete to be sponsored by Red Bull. In 1994, and as Red Bull expanded into markets outside of Austria, windsurfers Bjorn Dunkerbeck (Netherlands) and Robby Naish (USA) became the first international athletes to be sponsored by Red Bull.

Launching a Media Division

As part of the marketing strategy linking the Red Bull brand to extreme sports and engaging athletes to endorse the brand, the company followed the athletes it sponsored around the world to document their adventures. This resulted in the creation of a large body of video and media content. In an innovative strategy to capitalise on this content, the Red Bull Media House was launched in Salzburg in 2007, with a subsidiary company established in Los Angeles, California, in 2011. In 2011, Mateschitz claimed that this was 'our most important line extension so far. As a major content provider, it is our goal to communicate and distribute the "World of Red Bull" in all major media segments, from TV to print to new media to our music record label'.

Red Bull Media House describes itself as a 'multi-platform media company with a focus on sports, culture, and lifestyle'. It essentially acts as an umbrella brand to Red Bull by offering a range of media products and content across various media channels, including TV, mobile, digital, audio and print. Red Bull Media House also seeks partnerships with other companies, media outlets and affiliates in the areas of content distribution and licensing, brand partnerships and advertising.[4]

Both (companies) communicate 'The World of Red Bull'. Since the beginning it has been a brand philosophy and how to look upon the world, rather than pure marketing for consumer goods. In both areas we are talking about content distribution as a way to tell our consumers and friends what is new about our approximately 600 athletes worldwide, their achievements and next projects; another band launch or song hit from Red Bull Records; what is going on regarding nightlife, people, events, culture, Formula 1, etc. So it is both ways, the brand is supporting the sports and culture community, as well as the other way round. — Dietrich Mateschitz

Managing Director of Red Bull Media House Werner Brell contended that the media company was a natural progression for Red Bull

---

[4] http://www.redbullmediahouse.com/company.html

to leverage the media assets the company had been building over time. Brell explained: 'Everything we do pretty much pays back and powers the brand. The brand is why we do the things we do. We put life into the brand with all of the activities—whether they are sports activities or media activities.'

> Our roots are firmly planted in outdoor, extreme, adventure and motor sports. By becoming a global brand you have to adapt your marketing and media strategy accordingly…After 20 years the brand may have become a little more mainstream, but we still keep our individuality by staying true to our roots.
> — Dietrich Mateschitz

The popularity of the Austrian alpine region for outdoor and extreme sports meant that Red Bull could rub off some of the 'coolness' of that sporting community and extend it to its drinkers worldwide. This 'cool' community was more readily available in Austria than elsewhere and thus could serve as lead-users. Mateschitz found the niche and focused on it and in doing so managed to transplant that image of coolness to the brand. Austria is also home to other related industries, such as sports equipment companies, including Fischer, Blizzard Sport and Atomic Skis. What is remarkable is that Red Bull can now be seen as part of the larger sporting industry ecosystem.

Leveraging and Coping Strategies

Red Bull GmbH provides an example of a company that has succeeded on a global scale by adopting innovative marketing strategies to establish an international market for energy drinks and develop into a global extreme sports and counterculture brand. Its success stands as a testament to the importance of innovation and creativity in developing markets for new products and in doing so leveraging the competitive strengths of a location. While neither Austria as a whole nor the Salzburg region possessed a strong entrepreneurial culture or a high level of start-up activity, the location did afford Mateschitz access to the outdoor and active lifestyle he valued and to his social and professional networks. It also allowed him to tap into Austria's traditional manufacturing base of *mittlestand* located across regional areas. In addition to this, the European Commission (2012) reports that the Salzburg region performs relatively well in terms of marketing and organisational innovation, a competitive strength that aligns well with Red Bull's strategy.

Before expanding into international markets, Red Bull grew by building brand identity in its home market of Austria. It achieved this by leveraging the place surplus offered by Austria's natural environment, including its supply of fresh alpine water, the popularity of adventure sports and local community networks. Eschewing more traditional approaches to marketing which are popular with major soft drink companies, Mateschitz made the decision to build the Red Bull brand by developing an anti-brand ideology which used extreme sports and counterculture as a driver of its business model and enabled it to reach a broad audience of consumers.

As the company grew internationally, it was able to overcome locational deficits associated with being headquartered in a small Austrian town by adopting a bottom-up approach through decentralised sales and marketing teams at the local level (Chadwick et al. 2009). The company thus managed to tap into surpluses elsewhere and successfully establish strong brand awareness and loyalty across geographies and among consumers who were seeking to improve their physical or mental performance and were associated with extreme sports and counterculture.

Ultimately, the success of companies like Red Bull in places which are often not associated with start-up success seems to be largely the result of a good match between place surplus and a firm's desired competitive advantage. Therefore, it could be argued that the comparative advantage of a location is achieved only through a strategy which seeks to leverage that surplus. Thus, the quest for the next big success should involve a search for a good match between place surplus and strategy.

References

ABA-Invest in Austria. 2011. Austria: Headquarters location in the heart of Europe. ABA-Invest in Austria, 2010. http://investinaustria.at/uploads/ABA_Headquarters_Location_Austria_03_2011_11382_EN.pdf

Aiginger, K. 1994. Potential lessons from Austria for the restructuring process in eastern Europe. In *Eastern Europe in crisis and the way out*, ed. C.T. Saunders. London: Macmillan.

Chadwick, S., S. Gorse, and N. Burton. 2009. Entrepreneurship in Sport: How Dietrich Mateschitz Built the Red Bull Brand in a Day. The Centre for the International Business of Sport Working Paper Series No. 11, Coventry University, 2009. http://www.coventry.ac.uk/Global/05%20Research%20section%20assets/Research/Centre%20for%20the%20international%20Business%20of%20Sport/Working%20paper%20series/CIBS%20WP11.pdf

Dolan, K. A. 2012. Thai Red Bull Billionaire Chaleo Yoovidhya Dies. *Forbes*. http://www.forbes.com/sites/kerryadolan/2012/03/17/thai-red-bull-billionaire-yoovidhya-dies/. Accessed 17 Mar 2012.

Euromonitor International. 2013. Passport: Red Bull GMBH in Soft Drinks (World). Euromonitor International, Apr 2013. http://www.euromonitor.com/medialibrary/PDF/RedBull-Company-Profile-SWOT-Analysis.pdf

European Commission. 2012. *Regional innovation scoreboard 2012*. Belgium: European Commission. http://ec.europa.eu/enterprise/policies/innovation/files/ris-2012_en.pdf.

European Commission. 2014. Regional innovation monitor plus. http://ec.europa.eu/enterprise/policies/innovation/policy/regionalinnovation/monitor/index.cfm?q=p.baseline&r=AT32

Gorse, S., S. Chadwick, and N. Burton. 2010. Entrepreneurship through sports marketing: A case analysis of Red Bull in sport. *Journal of Sponsorship* 3(4). August 2010.

Indira, A. 2005. Red Bull gives you wings. ICMR Centre for Management Research, 505-063-1, India.

Lobo, R. 2013. Marketing with wings: Dietrich Mateschitz and the art of branding. European CEO. http://www.europeanceo.com/home/featured/2013/10/marketing-with-wings-dietrich-mateschitz-and-the-art-of-branding/. Accessed 16 Oct 2013.

Pangarkar, N. and M. Agarwal. 2013. 'The wind behind Red Bull's wings', Forbes., http://www.forbes.com/sites/forbesasia/2013/06/24/the-wind-behind-red-bulls-wings/print/. 24 June 2013.

Patnaik, R. 2006. Red Bull: Changing flavours? Case Study, IBS CDC, 2006.

Schibany, A. 1998. Co-operative behaviour of innovative firms in Austria, focus group: Innovative firm networks. A study prepared for the OECD project of National Innovation Systems, 1990, http://www.oecd.org/sti/inno/2368867.pdf

WEF. 2013a. The global competitiveness report 2013–2014. *World Economic Forum.* http://www.weforum.org/reports/global-competitiveness-report-2013–2014

WEF. 2013b. The travel and tourism competitiveness report 2013. *World EconomicForum,*2013.http://www.weforum.org/reports/travel-tourism-competitiveness-report-2013

World Bank. 2013. Doing business 2014. http://www.doingbusiness.org/reports/global-reports/doing-business-2014

8

TomTom in Amsterdam, Clogs and Cheese, but Also Transport and Logistics

Since the establishment of the Dutch East India Company in the early 1600s, the Netherlands has been a hub of trade, logistics and commerce. Strategically located at the nexus between Scandinavia and the rest of Europe, the country has Europe's largest port, Rotterdam. It also boasts a sophisticated banking system with which to finance international trade and lays claim to the title 'home of the world's first central bank', which commenced operations in Amsterdam in 1609, and of the first ever stock exchange (Kerrie 2013). For trade to flourish, its relatively small population of 17 million (CIA 2015) has been compelled to learn other languages, especially English. These combined strengths afford significant benefits to companies operating from within its borders.

Further competitive advantage is derived from a highly developed information and communications technology (ICT) sector. The Netherlands is reported to be the most IT-intensive economy in Europe after the UK, with an ICT sector estimated to be worth 55 billion euros and to grow by 2.6 % per year until 2015. It purportedly has the largest number of

© The Editor(s) (if applicable) and The Author(s) 2016
S. Mahroum, *Black Swan Start-ups*,
DOI 10.1057/978-1-137-57727-6_8

ICT consultants, who collectively constitute an informal platform for the sharing of information and ideas and are thus conducive to the development of further ICT products and services.[1]

In terms of innovation and entrepreneurship, the Netherlands is classified in the 2010 Global Entrepreneurship Monitor (Kelley et al. 2011) as an 'innovation-driven economy', with increasing levels of entrepreneurial activity progressively replacing the traditionally conservative job culture. Nevertheless, its rate of product and business innovation is modest compared with other innovation-driven economies, which may explain why in 2009 the European Innovation Scoreboard (EIS) classified the Netherlands as an 'innovation follower' rather than 'innovation leader'. According to the report, while it was above average in terms of efficiency in transforming innovation inputs into outputs, it needed to improve innovation in its economy by

- Strengthening the capacity for innovation in the economy to improve productivity,
- Increasing output and excellence in higher education and research, and
- Creating more room for innovative entrepreneurs by reducing 'bottlenecks' and 'improving access to capital, especially for start-ups and fast-growing companies'.[2]

Recognising these challenges and the vital role of innovation in strengthening a country's competitive position, the Dutch government has implemented a more flexible and customised approach aimed at assisting entrepreneurs and attracting innovative companies. For example, in 2007 it introduced an Innovation Box, which granted tax concessions to companies engaged in innovation and entrepreneurship (van Eck and Schreuders 2011). It also supports R&D and innovation through an Innovative BMKB scheme that offers to guarantee 60 % of bank loans for innovative companies.

---

[1] iAmsterdam.com
[2] InnovationEU.org

However, according to Jeroen van Duffelen of the Amsterdam Center for Entrepreneurship's (ACE) Venture Lab, an incubator attached to the University of Amsterdam, most government aid has been directed towards scientific research in priority areas such as health care and clean energy rather than to creative or Web-based initiatives.[3]

For high-tech start-ups, the country presents an attractive location for doing business and engaging in technology innovation. With one of Europe's strongest ICT sectors, the Netherlands offers tech companies significant competitive advantages, or what Roger Bolton (Bolton 2002) refers to as place surplus.

Nevertheless, a number of challenges detract from the utility that start-ups otherwise derive. According to the World Economic Forum's Global Competitiveness Report 2012–2014, there is room for improvement in terms of access to finance, restrictive labour market regulations, ease of starting a business, output of higher education, the level of university–industry collaboration and the supply of engineers and scientists. All of these are needed to enhance the Netherlands' place surplus with corresponding advantages for 'technopreneurs' operating in the country.

The Genesis of TomTom

The genesis of TomTom in Amsterdam resembles that of many Silicon Valley start-ups. In the early 1990s, the Dutch distributor for the UK computer manufacturer Psion asked some university friends to help him develop software to enable Psion to sell hardware to the Dutch market (Vigreux 2007). This resulted in the formation of a company that would become TomTom, one of a number of European technology companies to emerge as a result of collaboration between university students in a landscape which had been traditionally dominated by multinationals. It suggests that in the early days they enjoyed a specific locational advantage (or place surplus) from their proximity to like-minded people with similar interests and backgrounds, which could be leveraged to develop a business idea. TomTom's founders—Peter-Frans Pauwels, Pieter Geelen,

---

[3] Based on an interview for this book.

Harold Goddijn and Corinne Vigreux—were graduates of the University of Amsterdam (except Vigreux), so it could be said that the company was a product of the Dutch university system.

Pauwels recalled how the company struggled in its first 5 years. Working with Goddijn, who was then CEO of the computer division of Psion, the company formed a 'kind of joint venture to develop new software applications for the Psion accessories' (Turpin 2008). Building on the flow of new technology available in the early 1990s, TomTom focused on developing software for portable computers such as personal digital assistants (PDAs) and palmtops, as well as delivering software to businesses such as barcode and meter readers. Originally called 'Palmtop' (after the device of the same name), the company subsequently shifted its focus to the development of consumer software for PDAs in domains such as personal finance, dictionaries and games.

By 1998, thanks to the creation of applications such as Citymaps and EnRoute (later renamed Route Planner), TomTom had established itself as a market leader in this field. But despite its success, TomTom was 'bleeding to death' by the late 1990s and had to close its London office, firing a third of its employees and relocating the remainder to Amsterdam (Turpin 2008).

The Dutch government had started rolling out initiatives aimed at making the Netherlands more conducive to entrepreneurship and innovation. This included streamlining regulatory and administrative processes and introducing a Technopartner programme to promote high-tech entrepreneurship and support promising tech companies. As a result, interest in investing in technology start-ups grew, and working for promising young companies like TomTom became a more attractive option.

A Strategic Pivot

The early 2000s marked a major turning point for TomTom. Goddijn, who had been involved in founding the company, joined TomTom in 2001 as a fourth full partner. In 2002, recognising the opportunity presented by President Clinton's decision to declassify high-quality Global Positioning System (GPS) data—allowing civilian and commercial uses of GPS services—TomTom launched its first fully functioning in-car navigation system for PDAs, TomTom Navigator (Downes and Nunes 2013). This coincided with the arrival of PDAs with sufficient processing power to enable the use of navigation services. Initially sold as an add-on application for third-party PDAs, the TomTom Navigator could be purchased at a much lower price than was previously available for factory-fitted systems. This coincided with a growing demand for affordable, easy-to-use portable in-car navigation systems.

Launched in the Netherlands in 2002, TomTom Navigator was then rolled out in France, Germany and the UK. Key to the company's success was its ability to gain access to major retailers in Europe such as FNAC in France and Dixons in the UK. As a Dutch company, TomTom enjoyed few trade restrictions in Europe owing to the Netherlands' membership in the European Union (EU) (Samushonga 2011). By late 2002, it had entered the US market, establishing a sales and marketing office in Massachusetts (Turpin 2008).

In what Corinne Vigreux described as a 'eureka moment' (Karlsson 2013), TomTom invested in research and development (R&D) to develop software that would operate on its own hardware as well as third-party hardware platforms and operating systems.

With the launch, in 2004, of the TomTom Go, the company 'defined a new category of consumer electronics: the PND'. It was a user-friendly, all-in-one personal navigation device, and a far cry from existing hardware that comprised a cumbersome package of multiple units that needed to be connected.

Given the preference of Dutch venture capitalists to invest in later-stage companies with proven brands, Alexander Ribbink—who was appointed Chief Marketing Officer in 2003—was tasked with growing the TomTom brand among regional investors, particularly for proprietary navigation devices. Ribbink, a former executive at Mars, Inc. and Unilever NV, was also a graduate of the University of Amsterdam.

Thanks to TomTom Navigator, TomTom Go and TomTom Mobile (designed for smartphones), in 2004, the company experienced rapid growth in sales. Pauwels, co-founder and Chief Technology Officer, attributed the growth to TomTom's ability to reach customers through a well-developed distribution network (Turpin 2008). It had also kept developing navigation software for handheld devices, introducing the

Navigator 3 for Windows CE in March 2004. Expanding across Europe and North America, by 2005 it had sold 1.7 million PNDs, up from 250,000 in 2003.

Leveraging for Success

In May 2005, the company listed on the NYSE Euronext Amsterdam, accessing local equity markets to raise 125 million euros to fund further expansion and innovative R&D to maintain its leading edge.

Over the next few years, TomTom made several strategic investments and formed partnerships in businesses, products and technologies where it considered these complementary to its growth strategy. In August 2005, it expanded into fleet management services through the acquisition of the German telematics company Datafactory AG. In early 2006, it purchased Applied Generics, which specialised in the use of data from mobile networks for the advanced routing of vehicles. TomTom continued to expand rapidly in 2007, with revenue reaching 1.7 billion euros (TomTom 2007), securing 50 % of the European market and 30 % of the American market (Turpin 2011). Its expanding workforce was sourced from around 40 different countries to compete in international markets (Hoffman 2010).

The development of navigation devices had reached a point where they were cheap and small enough to be easily installed in a car. A GPS became the next gizmo that everyone wanted to own or gift, giving TomTom's sales an enormous boost. To further leverage the huge demand for PNDs, TomTom developed new and innovative features such as providing information about traffic and rerouting options (via a chargeable subscription service). This feature, developed before Google Maps, was designed to use the concentration of mobile phone signals to predict traffic jams in a specific location (The Economist 2007).

In 2008, the company made a strategic acquisition in purchasing the digital mapping company TeleAtlas, headquartered in the Netherlands. TeleAtlas was one of two leading providers of high-accuracy digital road-maps from which all navigation system vendors needed to source maps (the other was NAVTEQ in the USA) (Turpin 2008). TeleAtlas enabled

TomTom to speed up the release of new maps, increase accuracy, gain efficiencies in map production processing and deliver a superior customer experience. Above all, it enabled TomTom to provide global maps that could match the quality of new solutions such as Google Maps, given that TeleAtlas had previously worked with Google (Schonfeld 2008).

From an operational perspective, the company adopted a flexible and scalable business model whereby core activities—product design, software development, sales and marketing—were kept in-house, while non-core activities—hardware production, manufacturing logistics and distribution—were outsourced (TomTom 2007). For example, Taiwan became the hub from where relationships with contract manufacturers based in Asia were managed. In an effort to remain price competitive while maintaining profit margins, TomTom sought to reduce unit costs by re-engineering its products so that expensive components were replaced or eliminated.

Drawing on its strong technology base and centralised R&D resources, TomTom focused on developing friendly technical innovations to maintain its competitive advantage (Turpin 2008). Seeing customer involvement as particularly vital, it utilised several technologies and services to maintain customer loyalty, such as Oracle and RightNow services.[4] The RightNow-powered Web self-service system, for example, captured company and product knowledge and delivered it to customers when and how they needed it. This enabled TomTom to achieve high levels of customer satisfaction while containing contact centre costs. As a result, the company was able to handle an 800 % increase in operations with only a 100 % increase in e-mail and enquiry traffic (RightNow 2010).

Continuing Innovation

In 2008, TomTom responded to growing consumer demand for navigation systems across multiple platforms by launching its first connected products with bundled LIVE services offering traffic, local search and weather information. In 2009, the company entered the mass market for

---

[4] SpringSource, 'Case Study: TomTom Accelerates Development and Reserve Risk with Spring Roo'.

in-dash car navigation systems with the launch of its first fully integrated in-dash product with car manufacturer Renault. Similar agreements were made with Fiat, Toyota and Daimler (Karlsson 2013).

Subsequently it focused on developing innovations for its range of products and services, especially its LIVE services offering, forging a number of strategic partnerships and joint ventures. The launch in 2011 of the Nike SportWatch, powered by GPS supplied by TomTom, was one such initiative, which saw the company capture 25 % of the sports watch market within 18 months (Karlsson 2013). This was followed in 2012 by a partnership with Apple to produce an Apple Maps app, which, under a licensing agreement, was incorporated into all new iOS-based products (Steinglass 2012). While problems with Apple's iOS software negatively impacted sales of the Apple's Maps app, Vigreux reported that TomTom's smartphone app was one of the highest grossing in the App Store (Karlsson 2013).

Troubling Times for TomTom

Having seen impressive revenue growth since the move into navigation systems with TomTom Navigator in 2003, the company witnessed a decline in revenues from 2007 to 2012 of around 30 %. Sales were negatively affected by the fall in consumer confidence following the global financial crisis in 2008, which led to declining car sales and the associated demand for navigation systems. The need to constantly innovate was a challenge given the competition from new smartphones offering alternative navigation and location-based services—with apps often supplied free of charge. As consumers shifted away from PNDs and towards all-in-one devices (Downes and Nunes 2013), PND sales fell 10–15 % per year (Steinglass 2013b). Notwithstanding, during an interview in April 2013, Vigreux contended that PNDs remained popular as fit-for-purpose devices that provided the best-quality personal navigation services available on the market (Karlsson 2013).

Responding to changing consumer demands and competing technologies, TomTom shifted its strategic focus away from PNDs and towards software development and related services, concentrating on the sale of map data, built-in car satnav systems and business-to-business navigation services (Steinglass 2013a). Since 2008 it had maintained a comparably high level of R&D investment in order to develop innovative, high-quality and easy-to-use products and services—a strategy seen as critical to its future competitiveness. A milestone was reached in 2012, when over 50 % of group revenues were derived from non-PND sales. But this was not sufficient to offset the loss of market share due to the continuing decline in demand for PNDs, and group sales were still in decline in mid-2013. Positioning itself as the preferred supplier of location and navigation services, as well as focusing on business solutions for commercial fleet management—which recorded double-digit growth over 2012 (TomTom 2012)—it remained to be seen whether TomTom could restore revenue growth from non-PND sales and stem the decline in PND sales.

Despite prominent brand image and recognition, much would depend on its ability to keep pace with rapid changes in technology and shifting consumer preferences in a highly competitive market. Crucial to this was TomTom's capacity for sustainable innovation—to develop and commercialise innovative products and services which could compete in the marketplace. Returning to the spectacular growth of the mid-2000s would require disruptive new technologies which could change the competitive landscape, as with the introduction of the PND and, later, the smartphone. And could the place surplus derived from being headquartered in Amsterdam, and the ability to develop strategies to tap surpluses elsewhere, ensure its continued success?

Place Surplus in Amsterdam: An Emerging Innovation Hotspot?

Being in the Right Place to Succeed

Factors in the socioeconomic make-up of Amsterdam clearly played a role in the rise of TomTom. According to Bolton's (Bolton 2002) concept of place surplus, TomTom flourished because the city had a surplus of the resources and conditions needed to grow.

A particular location affords individuals or organisations utility, such as ICT infrastructure, supply of talent, transport linkages, formal and informal professional networks, advantageous taxation and regulatory frameworks and government policies. Utility can also include non-tradable assets such as clean air. Should the surplus and its corresponding utility diminish, Bolton argues, economic actors must make one of three decisions:

* **Exit** – because the combined tangible and intangible costs of staying are higher than any derived benefits;
* **Voice** – attempt to improve a deteriorating situation because the loss from exiting is perceived to be significant. 'People who get the greatest place surplus relative to the place they would move to if they exited will lose the most if they exit quickly' (Bolton).
* **Loyalty** – stay put for reasons linked to a sense of loyalty. This is determined by factors such as social capital and the presence of supportive community networks—the bonds between local actors who stick together despite adverse conditions. It represents a form of place surplus equivalent to the satisfaction derived from a location that would be lost on exit (an exit cost).

According to Bolton's concept, companies tend to succeed in places with surpluses that yield the type of utility that is most important to them. This is a function of the following comparative advantages:

* **Cost** of operating is significantly lower than elsewhere.
* **Convenience** of operating is significantly easier than elsewhere.
* **Calibre** (quality) of personnel and other resources are more closely aligned to the needs of the business than elsewhere.
* **Creative destruction** of the social, political or economic structure by technological or other innovation frees up resources and creates opportunities for businesses.
* **Community** (social capital) solidarity gives support to members in need of resources.

The utility derived from these five Cs individually and collectively generates a perceived competitive advantage for players operating in that locale.

We can apply Bolton's framework to understand the environment that supported TomTom in its infancy and as it evolved as a market leader in the provision of GPS-enabled navigation systems, as well as the dynamics behind the decision of its founders to remain headquartered in Amsterdam despite some locational disadvantages. For the purpose of our analysis, our focus is on locational factors. Internal factors, such as strategy, leadership and business management skills, though important to the success of enterprises, are not considered in detail.

How High-Tech Start-ups Derive Place Surplus in Amsterdam

Like many European cities, the Dutch capital is home to a number of well-known multinationals (Philips, ING Group and Heineken). It is said to host the offices of 60 % of all Forbes 2000 companies active in the ICT industry, including Google, Microsoft, Cisco, LinkedIn and IBM.[5] However, Amsterdam is less well known for entrepreneurship or high-tech start-ups. Clearly there is a distinct place surplus advantage for multinationals' headquarters, but does it pertain to high-tech start-ups and what supports them as they grow?

Transportation and Logistics Hub and Proximity to Markets

As a leading transportation and logistics hub, Amsterdam is home to a large community of companies operating in these sectors. Since these companies require innovative solutions to remain competitive, there are opportunities for innovative firms to supply new technologies which can improve their efficiency and the bottomline.

These firms also derive a direct advantage from Amsterdam's proximity to the major markets of Europe, including Germany, France, the UK and the Scandinavian countries. Moreover, the convenience and calibre

---

[5] iAmsterdam.com

of its transportation infrastructure makes access to these markets easy and quick (van Oterloo 2013). The Netherlands boasts world-class infrastructure, including Rotterdam, Europe's largest port, Amsterdam's Schiphol Airport, Europe's third largest airport,[6] and a major cargo and passenger hub, and an extensive network of road, rail, waterways and pipelines. These are supported by leading logistics service providers which utilise the country's excellent ICT infrastructure to deliver optimal supply chain solutions, especially in time-critical areas such as food and flowers.

The country's inland navigation sector operates as an extension of the Dutch maritime transport sector and is considered Europe's largest and most innovative and differentiated fleet. In this respect, the government hopes that under the Smart Cargo Hub for Europe initiative, Amsterdam will become the fastest, most reliable multimodal hub in Europe. It is perhaps not surprising that the 2010 European Cities Monitor ranked Amsterdam the fourth best European city for external transport and fourth for ease of access to markets.

Benefitting from Amsterdam's ICT Infrastructure

Fast and reliable Internet connection bandwidths are of crucial importance to high-tech companies. Growth in Amsterdam's high-tech sector was promoted by the development of the city's Internet Exchange (AMS-IX),[7] an Internet hub which is the largest in Europe and one of the largest in the world. As a result, the city is well connected not only geographically but also digitally—a significant place surplus for tech companies located in Amsterdam.

According to Michiel Eielts, Managing Director of Equinix Netherlands (the Dutch arm of the US-based Equinix), a provider of large-scale, global data centres, the presence of AMS-IS has made Amsterdam an important hub for networks serving Europe. With an increasing number of multinational corporations selecting the Netherlands as their base for serving the European market, the region is becoming a strategic market for premium data centre and interconnection services.

---

[6] InvestInHolland.com
[7] https://www.ams-ix.net/about/strategy

An Emerging Tech Scene

Dubbed Silicon Canal, Amsterdam is emerging as a vibrant technology hub in Europe and is home to a growing number of mobile app developers and other high-tech start-ups, particularly in the creative and Web-based sectors (Holland Herald 2012; van Royen 2010). In terms of community and calibre, it provides a valuable place surplus for start-ups looking to get established in the city.

A report published in *Wired UK* in October 2013 rated Amsterdam one of the ten most important tech start-up hubs in Europe. It noted that in 2008, Australian software company Atlassian chose Amsterdam as its European operations hub, because of the city's convenience and strong tech community, and reported that start-ups also benefitted from its international and socially tolerant culture and liberal tax laws that make it attractive to international investors (Armstrong 2013).

Former Apple employee Mike Lee, founder of Appsterdam, a non-profit organisation that has established a collaborative knowledge network that runs monthly events where app developers can network and share ideas, was attracted by the city's cultural advantages, including being home to 'the happiest people on earth'.[8] He extols Amsterdam's ease of access to the rest of Europe, the calibre and supply of designers and creative talent and (compared to Silicon Valley) easier immigration laws (Byrne 2011). Appsterdam, originally conceived as a joint effort between Sofa (a local software company), the University of Amsterdam (looking to develop a programme similar to that of Stanford University) and the city council, is evidence of successful private- and public-sector collaboration in the city (Hardawar 2011).

The growing place surplus was also reflected in the decision of the founder of Freedom of Creation, a pioneering design company which specialises in 3D printing technologies, to relocate from Helsinki (where the company was originally established in 2000) to Amsterdam in 2006. Janne Kyttanen, a Finnish graduate of the Gerrit Rieveld Academy in Amsterdam, was drawn to the calibre of the city's creative design community, the strength of its ICT sector and the network of like-minded people

---

[8] iAmsterdam.com

with a similar educational background (van Gool 2013b).[9] Amsterdam is home to a growing 3D printing sector, with 3D start-ups reportedly inspired by success stories, including Freedom of Creation, Shapeways and Ultimaker (van Gool 2013b).

A Great Place to Live

High-tech start-ups in Amsterdam benefit from the city's cultural diversity, socially tolerant atmosphere, creativity and arts heritage. Its attractiveness as a place to live and do business is evident in the Mercer Quality of Living survey that ranked Amsterdam the 12th most liveable city in the world in 2012 (Mercer 2014).

Herman Hulst, Managing Director and co-founder of Guerrilla Games, an Amsterdam-based game development company, claims that as an employer he has found it easy to attract people from overseas owing to the quality of life in the city. It was the city's spirit of independent thinking (people are not scared to innovate) that originally enticed him and his co-founders to set up shop in Amsterdam in 2000. Other technology-oriented companies that have made Amsterdam their headquarters include Yourkarma, Layar and eBuddy.

Collaborative Networks and Paying It Forward

Contributing to the supportive community for technopreneur start-ups in Amsterdam are events promoting collaborative networks. These include the annual Unite event for developers and publishers working with the Unity 3D platform, the Got Game conference which brings together industry professionals with novices and students, and the yearly weekend and monthly Hackers and Founders events. Nevertheless, some industry commentators have complained that events tend to be sporadic and one-off and, as a result, limit opportunities for building relationships necessary for collaboration to occur (O'Connell 2013). And while shared work spaces and collaborative communities such as The Hub Amsterdam,

---

[9] http://en.wikipedia.org/wiki/User:Jannekyttanen

Living Labs project space and Rocketstart Spaces promote collaboration and integration, more could be done to facilitate the establishment of additional co-working spaces.

Greater collaboration between universities, tech companies and start-ups would also help develop a more interconnected professional community (O'Connell 2013)—and thus place surplus—by promoting entrepreneurship among the student population. However, the country's technical and design universities are based outside of Amsterdam, a factor that Dr Patries Boekholt, Managing Director of Amsterdam-based Technopolis Group, claims hinders efforts in this respect. Moreover, Jeroen van Duffelen, of the ACE Venture Lab, claims that Dutch culture lacks a spirit of giving back and openness. Despite a growing level of bottom-up community support which is helping to increase networking and mentoring opportunities, he laments the Dutch failure to 'pay it forward'—or giving back to the community which has supported them— and sees this as the chief deficit of the current scene and one of the most serious challenges facing start-ups and technopreneurs in Amsterdam.

Talent Surplus or Deficit?

Contributing to Amsterdam's place surplus is its wealth of creative talent, the calibre of its well-educated workforce (including a large proportion of scientists and engineers) and cosmopolitan and multilingual population (van Oterloo 2013). According to i-Amsterdam, an Internet portal to Amsterdam, the city boasts the highest density of knowledge workers in the country, with 44 % estimated to have higher education. It is also reported to be successful in drawing talented workers from other EU countries. Around 90 % of the city's workforce speaks two or more languages, and with approximately 80 % speaking English, Amsterdam is the largest Anglophone city in continental Europe. In 2012, Co. Exist ranked Amsterdam third (after Copenhagen and Stockholm) in its Top 10 Smartest Cities in Europe (Cohen 2012). Despite the calibre of the city's workforce, however, Jeroen van Duffelen claims that most quality graduates can readily obtain employment among the city's established companies.[10] Hence few graduates consider entrepreneurship an attractive option. Without good connections to the country's universities, start-ups often struggle to recruit quality graduates.

Nevertheless, start-ups may recruit talent from outside the Netherlands, aided by the attractiveness of Amsterdam as a place to live, as well as the opening in 2008 of the Expatcenter in Amsterdam, which offers accelerated procedures for arranging residency and municipal registration of highly skilled migrants and accompanying family members. Nevertheless, immigration policies and visa requirements continue to make it difficult to source talent from outside the EU. The high cost of work visas is prohibitive for all but the major companies.[11]

A Venture Capital Deficit

Dutch venture capitalists, like many of their European counterparts, typically show a preference for investing in later-stage start-ups with proven track records. A lack of big success stories has hindered confidence and growth in the Dutch venture capital (VC) market, according to Jeroen van Duffelen. While there are a growing number of small-scale VC investors, funding remains limited and follow-through finance is lacking. Meanwhile, seed investment by the government is typically directed towards sectors such as health care and clean energy rather than ICT companies, prompting many high-tech start-ups to look overseas for funding and others to relocate to places more conducive in this respect (van Gool 2013a). For example, according to a *Wired* report on European start-up hubs, the Dutch enterprise application platform Mendix was founded in Amsterdam in 2005 but subsequently relocated to Boston in 2008, where it raised US$13 million in Series A funding (Armstrong 2013). Wercker—a Dutch start-up that has been successful in fund-raising in both Amsterdam and Silicon Valley—claimed that the US investors were better able to look at the longer-term, big picture, while European investors were more focused on short-term gains.

---

[10] Based on interview with INSEAD.
[11] Based on interview with Dr Patries Boekholt, Managing Director, Technopolis Group.

The company has relocated its operations to Silicon Valley while retaining its development team in Amsterdam, thereby leveraging the place surplus in each location (van Oterloo 2013).

Overall, Amsterdam's place surplus for high-tech start-ups is primarily in terms of community, calibre and convenience thanks to its position as a key transportation and logistics hub in Europe, ICT infrastructure, quality of life, creative culture, global outlook, technical IT talent pool and nascent tech scene. But it must also develop strategies to mitigate the deficits of the location: a lack of entrepreneurial culture amongst university graduates who traditionally gravitate towards established companies, a shortage of early-stage VC, an absence of technology universities in the city and a relative paucity of collaborative networks and mentoring opportunities.

How Did TomTom Derive Place Surplus in Amsterdam? Coping and Leveraging Strategies

Analysing TomTom's extraordinary success following the launch of its navigation systems and PNDs raises questions about the competitive advantage the company has derived from being headquartered in Amsterdam. Has it provided TomTom with an environment conducive to growth in the high-tech sector both during its start-up phase and as it has evolved over time? And how has being headquartered in Amsterdam affected TomTom's more recent efforts to reposition itself through investment in R&D to develop new product and service solutions?

It could be argued that the driving force behind TomTom's evolution as a leading provider of navigation- and location-based products and services has been its ability to leverage the business community, which derives most value from its innovations, namely transport and logistics. This, combined with the city's impressive ICT infrastructure, has provided significant advantages, firstly as a software developer for portable computers and PDAs and secondly as a provider of navigation systems. Indeed, the strength of the Netherlands as a strategic European transportation and logistics hub has provided an environment highly receptive to new technologies offering innovative solutions which improve efficiency in these sectors.

Accordingly, TomTom's more recent venture into fleet management services, a sector which is growing strongly and in which TomTom is a lead player,[12] has also provided a logical extension for the company's service offerings. For example, TomTom's WEBFLEET app takes data directly from vehicles to measure their fuel efficiency and carbon footprint in order to reduce both financial and environmental costs.[13] In this way, the company has managed to successfully wed Amsterdam's place surpluses in both ICT and transport infrastructure.

Indeed the Netherlands' relatively tech-savvy, well-educated and prosperous population presented TomTom with a convenient opportunity in 2003 to experiment with selling its dedicated navigation devices on a small scale. Despite the country's relatively small size, the market generated more than eight million euros in sales.

TomTom has also been able to attract highly skilled talent not only from the local market but from neighbouring countries as well, aided by the EU's open migration policy, which enabled it to keep pace with demand and grow from 30 to 3500 employees in less than a decade.

It could be argued that the original decision by the founders to establish the company in Amsterdam in the early 1990s was the result of a combination of convenience and community advantages as three of them were part of a network of graduates from the University of Amsterdam. These networks—including the founders' connections with the Dutch distributor for Psion—played an important role in gaining access to major European retailers when TomTom Navigator was first launched in 2002. They provided a sense of place loyalty, which helps to explain why TomTom has remained headquartered in Amsterdam despite its growth in international markets.

As a fledgling start-up, TomTom had difficulties accessing VC because Dutch venture capitalists tended to invest in more established companies. It was, however, able to leverage its network of university alumni to form a joint venture with the UK-based Psion, where Harold Goddjin was working at the time, to undertake software development, which partially addressed its early-stage funding needs (Turpin 2008).

---

[12] http://finance.yahoo.com/news/research-markets-global-fleet-management-180000620.html
[13] http://business.tomtom.com/en_gb/products/webfleet/highlights/

As the company expanded and established the brand, it was able to access the Dutch equity market to raise capital for a number of strategic acquisitions, the most important being the purchase of TeleAtlas, one of the two leading suppliers of digital mapping data on which sellers of navigation systems depend. TeleAtlas also happened to be headquartered in Amsterdam, furthering TomTom's connectedness to the city.

While Amsterdam provided TomTom with convenient access to many creative and talented people with technical skills, by establishing sales offices and logistics operations in key markets such as the USA and outsourcing its manufacturing operations to Asia, TomTom was also able to tap into surpluses in other locations.

It is unclear how successful TomTom will be going forward in terms of its ability to innovate and commercialise new products and services and re-create the kind of disruptive change to the market which underpinned its explosive growth when it first introduced navigation systems and PNDs. TomTom can be expected to continue to derive place surplus from its proximity to Amsterdam's transport and logistics community, as well as from the calibre of the city's technology base and skilled workforce. Thanks to the networks it has developed, its customers' loyalty is assured, particularly if it continues to leverage its international networks and form new alliances through which to launch products such as the Nike SportWatch and the Apple Maps app.

In Conclusion

The success of companies like TomTom, Rovio, Skype, SoundCloud and others in places which are often not associated with start-up success seems to be largely the result of a good match between place surplus and a firm's desired competitive advantage. Therefore, it can be argued that the comparative advantage of a location is achieved only through a strategy which seeks to leverage that surplus. Thus, the quest for the next big success should involve the search for a good match between place surplus and strategy. At the same time, TomTom has successfully developed strategies to overcome place deficits by effectively tapping into surpluses elsewhere.

In an observation relevant to locational decision-making, Peter van Meersbergen, Managing Partner of Investormatch, a Dutch investment platform, contends that companies have a better chance of raising funds in locations which specialise in the same sector as their operations. For example, start-ups in the transport, design or agricultural sectors have more success raising VC in the Netherlands, while ICT start-ups are more likely to be successful in Silicon Valley (Saberi 2013). It could be argued that Dutch investors are more familiar with the transportation sector and perceive it as offering relatively lower risk investment opportunities than the technology sector. Hence, place matters, but companies can mitigate place deficit by adopting strategies that tap into the surpluses of other places or exit.

Despite the challenges confronting high-tech start-ups in Amsterdam, the emergence of a tech scene—evidenced by a growing number of successful high-tech start-ups such as Guerrilla Games, eBuddy and Layar—indicates how a confluence of technology, creativity, talent and location has provided place surplus in a city better known for its multinationals. However, start-ups unable to develop effective strategies to overcome deficits, such as a lack of VC, or which perceive the place surplus to be greater elsewhere, such as Mendix and Wercker, are likely to exit. It is therefore critical that the government, higher education institutions and the business community work together to develop and implement policies that support the ongoing evolution of the city's nascent high-tech start-up landscape and contribute to the place surplus offered by Amsterdam.

References

Armstrong, S. 2013. Europe's hottest startup capitals: Amsterdam. Wired. co.uk, 1 Oct 2013. Sourced from: http://www.wired.co.uk/magazine/archive/2013/11/european-startups/amsterdam

Bolton, R. 2002. Place surplus, exit, voice, and loyalty. In *Regional policies and comparative advantage*, ed. Johansson Borje et al. Northampton, MA: Edward Elgar.

Byrne, C. 2011. Appsterdam: A haven for indie app makers?. Venture Beat, 27 June 2011. Sourced from: http://venturebeat.com/2011/06/27/appsterdam-a-haven-for-indie-developers/

CIA. 2015. The world factbook: Netherlands. At: https://www.cia.gov/library/publications/the-world-factbook/geos/nl.html. Accessed 9 Oct 2015.

Cohen, B. 2012. The top 10 smartest European cities. CoExist, 11 Nov 2012. Sourced from: http://www.fastcoexist.com/1680856/the-top-10-smartest-european-cities

Downes, L., and P. F. Nunes. 2013. The big idea: Big-bang disruption - A new kind of innovator can wipe out incumbents in a flash. *Harvard Business Review*, Mar 2013.

Hardawar, D. 2011. Say hello to Appsterdam: Developers aim to move the valley to Amsterdam. Venture Beat. 24 June 2011. Sourced from: http://venturebeat.com/2011/06/24/say-hello-to-appsterdam-developers-aim-to-move-the-valley-to-amsterdam/

Hoffman, A. N. 2010. TomTom: New competition everywhere!. Rotterdam chool of Management, Erasmus University and Bentley University. 310-104-1, 2011.

Holland Herald. 2012. Silicon canals. Holland Herald, 25 Oct 2012. Sourced from: http://holland-herald.com/2012/09/silicon-canals/

iAmsterdam.com. Why choose Amsterdam?. iAmsterdam.com. Sourced from: http://www.iamsterdam.com/en-GB/business/setting-up-your-business/Your-industry/ICT/Why-choose-Amsterdam

InvestInHolland.com. Why invest in Holland. Sourced at: https://startupjuncture.com/2013/03/08/four-reasons-to-move-your-startup-to-amsterdam-and-2-challenges/

InnovationEU. Innovation EU: The Netherlands. Vol. 1–1. Sourced from: http://innovationeu.org/news/innovation-eu-vol1-1/0101-netherlands.html

Janssen, R. T. A. and Niaba. n.d. Highlights: The Netherlands. nature.com. Sourced at: http://www.nature.com/naturejobs/science/articles/10.1038/nj0097

Karlsson, M. 2013. Corinne Vigreux, co-founder of navigation company TomTom. France24, 29 Apr 2013. Sourced at: http://www.france24.com/en/20130426-2013-04-27-2143-wb-en-business-interview

Kelley, D., N. Bosma., and J. E. Amoros. 2011. Global entrepreneurship monitor: 2010 global report. GEM Consortium. 2011. Sourced at: http://www.gemconsortium.org/report

Kerrie, F. 2013. *Innovation? It's in Amsterdam's DNA*. Amsterdam: FinchFactor.

Lee, M. n.d. Citytalk #28 Mike Lee, Mayor of Amsterdam. Sebastiaan Capel. Sourced from: http://sebastiaancapel.nl/Stadsgesprekken/post/citytalk_28_mike_lee_mayor_of_appsterdam

Mercer. 2014. 2014 quality of living worldwide city rankings – mercer survey. Mercer, 19 Feb 2014. Sourced from: http://www.mercer.com/newsroom/2014-quality-of-living-survey.html

O'Connell, P. 2013. Amsterdam's startup manifesto. Medium.com, 11 Sept 2013. Sourced from: https://medium.com/@paulmoconnell/amsterdams-startup-manifesto-8656836beb94

RightNow. 2010. Case study: TomTom. RightNow.com. 2010. Sourced from: http://www.rightnow.com/files/casestudy/TomTom-Case-Study.pdf

Saberi, S. 2013. Good business ideas always get funded. Even in the Netherlands. Startup Juncture, 3 Apr 2013. Sourced from: https://startupjuncture.com/2013/04/03/good-business-ideas-always-get-funded-even-in-the-netherlands/

Samushonga, K. 2011. TomTom's initial public offering: Dud or nugget?. Switzerland: IMD Lausanne. 12.04.2011, IMD-1-0273.

Schonfeld, E. 2008. In a new deal with tele atlas. Google maps sends data back. The Washington Post: TechCrunch. 30 June 2008. Sourced from: http://www.washingtonpost.com/wp-dyn/content/article/2008/06/30/AR2008063000799.html

SpringSource. Case Study: TomTom accelerates development and reserve risk with spring roo. SpringSource. Sourced from: http://assets.spring.io/drupal/files/uploads/all/pdf_files/customer/S2_CaseStudy_TomTom.pdf

Steinglass, M. 2012. TomTom steers 'solid' course. *Financial Times*, 30 Oct 2012.

Steinglass, M. 2013a. TomTom off course after satnav demand dips. *Financial Times*, 12 Feb 2013.

Steinglass, M. 2013b. TomTom denies reports it is considering sale of consumer arm. *Financial Times*, 1 July 2013.

The Economist. 2007. GPS changes direction. The Economist: Tech View, 14 Dec 2007. Sourced from: http://www.economist.com/node/10309011

TomTom. 2007. TomTom annual report and accounts 2007. TomTom.com. Sourced from: http://ar2007.tomtom.com/pdf/tomtom_Ar07.pdf

TomTom. 2012. TomTom annual report 2012. TomTom.com. Sourced from: http://files.shareholder.com/downloads/TOMTOM/832973783x0x638911/86013D50-A248-483B-BDC2-7C8391123481/TomTom_Annual_Report_2012.pdf

Turpin, D. 2008. TomTom: Building & marketing a new business concept. Switzerland: IMD Lausanne. 10.04.2008, IMD-5-0735.

Turpin, D. 2011. Case study: Why TomTom is a map for mastering international markets. Business Spectator, 16 Mar 2011. Sourced from: http://www.businessspectator.com.au/article/2011/3/16/resources-and-energy/case-study-why-tomtom-map-mastering-international-markets

van Eck, K., and K. Schreuders. 2011. The Netherlands: The innovation box. Bird and Bird, 31 Jan 2011. Sourced at: http://www.twobirds.com/en/news/articles/2012/the-netherlands-the-innovation-box

van Gool, L. 2013a. Why Dutch startups are not Europe's hottest. Startup Juncture, 3 Sept 2013. Sourced from: https://startupjuncture.com/2013/09/03/are-dutch-startups-missing-in-this-euro-tech-scene-infographic/

van Gool, L. 2013b. Why 3D startups thrive so well in the Netherlands. Startup Juncture, 15 Oct 2013. Sourced from: https://startupjuncture.com/2013/10/15/why-3d-startups-thrive-so-well-in-the-netherlands/

van Oterloo, S. 2013. Four reasons to move your startup to Amsterdam (and 2 Challenges). Startup Juncture, 8 Mar 2013. Sourced at: https://startupjuncture.com/2013/03/08/four-reasons-to-move-your-startup-to-amsterdam-and-2-challenges/

van Royen, E. 2010. Guest post: Silicon canals and red lights: Amsterdam as a technology hub. TechCrunch, 30 Dec 2010. Sourced from: http://techcrunch.com/2010/12/30/silicon-canals-and-red-light-ruby-amsterdam-as-a-technology-hub/

Vigreux, C. 2007. TomTom – The movie!. TomTomJonJon, 8 May 2007. Sourced from: https://www.youtube.com/watch?v=x-Nk2IQ8hes

9

MAKTOOB in Amman: A Rose Between a Rock and a Hard Place

Maktoob launched the first Arabic-language Web site to offer an online e-mail service in 2000. At the time, the Web barely existed in the Arab world, and there were fewer than one million Arab-speaking Internet users. As the popularity of the Internet grew rapidly in the Middle East, Maktoob expanded to include messaging services, news, entertainment and other services tailored to the Arabic-speaking market.

The company's Jordanian founders, Samih Toukan and Hussam Khoury, initially adopted a cautious growth strategy before expanding rapidly, prompted by a burgeoning increase in Internet use, revealing the commercial possibilities of the Arabic-speaking market. Between 2000 and 2010, the number of Internet users in the Middle East and North Africa (MENA) region grew tenfold to more than 100 million users (Sweis 2012).

Maktoob had an estimated 16 million unique users[1] when it was acquired by Yahoo! in August 2009 for an estimated US$164 million—

---

[1] The term *unique user* refers to a unique IP address on incoming requests that a Web site receives. Hence, if a user visits a site one or more times during a measurement period, it is counted as one unique user. Source: http://www.pcmag.com/encyclopedia/term/53438/unique-visitors

© The Editor(s) (if applicable) and The Author(s) 2016
S. Mahroum, *Black Swan Start-ups*,
DOI 10.1057/978-1-137-57727-6_9

the first acquisition by an international media company of an Arab Web portal—creating a new division named Yahoo! Maktoob and inspiring a generation of technological entrepreneurs in the Arab region.

Aramex's Fadi Ghandoor, an original investor in Maktoob, contends that prior to the success of Maktoob few in the Middle East believed local high-tech companies could succeed (Rusli 2010). Yet despite the ongoing funding challenges encountered by start-ups and SMEs in the MENA region, Yahoo's purchase of Maktoob in 2009 has played a pivotal role in encouraging investments in online start-ups (Ghandour 2009; Sweis 2012).

Excluded from the Yahoo! deal were other areas of operations within the Maktoob group of companies, such as its e-commerce portal, Souq.com, online payment system, CashU, and Arabic search engine, Araby.com. These companies were retained by Toukan and Khoury within a newly established investment company, the Jabbar Internet Group. This company was established to focus on, among other things, e-commerce and online gaming, into which Toukan and Khoury invested proceeds from the Maktoob sale (Anzur 2010).

Jordan: Striving to Succeed

The Hashemite Kingdom of Jordan is considered the most evolved high-tech start-up hub in the MENA region. A report by the MENA Private Equity Association indicates that Jordan was ranked first in terms of the number of technology deals funded in the region and second in terms of the level of funding received (Wamda 2013).

However, Jordan presents many challenges for would-be entrepreneurs and those wishing to use the country as a base from which to launch a high-growth company. A poor nation lacking in natural resources and suffering from severe water scarcity and a harsh and arid climate, Jordan presents a tough physical environment for its inhabitants.

At the crossroads of several unstable and worn-torn countries, Jordan has been the recipient of a large number of refugees from Palestine, Kuwait, Iraq and Syria. This places enormous pressures on the country's limited resources (Mahroum et al. 2013). Not surprisingly, Jordan's position in a historically turbulent geopolitical region has created a difficult and some-times unstable business environment for would-be entrepreneurs.

Jordan faces many other pressing challenges, including the need to tackle large external and fiscal imbalances. These, in part, reflect the country's dependence on food and energy imports and remittances from its large diaspora living overseas, as well as the pressure on public finances resulting from the influx of refugees. Total government debt totaled more than three-fourths of gross domestic product (GDP) in 2011, while the country's current account deficit hovers near 20 % of GDP. These twin deficits illustrate the vulnerability of Jordan to external shocks (World Bank 2013).

Jordan has historically lacked a strong tradition of entrepreneurship stemming in a large part from cultural barriers to risk-taking and busi-ness failure (Mahroum et al. 2013). It was ranked a relatively low 73rd out of 121 countries by the Global Entrepreneurship and Development Institute Index in 2014 and was 70th out of 142 countries for new busi-ness density, according to the Global Innovation Index 2013.

The Brain Drain

Jordan has also suffered from a significant 'brain drain' as a result of its high level of unemployment, low salaries and better employment oppor-tunities elsewhere.[2] Unemployment is especially high among the coun-try's large youth population, with over 50 %of Jordanians aged 24 years or under out of work. High levels of economic activity and employment growth are necessary to absorb the estimated 60,000 new entrants join-ing Jordan's labour market each year (WEF 2013b). Unlike many of their neighbours in the richer Gulf States, Jordanians cannot rely on well-paid government jobs as a means of employment; rather, economic necessity requires that they seek employment opportunities elsewhere.

Many talented Jordanians relocate elsewhere in the region or internation-ally. As a result, Jordan has a large diaspora living abroad. This trend has been amplified by the tendency for university graduates to study overseas

---

[2] http://entrepreneurship.intel.com/problem/youth-unemployment-jordan

at the postgraduate level and subsequently find employment opportunities and settle in these countries (Mahroum et al. 2013). Of note, the WEF's Global Competitiveness Index (GCI) 2013–2014 ranked Jordan a relatively low 53rd out of 148 countries for its capacity to retain talent and 57th for its capacity to attract talent (WEF 2013a). Furthermore, a quality-of-life survey conducted by Mercer in 2012 ranked the capital Amman 124th out of 221 cities, indicating that lifestyle considerations are likely to detract from the desirability of Amman as a place of employment. These factors suggest that start-ups and high-growth companies located in Jordan may encounter difficulties sourcing skilled talent locally or attracting talent from elsewhere.

Education

Jordan is widely regarded within the MENA region as having a well-educated and highly literate population. Considerable attention has been focused on the development of Jordan's education system through reforms introduced in the 1990s aimed at improving the quality of the education system that historically focused on rote learning. Various initiatives have been introduced by King Abdullah II to improve the application of technology in the classroom, to develop skill sets that better meet the needs of the growing information and communications technology (ICT) sector and to provide the country's youth with the skills they need to develop Jordan as a knowledge-based economy more generally.

Deregulation of the telecommunications industry led to job creation in the ICT sector, which in turn encouraged students to enrol in ICT programmes. Universities such as the Princess Sumaya University of Technology responded by offering ICT courses and providing a supply of quality ICT talent that tech start-ups can leverage.

Nevertheless, concerns have been reported regarding levels of funding, academic standards and the quality of graduates (Mahroum et al. 2013). Importantly, and on a broader level, a lack of local talent has been cited as posing a challenge to founders of Arabic online start-ups, with schools and universities in the MENA region reportedly still failing to produce enough technically trained and independent-minded graduates (Sweis 2012).

Money Woes in the Early Days

The region continues to lack sufficient early-stage angel investors. Maktoob's Toukan claims that local angel investors require a better understanding of the need to invest in many companies while accepting that only a few will succeed (Anzur 2010). Otherwise, local investors prefer safe, tangible investments such as property and factories over high-risk start-ups; this in turn has led to several start-ups in Amman shutting down.

A report by the World Bank and the Union of Arab Banks found that loans to SMEs represented less than 8 % of total loans by MENA banks; in Jordan, loans to SMEs were slightly higher at just over 10 %. And while the study found that state banks partly compensated for the low level of involvement of private banks in SME finance, lending to SMEs in the region was noticeably lower than in OECD countries where bank lending to SMEs stood at close to 27 % of total bank loans (Rocha et al. 2011).

Arab Spring Impact

National security issues centring on the unrest of the Arab Spring have diverted government funds from investment in ICT starting in 2011. The country's ICT industry contracted in 2012, with year-on-year revenue growth reported to have declined by 16 %. Subsequent tax increases (including a 100 % increase in mobile phone taxes), a hike in electricity prices and new censorship laws are also reported to have negatively impacted the ICT industry.

In an unexpected positive twist, the unrest resulting from the Arab Spring was reported to have encouraged the growth of Internet start-ups. The Arab Spring gave people in the region a sense that they could reach goals they had previously thought to be unattainable, including establishing new companies. In discussing the growing interest in online start-ups, Omar Christidis, founder of ArabNet—an Internet news service for professionals and entrepreneurs—explained the situation: 'It's an alternative path for us to have an impact on economies and societies which is not tied to the government' (Sweis 2012). A further spin-off of the Arab Spring has been a relocation of high-tech start-ups to Jordan from Syria, with Oasis 500 actively recruiting technological entrepreneurs displaced by the war in their home country (Clark and Topol 2013). Jordan's connections within the region are also deepened through its large population of refugees who not only bring their skills to Jordan but also their connections and networks with their home countries.

Businesses operating in Jordan benefit from the country's relative political stability in a region plagued by sociopolitical unrest. This can be attributed largely to the strong leadership provided by Jordan's reigning monarch, His Majesty King Abdullah II, who succeeded to the throne in 1999. The king has also accelerated Jordan's economic liberalisation programme first started in the late 1980s. Jordan's accession to the World Trade Organisation in 2000 saw the introduction of economic reforms, the liberalisation of Jordan's service sectors and a reduction in tariffs on traded goods. Jordan's goods and services also gained improved access to foreign markets. New laws also allow foreigners to own 100 % of Jordanian companies.

Rasha Manna, Managing Director of Endeavor Jordan, claims that many start-ups build a track record in Jordan and then expand their businesses to Dubai and Saudi Arabia, countries characterized by superior infrastructure and accessibility to the Internet and providing consumers markets with higher disposable incomes. These factors highlight the challenging environment for businesses operating in Jordan which industry commentators contend causes some companies to consider leaving Jordan.

How They Did It

Maktoob's founders, Hussam Khoury and Samih Toukan, launched their first business, a start-up, Business Optimization Consultants (BOC), an Internet and technology consulting firm, in Jordan in the mid-1990s. The ecosystem for technology start-ups in Jordan was challenging at the time, recalls Khoury. 'The local authorities could not understand the concept and continuously needed clarification on the matter. On the financing side, there were no incubators, no accelerators, no funds looking at tech, no tech scene and definitely a wary and non-serious feeling towards the Internet, let alone making a living off it.'

During an interview with TechCrunch TV (Rusli 2010), Fadi Ghandour, founder and vice chairman of Aramex and executive chairman of Wamda Capital,[3] recounted his first meeting with Khoury and Toukan in the mid-1990s when they were employed by Andersen Consulting to work on a sales re-engineering project at Aramex. Both had experience studying and working overseas and, filled with ambition, approached Ghandour with the idea of establishing their own consulting firm. Khoury claims Ghandour was 'a visionary, a risk taker, a believer, a mentor and a dear friend'. Aramex was BOC's first client when it was hired to develop the Aramex Web site–the first ever Arabic-language corporate Web site.

Ghandour indicates that the start-up initially fell under the Aramex group of companies. However, when the decision was made to publicly list Aramex on NASDAQ in 1997, investment bankers did not consider BOC a good fit within Aramex's portfolio of companies. Consequently, Ghandour purchased Aramex's equity share in the not-yet-profitable start-up (Rusli 2010).

'Around 1999, Maktoob was launched as a small e-mail application under BOC', says Khoury. Recounting its genesis, he explains: 'As Maktoob grew it started to take up more and more time and resources. It became the only project internally that we focused on, and naturally BOC evolved into it.' Initial seed capital for the start-up came from the founders' fathers and Ghandour. 'Start-ups need guidance and mentorship, especially when the founders are young and just starting. Fadi [Ghandour] provided that support and guidance, in addition to our fathers who were also supportive', explains Khoury.

The First Arabic Internet Service

In launching what amounted to the world's first Arabic e-mail service, Toukan explains that the duo felt that if the Internet was going to 'spread to the masses, Arabic was going to be key'. While there were an estimated 320 million Arabic speakers globally, of which around 50 million were

---

[3] http://www.wamda.com/about

Internet users (approximately 5 % of total Internet users), Arabic represented less than 1 % of all online content. The founders also considered that e-mails represented the most important Internet service available to users and that an Arabic e-mail service would be instrumental to ensuring that the Arabic language was promoted effectively on the Internet (Anzur 2010). They also made the decision to keep the service free in order to grow their user base (Wamda 2013).

They chose the name Maktoob for the company, which in Arabic means *letter* or *destiny*.

In an early innovation, Maktoob provided users who did not have access to Arabic keyboards (many users in the USA and Europe) with virtual keyboards using Java technology. They also mailed stickers to subscribers that could be attached to existing keyboards. When Maktoob was first launched, Toukan claims that there were only a few thousand users in the Arab world. Existing ICT infrastructure also required the use of dial-up modems to connect to the Internet. Fortunately, broadband Internet access and Internet penetration grew rapidly in the region over the ensuing years and facilitated the growth of the Arabic language portal. The company also expanded the portal by including a growing range of services and in doing so successfully attracted an increasing number of users (Anzur 2010).

In terms of geographical location, Maktoob established what Toukan described as a 'double head office', with one office located in Amman and the other in Dubai (Anzur 2010). According to Khoury: 'It soon became apparent that if we were to start bringing in serious revenue we needed to have a physical presence in Dubai where all of the serious ad spend of the region is controlled. Gradually, the Dubai office grew into the commercial side of the business, whereas Amman matured to the back office and tech side of the business. We never could really justify moving our tech side of the business to Dubai in those days.' So while 'anything not revenue generating was based in Amman', Maktoob's business model, which was '80 % ad revenue based', necessitated a dual head office in Dubai, explained Khoury.

Toukan also claims it was important to be in both places. Jordan was a good place for back-office operations as the country offered a good supply of highly skilled people, while Dubai was a major regional hub (Anzur 2010) and, hence, better suited to sales and marketing activities.

'For the first 2 years of operations, the company was funded by friends (Fadi Ghandour) and family (our parents).' The priority in establishing Maktoob was to build the value of the company by reinvesting profits and tapping into available investment funding. Growing the company and developing a bigger user base was more important in the early years than making a profit. Nevertheless, Toukan claims that within 3 years the company was profitable (Anzur 2010).

Slow and Steady Wins the Day

The founders avoided overly ambitious growth agendas and overspending so that the company never overextended itself (Gara 2012). In justifying this approach, Toukan posits: 'We did it differently: start small, grow smartly and expand into a complete portal. Even our investors were saying to me "why are you keeping money in the bank?".'

Toukan believes that this cautious strategy enabled the company to survive the difficult years as the Internet established a viable user base in the Arab world. It also meant that it was well placed to respond to emerging opportunities as the popularity of the Internet in the region grew and the potential for generating revenue streams emerged. Consequently, Maktoob was in a strong financial position when the time was right to purchase a number of smaller Web sites in a process which collectively added millions of new users to its audience base. In contrast, other competitors came and went, the most significant being Arabia Online, a start-up established by other Jordanian entrepreneurs and launched as a pan-regional Web portal—and Maktoob's main rival.

Maktoob also launched several companies. For example, in 2002, to address the needs of the region's sizable young population which had limited access to credit card facilities, Maktoob launched CashU, an alternative payment method that supports online shopping (including online gamers). CashU indicates that it provides online shoppers in Arabic-speaking countries a secure, accessible and easy-to-use prepaid payment solution that does not discriminate based on income, nationality or banking contacts. It also provides a secure payment platform that merchants can use to grow their businesses in the MENA region. Maktoob also pioneered online shopping and e-commerce in the MENA region with the 2005 launch of an auction site (later to include a marketplace with a fixed price model) linked to the Maktoob portal called Souq.com. This grew into the largest online shopping Web site in the Arab world.

Following an introduction by Ghandour, the company was able to raise a second round of funding that saw Dubai-based Abraaj Capital purchase a 40 % stake in Maktoob for US\$5.2 million in 2005. In late 2007, Abraaj sold its stake for an undisclosed amount to US-based hedge fund Tiger Global Management (Tiger), in what represented a third round of venture capital (VC) funding (Anzur 2010). By this stage, Khoury explains that Maktoob was an established brand and a market leader in the regional Internet industry. This attracted Tiger, which, according to Khoury, 'pumped in a serious amount of money as growth capital, which was badly needed by us to expand and to cope with the massive traffic numbers we were achieving then'.

Yahoo! Buys Maktoob

The purchase of Maktoob provided Yahoo! with a strategic vehicle for increasing its presence in this emerging market of Arabic-speaking Internet users. If Yahoo! was to tackle effectively the challenges of catering to a market of over 300 million people located across 22 countries, it needed to understand the region's various cultural sensitivities, customs, laws and regulations—all of which demanded customised strategies. 'The Maktoob team has learnt to deal with these situations and understand[s] the local environments very well and that is one of our major differentiators', asserted Toukan in discussing the benefits of the deal (Abdelkader 2010).

The Yahoo! deal also came at a time when Internet advertising expenditure was declining in North American and Europe (Boutin 2009). Additionally, Yahoo! already had 44 million unique users in the region yet provided no Arabic content. Keith Nilsson, Senior Vice President of Emerging Markets at Yahoo!, explained that the strong potential for growth of the Arabic-speaking market (which was growing between 25 % and 50 % per annum) was a key factor behind Yahoo!'s decision to acquire the Arabic portal.

The purchase provided Yahoo! not only with access to Maktoob's Arabic content and online community but also the capacity to translate existing Yahoo! products into Arabic and tailor them to the local market. At the same time, Maktoob's users gained access to Yahoo!'s world-class platform providing mail, messenger, a search engine, news, finance and entertainment. Following the sale, Nilsson indicated that Yahoo! intended to partner with regional media companies and to syndicate media content such as Yahoo! News and to invest in the local consumer product experience, reflecting the potential for growth in regional advertising revenues.

At the time of purchase the intention was to retain the development team in Amman, while Maktoob's general manager, Ahmed Nassef, remained at the helm of the newly created division, with Yahoo! to oversee the integration process, and also continued to work as consultants to Yahoo! for a further 2 years following the completion of the initial integration process (Anzur 2010).

Eighteen months after the acquisition of Maktoob, Nassef claimed the combined Yahoo! Maktoob regional reach had grown to 50 million unique users (Ferris-Lay 2011). The Middle East was also one of the highest revenue growth regions within the Yahoo! group. Advertising revenue was recording double-digit growth despite the unrest in the region. By late 2012, based on data provided by the American Internet analytics company comScore, the estimated number of Internet users in the MENA region had grown to 135 million, with Yahoo! the fourth most visited site (68.5 million monthly visitors) after Google, Facebook and Microsoft.

Signs of an improving VC funding environment in Jordan were evident during an entrepreneurship forum held in Amman in 2012. Local investors indicated that they were ready to invest as much as US$500 million as seed money in new businesses that were tapping into the fast-growing regional markets for Internet and mobile telecommunications applications. This increased interest was reflected in a rise in the total value of VC funding of technology start-ups in the Arab world, which was estimated to have increased from US$9.7 million in 2010 to US$123.9 million in 2011. Nevertheless, the largest VC investors were sourced from outside of the region, pointing to a continuing weakness in the local industry (Sindibad 2012). Endeavor Jordan's Manna warns that it has been awhile since the Maktoob exit, and many investors are on the sidelines awaiting another successful exit before their 'appetite' for investing in local start-ups is restored.

How Did Maktoob Cope with and Leverage Place Surplus and Deficit in Amman?

In discussing the lessons from Maktoob's journey, the company's first investor and mentor to its founders, Fadi Ghandour, wrote the following on his blog (Ghandour 2009): 'It is not about vision; it is about a tedious process of discovery. It is about a unique product at the right time for the right geography. Maktoob started as a consulting company, then changed to become one of the first (if not the first) Arab Website developers, and then moved on to inventing Arabic Web email. They saw the niche and they went all the way, building everything around that niche.'

In selecting Amman as the location of their start-up venture, Maktoob's founders were able to identify and successfully leverage the unique characteristics, or place surplus, of Amman to derive competitive advantage. The founders were able to effectively leverage three key areas of competitive advantage in order to succeed: cost, convenience and community surpluses.

Cost

Compared to alternative ICT hubs in locations such as the UAE or further afield in Europe or Silicon Valley, Jordan provides companies a relative low-cost environment which makes establishing and running a development team in Jordan an attractive business proposition. Cost was a key factor behind the decisions of other start-ups to also locate in Amman, including the micro-savings platform Bluelight and the development team of online recruitment company Bayt.com.[4]

---

[4] According to information provided during an interview conducted by INSEAD with Bayt.com's CEO, Rabea Ataya, in March 2014.

Convenience

When Maktoob was first launched in 1999, the number of Internet users in the Arab world was very low but growing rapidly (Sweis 2012). While this presented a challenge for the Internet start-up, Maktoob's founders also recognised the opportunity this growing market of potential customers in the emerging market of Arabic-speaking Internet users presented, which at the time was largely untapped. By locating their start-up in Amman the founders were afforded convenient access to this fast-growing market across the MENA region. Compared to its Levantine neighbours, the Jordanian capital also afforded Maktoob a relatively moderate and stable political business environment. Moreover, Maktoob's Khoury claims that for much of the company's journey, Jordan was ahead of other countries in the region owing to the openness and relatively low level of regulation of the Internet. Nevertheless, he considered more recent changes to censorship and taxation laws as being 'not a step in the right direction'.

By maintaining its development team and back-office operations in Amman, Maktoob was also able to derive competitive advantage by having ready access to Jordan's large number of bilingual Arabic–English speakers, a skill that benefits ICT-based companies in establishing a presence in the global ICT industry (WEF 2013b). English language skills are also important for companies trying to connect to opportunities in international markets and to access offshore funding. Accordingly, bilingual skills would facilitate the founders' successful exit when Maktoob was sold to the American Internet company, Yahoo!.

As Maktoob grew, Jordan's young, tech-savvy and educated population also provided the company with convenient access to a pool of engineers and programmers necessary to develop and grow the Arabic/English Internet portal (Mahroum et al. 2013; WEF 2013a). His Majesty King Abdullah's early support of the ICT sector and technology start-ups led to the introduction of technology into the classroom and the development of ICT skills that contributed to the local talent pool. Nevertheless, Khoury explains that 'the technologies, methods and development languages that we were using were leading edge and not available in the local market'. This presented Maktoob with one of its biggest challenges as it needed to invest considerable resources in training new employees. This in turn made them valuable on the market, and many were head-hunted by rival Web companies. Khoury claims that Maktoob became known as 'the place to hire the best from'. Hence, while the convenience and cost factors clearly played a key role in Maktoob's decision to maintain its development team in Amman, the calibre of talent presented a challenge.

Community

Maktoob's Amman location also gave the founders the advantage of community since Jordan was their country of origin. The location afforded Toukan and Khoury the benefit of immediate access to their existing networks in Jordan, including the connections and experience Khoury had developed establishing previous business ventures in Amman, as well as the important mentor–mentee relationship they established with Aramex's Fadi Ghandour. During an interview following the sale of Maktoob to Yahoo!, Toukan claimed that the biggest inspiration for starting Maktoob had come from their mentor, Ghandour. Moreover, they saw Aramex, a company Ghandour had co-founded, as providing an inspiring example of successful entrepreneurship in the Arab world (Abdelkader 2010). Ghandour also granted the founders access to his established networks across the region and his international connections and experience.

The company's relationships and networks in the region also provided Maktoob with a competitive advantage for addressing the challenges of servicing a market of over 300 million people spread over 22 Arab countries, each with differing cultural sensitivities, customs, laws and regulations. Yahoo! recognised this strength as being of key importance, and it was a critical factor in its decision to acquire Maktoob in 2009 as part of its growth strategy in Arabic-speaking markets (MacMillan 2009).

It could be argued that Maktoob's connections with the Jordanian community and the Arab world provided it with a sense of loyalty and place. Ultimately, these connections help to explain why Maktoob remained headquartered in Amman despite its growth throughout the Arab world, including in larger markets such as Saudi Arabia, and despite the fact that other locations offered relatively high levels of stability. These connections were also valuable for Yahoo! not only in providing localised content but also for gaining acceptance in the Arab world and overcoming any anti-American sentiments associated with the Yahoo! brand.

Adopting Strategies to Tackle Locational Deficits by Seeking Advantages Outside of Jordan

Maktoob was also able to tap into surpluses in other locations by establishing a dual head office in Dubai, a recognised regional hub that provided an excellent base for the company's marketing and sales opportunities. Maktoob also established offices in Egypt, Saudi Arabia and Kuwait in order to gain a stronger regional reach and improved local knowledge. This strategy enabled Maktoob to better cater to the specific needs of the diverse range of countries in the Arab region.

As Maktoob grew, it was also able to use its regional and international networks to overcome a lack of VC in Jordan. The start-up was able to obtain an initial round of funding through the Egyptian investment bank EFG-Hermes, followed by a second funding round from Dubai-based Abraaj Capital, and a third round from US hedge fund Tiger Global Management. In this way the company was able to leverage its networks to circumvent locational disadvantages associated with Jordan.

In Conclusion

This case study demonstrates how Maktoob benefited from the place surplus offered by Amman, including its low cost base, the convenience of close proximity to the country's ICT talent pool, the opportunities offered by the growing market of Arabic-speaking Internet users to which Jordanian companies have ready access, and the value of local, regional and international networks. However, these benefits must be offset against a number of challenges high-tech start-ups face operating in the Jordanian capital. These place deficits include the cost and inconvenience of high levels of sociopolitical unrest and war in the region, large and regular influxes of refugees from neighbouring countries, poverty, a scarcity of water, a dependence on energy and food imports, and high rates of youth unemployment. Added to this, start-ups must contend with a historical lack of an entrepreneurial culture and limited access to seed and venture capital.

In the case of Maktoob, it was also necessary to train new employees in the cutting-edge technologies and methodologies the company was using in the development of its Arabic portal. Start-ups unable to develop effective strategies to overcome these place deficits, or that perceive place surplus to be greater elsewhere, are likely to exit. It is therefore critical that the government, education institutions and business community work together to develop and implement policies that support the ongoing evolution of Jordan's nascent high-tech start-up landscape and contribute to the place surplus offered by the country.

References

Abdelkader, R. 2010. Meet the chief yahoo! of the Arab world. Dinar Standard, 5Oct2010.http://rimaabdelkader.journalism.cuny.edu/2009/10/06/meet-the-chief-yahoo-of-the-arab-world/

Anzur, A. 2010. Lessons from creating the largest internet company in the Arab World: Samih Toukan. Webpreneur University, 15 Dec 2010. http://www.youtube.com/watch?v=7vozm-8DHaA#aid=P6i5FjufVpA

Boutin, P. 2009. Yahoo acquires maktoob, jumps into fast-growing Arabic ad market. Venture Beat, 25 Aug 2009. http://venturebeat.com/2009/08/25/yahoo-acquires-maktoob-jumps-into-fast-growing-arabic-ad-market/

Clark, P., and S. A. Topol. 2013. Syria's tech start-ups find refuge in Jordan. Bloomberg Businessweek, 29 Apr 2013. http://www.businessweek.com/printer/articles/113872-syrias-tech-startups-find-a-refuge-in-jordan.

Ferris-Lay, C. 2011. Yahoo to double its staff in MENA, say CEO. Arabian Business, 9 June 2011. http://www.arabianbusiness.com/yahoo-double-its-staff-in-mena-says-ceo--404392.html

Gara, T. 2012. Tea with FT Middle East: Samih Toukan. Financial Times, 9 July 2012. http://www.ft.com/intl/cms/s/0/8d8028c4-c9d5-11e1-844e-00144feabdc0.html#axzz2w6csFZ88

Ghandour, F. 2009. The Samih and Hussam Maktoob story is even more relevant today. Fadi Ghandour Blog, 27 Aug 2009. http://www.fadighandour.com/samih-and-hussam-maktoob-story-is-so-relevant-today

MacMillan, D. 2009. Yahoo's bold advance into the Middle East. Business Week, 27 Aug 2009. http://www.businessweek.com/technology/content/aug2009/tc20090826_150597.htm

Mahroum, S., J. M. Al-Bdour., E. Scott., S. Shouqar., and A. Arafat. 2013. Jordan: The atlas of Islamic world science and innovation case study. Royal Society & Organisation of the Islamic Conference. 2013. http://royalsociety.org/uploadedFiles/Royal_Society_Content/policy/projects/atlas-islamic-world/Atlas_Jordan.pdf

Rocha, R., S. Farazi., R. Khouri., and R. Pearce. 2011. The status of bank lending to SMEs in the middle East and North Africa region: Results of a joint survey of the union of Arab bank. Policy Research Working Paper 5607, The World Bank &The Union of Arab Banks, Mar 2011. http://elibrary.worldbank.org/doi/pdf/10.1596/1813-9450-5607.

Rusli, E. 2010. Entrepreneur to entrepreneur: Meet the ron conway of the middle East (TCTV). TechCrunch, 16 Sept 2013. http://techcrunch.com/2010/09/16/middle-east-ron-conway-fadi-ghandour-shervin-pishevar/

Sindibad. 2012. Investment report in internet & technology startups in the Arab world: 2012 update. A Sindibad Business Report. 2012. http://static.wamda.com/web/uploads/resources/Sindibad-Investment-Report_Oct_20111.pdf

Sweis, R. 2012. Unrest encourages start-up funding for the middle East. The New York Times, 6 June 2012. http://www.nytimes.com/2012/06/07/world/middleeast/unrest-encourages-start-up-funding-for-the-middle-east.html?_r=2&& pagewanted=print.

Wamda. 2013. The story of yahoo's acquisition of maktoob [Case Study]. Wamda, 13 Oct 2013. http://www.wamda.com/2013/10/case-study-yahoo-acquisition-maktoob

Wamda (2013) '5 Trends Driving VC Investment in the Arab World [Report]', Wamda, 6th November 2013, http://www.wamda.com/2013/11/venture-capital-vc-investment-arab-world-report.

WEF. 2013a. The global competitiveness report 2013-2014. World Economic Forum. http://www.weforum.org/reports/global-competitiveness-report-2013-2014

WEF. 2013b. The Arab world competitiveness report 2013. European Bank of Reconstruction and Development & World Economic Forum. Geneva, May 2013. http://www.weforum.org/reports/arab-world-competitiveness-report-2013

World Bank. 2013. Jordan economic monitor: Maintaining stability and fostering shared prosperity amid regional turmoil. The World Bank, Spring 2013. file:///F:/1%20Innovation%20-%20IPI%20Sami%202013/1%20 Silicon%20Valley%20Project/1%20Maktoob/Lit%20review/WB%20 report%20Spring%202013%20Jordan_EM_Spring_2013.pdf

10

Stormgeo in Bergen Does It Again and Reinvents Weather

With reported global revenues of 330 million Norwegian krone (US$56 million) in 2013, StormGeo is now an international company employing over 320 staff in 22 offices located across 14 countries. The success of StormGeo in becoming an international leader in the provision of private weather forecasting services in a country better known for its high cost of living and prohibitive taxes puts to question many of our established assumptions on what makes a place business-friendly. Not only did StormGeo achieve international success out of Norway, but it did so out of Norway's relatively isolated second city, Bergen, known for its heavy rain and for being sealed in by seven surrounding mountains. How did Siri Kalvig succeed against the adversaries of geography and a socioeconomic system that is entrenched in deeply rooted socialism?

© The Editor(s) (if applicable) and The Author(s) 2016
S. Mahroum, *Black Swan Start-ups*,
DOI 10.1057/978-1-137-57727-6_10

Norway: Not for Entrepreneurs?

Norway is not considered a hotbed of entrepreneurial activity. As Silicon Valley serial entrepreneur Ryan Blair put it in his keynote address to the Norwegian International Entrepreneurship Conference in 2011, the Norwegian entrepreneurial ecosystem is puzzling:

> One of the things that I am constantly thinking about is why Norway isn't the Silicon Valley of the world. You know, the economics, the capital, the available collaboration environment, the management culture, everything should yield significant participants. There are some great and significant companies, but it is interesting to me why there isn't more entrepreneurship and more innovation here because of the environment. In America we have our Silicon Valley. I think Norway should probably be the Silicon Valley of the world.[1]

Overall, Blair contended that Norway lacked both necessity-driven and opportunity-driven forms of entrepreneurship. Norwegians were seemingly too comfortable in their lives and with existing opportunity to take the 'next step' and start new business ventures.

Norway's system of state capitalism and social welfare provides a significant safety net that, on the one hand, reduces the cost of new business failures but on the other appears to negate necessity-driven entrepreneurship. Indeed, Norway recorded the lowest level of necessity-driven entrepreneurship of any country surveyed by the GEM 2013, accounting for just 4 % of all early-stage start-up activity (Amorós and Bosma, 2014).

While allegedly accessing pre-seed funding from the government is generally not difficult to obtain, subsequent rounds of funding are much more difficult to access, with long-term and high-risk capital from private sources, especially scarce (Napier et al. 2013).

To better understand these apparent contradictions it is important to analyse Norway's entrepreneurial ecosystem within the context of the country's model of state capitalism and generous social welfare system.

---

[1] http://www.grundertv.com/episoder/giving-mark-zuckerberg-a-run-for-his-money-ryan-blair-part-2

Once one of Europe's poorer nations, by the early twenty-first century, Norway had become one of the wealthiest nations in the world (Fagerberg et al. 2009), and today, Norwegians enjoy one of the highest levels of per capita gross domestic product (GDP) in the world. Unemployment is also low, while the demand for highly skilled labour, especially in the ICT sector, is high.

Norway's current blue print has its roots in the post-World War II period when the Norwegian government nationalised German business interests and gained a large and sometimes controlling interest in many Norwegian companies. This also saw the government develop a preference for exercising control through equity interests rather than regulation (The Economist 2013) and has translated into a relatively temperate regulatory environment—with the notable exceptions of tax and labour regulation—reflected in Norway's ranking of 9th out of 189 countries for ease of doing business (World Bank 2013).

The discovery of oil in 1969 (oil and gas account for more than 20 % of GDP) enabled the government to pursue expansionary fiscal and monetary policies, with public-sector growth currently accounting for over 30 % of employment in Norway (OECD 2014). Much of the significant revenue generated from oil and gas production in Norway has been managed through a sovereign wealth fund, known as the Government Petroleum Fund (Chafkin 2011; OECD 2014) and invested primarily offshore. As such, the country's considerable oil fortune has not been directed towards domestic investment, which includes the funding of entrepreneurial venture activity.

Norwegian entrepreneur and blogger Tor Grønsund argues that government funding has become a 'sleeping pillow' for many aspiring entrepreneurs who direct their efforts towards chasing government funding rather than customers (Grønsund 2012). Further to this, the country's oil and gas sector is reported to often squeeze out tech start-ups in the competition for venture capital (VC) funding, capturing around one-third of all VC investment in 2012. Compared to the USA, the UK, and its European neighbours, and despite its oil wealth, Norway's ratio of research and development (R&D) to GDP ratio of 1.7 % (both public- and private-sector expenditures in 2011) is also relatively low, reducing its capacity to generate new knowledge and commercialise innovations (World Bank 2014).

At the same time, Norway's oil sector has become a major employer of engineers, effectively monopolising the nation's technical talent (The Economist 2013). Consequently, seemingly high-risk start-ups have had to compete with a relatively large and low-risk government sector for new talent.

And there's another impediment: because the Nordic social model requires that wages, subsidies and taxes be agreed upon through collective bargaining and consensus, Norwegian start-ups confront significant barriers, including high tax rates, restrictive labour regulations and a small domestic market—issues that are all largely absent in North America.

Support of entrepreneurs in Norway does not appear to match the country's potential. International indicators of entrepreneurial activity suggest that Norway has a relatively favourable ecosystem for entrepreneurs. The Global Entrepreneurship and Development Index 2014 (GEDI 2014) ranked Norway 16th out of 118 countries, while the Global Innovation Index 2013 ranked it 20th out of 142 countries for new-business density (Cornell, INSEAD and WIPO 2013; GEDI 2014).

Additionally, Norway has been ranked comparatively well in terms of global competitiveness, with the World Economic Forum's (WEF') Global Competitiveness Index (GCI) placing Norway 11th out of 148 countries in 2013–2014 (WEF 2013). In this regard, the European Union's Innovation Union Scorecard 2013 reports some improvement in Norway's innovation performance (EC 2013).

At the same time, the Global Entrepreneurship Monitor 2013 (GEM 2013) found that close to two-thirds of Norwegians saw opportunities for new businesses, ranked second only to Sweden in all of Europe.

Despite these findings, the GEM 2013 study also found that Norway lagged many of its European neighbours in terms of the perceived entrepreneurial capability, entrepreneurial intention and early-stage entrepreneurial activity of its population (Amorós and Bosma 2014). A lack of self-confidence could be one of the root problems. A GEM study of entrepreneurship around the globe determined that while Norwegians generally appear to see good opportunities for entrepreneurship, a relatively small proportion consider that they have the requisite skills to be entrepreneurs; moreover, government policies to promote entrepreneurship are reported to have had little impact on levels of start-up activity (Bosma et al. 2012; OECD 2014).

The Siri Kalvig Story

Siri Kalvig—founder and first CEO of StormGeo—was drawn to the Norwegian coastal city of Bergen like a bee to honey. Not only was she captivated by the city's charm, its excellent university and its new, private TV station, but there were the 'ghosts and legends of meteorologists past'.

Henrik Mohn, the Norwegian astronomer and meteorologist who co-founded the Norwegian Meteorological Institute in 1866, was born in Bergen, Norway's second city with a population of some 400,000 people. Along with another Norwegian meteorologist, Vilhelm Bjerknes, Mohn is widely credited with being one of the founding fathers of modern meteorology and weather forecasting. Together, Mohn and Bjerknes played a key role in the establishment of the Geophysical Institute at the University of Bergen and the Bergen School of Meteorology. This institution is credited with developing a weather forecasting approach that subsequently influenced post-World War I international efforts to develop meteorological practices (Jewell 1981).

Bjerknes was actually working in Leipzig—at the Geophysics Institute at the University of Leipzig—during World War I when the difficulties of living in the war-torn country prompted him to accept a professorship at the newly created Geophysics Institute in Bergen in 1917. Necessity stepped in to advance the profession of meteorology: Norway was in the grasp of a severe food shortage following a poor harvest. The agriculture sector was calling for more and better weather forecasts.

In response, the Norwegian government called on Bjerknes to establish a weather forecasting service for western Norway, and the Bergen School of Meteorology was born. It soon drew international recognition for its cutting-edge research in meteorology, and its forecasts had immediate applicability: the local Norwegian fishing community came to rely upon the daily forecasts to better cope with the strong winds and waves along Norway's rocky coastline. By 1919, weather forecasts had become an accepted tool for improving safety at sea, not only for the fishing industry but also for transatlantic shipping (Jewell 1981).

Bergen was at the epicenter of all this activity. So it comes as no surprise that Siri Kalvig—a graduate in geophysics from the University of Oslo—would enrol in the University of Bergen's Geophysical Institute for her postgraduate studies. She graduated in 1995 with a Master's degree in Meteorology, began looking for work and found it at Norway's first public TV channel, TV2, created by industry deregulation in 1992, making history by becoming the country's first on-air female meteorologist and weather presenter. This was only the beginning of the changes she would wreak.

Many technological changes had taken place in weather forecasting and reporting since the days of Bjerknes et al. In the late 1940s, computers were first introduced as a tool in calculating weather forecasts. A decade later, weather surveillance radar was being used to collect data on local atmospheric conditions, and since then meteorological satellites have collected broader data that supplement this. Moreover, since the late 1950s, improved computing technology had made possible the numerical weather prediction modelling of vast bodies of meteorological data, permitting more accurate and timely weather forecasts. Hence, a competitive weather industry emerged to meet the demand for so-called value-added content from government agencies, which owned and operated a vast weather forecasting infrastructure such as satellites, radar equipment and supercomputers

Some 40 years later, Kalvig, while presenting sophisticated weather forecasts at TV2, identified an opportunity to revolutionise the way weather forecasts were delivered by the Norwegian Meteorological Institute, which at the time involved—in her words—'uninspiring men in dark suits with pointers'. In 1993, she and TV2 again made history by being the first broadcaster globally to incorporate graphic animation and numerical weather information (including isobars and low- and high-pressure systems) to deliver a visually superior and more engaging view of developing weather patterns. With her good looks and youthful style, Kalvig soon gained celebrity status in Norway, rivalling the government's own weather forecasting service (Rugland 2009).

Her fame and visibility brought more rewards: the country's largest newspaper, VG, approached Kalvig to write a weather column. Kalvig realized that with two media clients—VG and TV2—she could establish a private weather services company.

In 1997, Kalvig and TV2 collaborated to launch StormGeo as a spin-off of TV2, with a view to transforming the way weather was presented. Additional talent came from the University of Bergen, and in the early days

Kalvig recalls that she hired most of her student cohort to work at StormGeo. She was particularly pleased when the start-up managed to attract a highly skilled meteorologist from the Meteorological Institute who believed in the founders' vision and was prepared to make the leap of faith and leave a well-paid and secure government job to work for their new venture.

Why StormGeo Succeeded Anyway

StormGeo's success is more akin to the successes found in Silicon Valley and serves as testimony to the efficacy of place surplus in the launch of a new business. Bergen, with its history and educational resources, proved to be an important factor in the funding growth and evolution of StormGeo. More specifically, Bergen had a strong place surplus for Siri and StormGeo in terms of the calibre of its meteorological science and talent, the convenience of the local presence of a main client and the community of practitioners that surrounded its meteorological activities.

With Kalvig at the helm as CEO, and with two customers, TV2 and VG, StormGeo was profitable from the outset. In establishing StormGeo, the founders invested one million Norwegian krone, with TV2 holding a 90.5 % equity stake in the start-up and Kalvig the balance of 9.5 %. Combined with the profits the company was generating, StormGeo was able to self-fund expansion in the early years, which was largely based on organic growth.

For the first 3 months, the company repackaged the government's forecasts, providing services to media-related industries in Norway. This was quickly expanded by capitalising on opportunities to provide other customised weather forecasts to Norway's hydroelectric power industry, and shortly thereafter to the country's oil and gas sectors as well. As StormGeo established a regular revenue stream, the decision was made to hire three meteorologists to generate in-house weather forecasts.

StormGeo was breaking the government monopoly on weather forecasting in Norway. But it still had to purchase raw data from the very organisation with which it was competing: the Norwegian Meteorological Institute. Indeed, Kalvig maintains that for many years this was a key challenge for the company.

Being able to collaborate with the university and recruit skilled talent graduating from its Geophysics Institute was a significant asset to the company. The university's leading-edge research into fine-scale, high-resolution atmospheric modelling was extremely important to StormGeo's R&D programme and the development of technological innovations necessary to carve itself a niche market as a commercial weather service.

As StormGeo developed its forecasting capabilities, including the use of sophisticated numerical modelling techniques, it recognised opportunities to offer customised analyses of the effects of weather on business and industry by developing meteorological systems which incorporated a unique understanding of client operations (TV2 2014). In 1998, StormGeo introduced customised weather forecasting services for the hydroelectric power industry, which had been recently liberalised.

Diversifying the Portfolio

Along with deregulation, the Nordic Power Exchange was established to enable the trading of electricity in the Nordic region. Kalvig noticed that her evening weather forecasts were impacting electricity prices on the exchange the following day and approached two power companies to offer them exclusive access to her weather forecasts 6 h ahead of the evening broadcast. This proved to be a very profitable venture. It also afforded StormGeo the opportunity to develop a good understanding of the hydroelectric power industry and how the weather impacted electricity production.

Later that year, StormGeo expanded into the broader energy market, including oil and gas and other offshore operations, such as wind turbines, all of which relied heavily on accurate weather and sea forecasts to ensure safe and efficient operations. As the company expanded, its main industries of focus became the media, renewables (onshore wind power and hydropower) and offshore industries. The customised weather analyses and forecasts provided by StormGeo soon became an important part of its clients' decision-making processes. Norway's oil and gas sector, concentrated on the country's west coast, provided the company with a particularly strong revenue stream.

By 2004, the company had established itself as the largest offshore weather service provider in Scandinavia. But by this time, Kalvig had moved out of the CEO office.

In 2000, Kalvig was a first-time mother, a role she juggled with running the growing company. Her husband's job also required that the family relocate to Stavanger, also on Norway's west coast, but a distance from StormGeo's Bergen headquarters. Kalvig made the difficult decision to step down as CEO and was replaced by TV2 colleague Mette Krohn-Hansen, who valued Kalvig's vision and strategic foresight. They soon formed a strong working relationship, with Krohn-Hansen handling the company's day-to-day operations and finance and Kalvig remaining the company's public face. Kalvig also assumed an active role within the company, including in marketing, offshore development and R&D. As the company positioned itself for a period of strong international expansion, Khron-Hansen decided to step down as CEO while continuing to maintain an active role in the company's growth trajectory, but in roles that did not require extensive international travel. She was replaced as CEO by Kent Zehetner in 2009.

StormGeo Takes Off Internationally

In 2008, Erik Langaker was appointed Chairman of StormGeo. Langaker had a strong background in finance and investment and was keen to drive StormGeo's international expansion into new areas such as shipping— a strategy which was largely acquisition-based. Langaker's investment company, Idèkapital AS, acquired a 42.5 % strategic stake in StormGeo. Langaker explained: 'We spent nearly 3 years preparing for international expansion by gradually shifting our focus towards products and services that can be sold anywhere in the world. But in order to achieve that, we realised that we needed a new ownership structure that supported our growth and globalisation ambitions.'

Subsequent investments in StormGeo by the Norwegian private equity firm Reiten & Co., the Norwegian company DNV, and later by EQT, an investment company originally founded in Sweden, facilitated further expansion. In 2012, StormGeo entered a strategic partnership with DNV

Group, a maritime classification and risk management company, in a deal which included DNV acquiring the right to purchase a 22.7 % stake in StormGeo.

This partnership significantly increased StormGeo's growth prospects and distribution power by providing it with access to DNV's global network of over 300 offices in 100 countries and its 80,000-strong base of customers, which were in similar industry groups. At the same time, DNV indicated that the deal gave it access to StormGeo's 'competence and ability to communicate complex issues in a simple and elegant way', while it also benefited from StormGeo's products and services, which extended DNV's existing portfolio. The deal also provided StormGeo with access to DNV's 'world class technical and business knowledge combined with strong growth ambitions'.

Both companies placed strong emphasis on investing in innovation and R&D and signalled the intention to collaborate in the further development of best practice meteorology solutions and products to optimise the efficiency and safety of clients' operations. The continued focus on the strategic role of R&D furthered the importance of Bergen as a location with a high calibre of scientific institutions and personnel. In fact, Bergen was quickly becoming the centre of the global weather forecasting business. StormGeo's purchase in 2010 of the Swedish company Seaware AB, a leading provider of on-board ship-routing solutions, saw the company expand its product and service line as well as its geographic reach. Over the next 3 years, StormGeo opened offices in Denmark, Sweden, the UK and the USA.

Continuing its global expansion, later in 2012 StormGeo acquired the outstanding shares of ImpactWeather Inc., a leading Houston-based provider of weather monitoring, forecasting and alerting services in a move which extended its presence in the North American market, including the Gulf of Mexico, and its offerings to operators in key industries affected by harsh weather and climate change.

StormGeo also formed a joint venture with shipping companies Wihelmensen ASA and Wallenius Marine AB to develop a range of innovative software solutions to improve the fuel efficiency of clients in the shipping industry. Further, by late 2013, StormGeo began offering services to the aviation industry when it became the first private weather services company to be certified by the Civil Aviation Authorities in Norway and the UK to provide official aviation forecasts.

As the company expanded its offerings and geographical reach, it successfully established itself as an active partner in large, weather-sensitive businesses and operations and became an integral part of its clients' decision-making systems. This included working with them to help prevent weather-related accidents, increase fuel and operational efficiencies, determine the optimal placement of wind turbines, aid in the safe operation of oil installations and collaborate in environmental risk analyses, especially where clients were operating under extreme weather conditions (Rugland 2009; TV2 2014).

Continuing investments in R&D saw the company announce the launch in 2014 of an environment monitoring service that involved a new and innovative approach to forecasting underwater currents. This service was seen as being particularly important for the management of oil spills in the oil and gas sector. The strategic importance of R&D for StormGeo and the weather forecast business in general has meant that the place surplus that Bergen offered in terms of scientific calibre and weather practitioners' community presence outweighed the adversity of high living costs, high taxes and geographic isolation.

Early 2014 saw StormGeo continue to expand through the strategic acquisition of Silicon Valley-based Applied Weather Technology, Inc. (AWT) in a deal that resulted in the company emerging as the global leader in the provision of decision support services to the shipping and offshore industries. Reiten & Co. sold its stake in StormGeo for an undisclosed amount in March 2014 to private equity firm EQT Mid Market, which then became the company's majority shareholder, while DNV also increased its stake in the company. Reiten & Co. indicated at the time that its investment in StormGeo had provided its investors with strong returns in a relatively short time period.

The Future of Weather Forecasting

Continually improving technology has resulted in faster supercomputers which use advanced computer modelling techniques to process billions of grid points of data on weather and environmental conditions (such as temperature, barometric pressure, humidity, wind speed and direction) from increasingly sophisticated radar and satellite technologies. Data are constantly updated from observation points around the globe to maximise the accuracy and speed of weather forecasts (Lubchenco and Hayes 2012). For example, it has been estimated that the supercomputer currently used by the UK's National Weather Service performs more than 1000 trillion calculations per second and runs an atmospheric model containing more than a million lines of code.

By 2013, the commercial weather industry in the USA alone was estimated to generate annual revenues of US$3 billion, representing 50 % growth over the previous 2 years (Knowledge@Wharton 2013). This compares to estimated annual revenue of US$500 million in 2003.

Fuelling growth has been a growing public appetite for weather information (a US study in 2009 found that people were accessing 300 billion weather forecasts annually) but also increasing awareness in industry of the potential economic impact of weather events on commercial operations and the need to minimise weather related risks; around one-third of US GDP is estimated to be either directly or indirectly affected by the weather. Weather events, including floods, hurricanes, blizzards and sandstorms, can negatively impact a diverse range of industries, including agriculture, transportation, energy, construction, manufacturing and sporting events. Even retailers are using weather forecasts to tailor advertising campaigns.

The media industry has also become a large consumer of private weather forecasting services (weather portals) to capitalise on growing public interest. Climate change has also put weather on political agendas. As a result, private companies ranging from small consultancy firms to large commercial forecasters have emerged to meet the needs of a diverse range of consumers demanding customised weather forecasting services to inform decision-making processes (Brin 2011; Mandel and Noyes 2012).

How Did StormGeo Do It?

In launching StormGeo in 1997, Kalvig and TV2 were able to clearly identify and effectively leverage the unique resources and characteristics offered by the Norwegian city of Bergen. This enabled them to derive the competitive advantage the start-up required to grow and compete effectively in the global market for commercial weather forecasting services. Kalvig contends that being headquartered in Bergen presented few challenges while the company was able to leverage the important surpluses offered by the city. These were in three key areas: the convenience of proximity to first clients, the high calibre of the relevant scientific talent in the city and the long-standing presence of a meteorological community in the region.

R&D played an important role in the company's ability to develop 'next-generation' products and services, and Kalvig acknowledges that being headquartered in Bergen meant the company was able 'to access talent that could do numerical modelling. We knew that the town was at the leading edge of atmospheric modelling, and this was particularly important during the company's start-up phase.' Indeed, according to Casper Lund from the Bergen Teknologioverføring, StormGeo has recruited most of the talent which has graduated with qualifications in geophysics and meteorology from the University of Bergen.

Kalvig also chose to found StormGeo in the city where she lived and worked. Hence, Bergen afforded her the convenience of familiarity and established social and professional networks, an important factor in the locational choices of many founders of high-growth companies (Morris 2013). Also noteworthy, Kalvig valued the support provided by the University of Bergen to the new weather forecasting start-up, while TV2 was a source of both support and talent, including future CEO Mette Krohn-Hansen.

Potential problems associated with Bergen's geographical distance from key markets such as the USA and Middle East were overcome by opening offices across the globe. In doing so, Kalvig explained that StormGeo was able to forge stronger relations with clients and stakeholders in key international markets and engage in important dialogue with foreign governments regarding the value of having access to important meteorological data for weather forecasting. In addition to this, StormGeo's strategic partnership with DNV provided the company with access to DNV's extensive global network and customer base, while its acquisition of US-based ImpactWeather, Inc., extended its reach into the North American market.

And while Norwegian start-ups must contend with a lack of growth capital, StormGeo was profitable from the outset and initially able to self-fund expansion. When the company decided to expand internationally, primarily through a series of strategic acquisitions in new businesses and geographies, this was achieved through equity financing facilitated by private equity partners located in the region. And in what represented a very Norwegian approach to funding investments in R&D and innovation, StormGeo entered into joint ventures and strategic alliances to undertake R&D and pursue the technological advancements necessary to ensure that the StormGeo group remained competitive in the global marketplace.

References

Amorós, J, E., and., N. Bosma. 2014. Global entrepreneurship monitor 2013 global report. US: GEM Consortium: Babson College; Chile: Universidad del Desarrollo; Malaysia: Universiti Tun Abdul Razak; UK: London Business School. http://www.gemconsortium.org/docs/download/3106

Bosma, N., S. Wennekers., and J. E. Amorós. 2012. Global entrepreneurship monitor extended report 2011: Entrepreneurs and entrepreneurial employees across the global. US: GEM Consortium: Babson College; Chile: Universidad del Desarrollo, Malaysia: Universiti Tun Abdul Razak; UK: London Business School. http://www.gemconsortium.org/docs/download/2200

Brin, D. W. 2011. Weather services become big business. CNBC, 1 Aug 2011. http://www.cnbc.com/id/43672839.

Chafkin, M. 2011. In Norway, start-ups say Ja to Socialism. Inc., 20 Jan 2011. http://www.inc.com/magazine/20110201/in-norway-start-ups-say-ja-to-socialism.html

Cornell, INSEAD, and WIPO. 2013. The global innovation index 2013. Johnson Cornell University, INSEAD, & World Intellectual Property Organisation (UN). http://www.globalinnovationindex.org/content.aspx?page=GII-Home

EC. 2013. Innovation scoreboard 2013. European Commission. Belgium. http://ec.europa.eu/enterprise/policies/innovation/files/ius-2013_en.pdf

Fagerberg, J., D. C. Mowery , and B. Verspagen. 2009. The evolution of Norway's national innovation system. *Science and Public Policy* 36(6):

431–444, July 2009. http://mpra.ub.uni-muenchen.de/19330/1/MPRA_paper_19330.pdf

GEDI. 2014. GEDI index. The Global Entrepreneurship and Development Institute. http://www.thegedi.org/research/gedi-index/

Global Entrepreneurship Monitor (GEM). 2013. TEA at its highest since 2005; a high proportion of entrepreneurs expect to become employers [WWW]. http://www.gemconsortium.org/country-profile/72.

Grønsund, T. 2012. Is the Norwegian start-up scene hot or not?. Arctic Startup, 8 May 2012. http://www.arcticstartup.com/2012/05/08/is-the-norwegian-startup-scene-hot-or-not

Jewell, R. 1981. The Bergen school of meteorology. *Bulletin American Meteorological Society* 62(6): 824–830, June 1981. http://climate.envsci.rutgers.edu/pdf/JewellBAMS.pdf

Knowledge@Wharton. 2013. Today's forecast for the weather business: Increased revenues and a focus on innovation. Knowledge@Wharton, 10 Apr 2013. http://knowledge.wharton.upenn.edu/article/todays-forecast-for-the-weather-business-increased-revenues-and-a-focus-on-innovation/

Lubchenco, J., and J. Hayes. 2012. New technology allows better extreme weather forecasts. *Scientific American* 306(5), 1 May 2012. http://www.scientificamerican.com/article/a-better-eye-on-the-storm/?print=true

Mandel, R., and E. Noyes. 2012. Beyond the NWS: Inside the thriving private weather forecasting industry. Weatherwise. Sept/Oct 2012. http://www.weatherwise.org/Archives/Back%20Issues/2013/January-February%202013/beyond-nws-full.html

Morris, R. 2013. What do the best entrepreneurs want in a city? Lessons from the Founders of America's fastest-growing companies. Endeavor Insight. http://issuu.com/endeavorglobal1/docs/what_do_the_best_entrepreneurs_want?e=0/6600427

Napier, G., P. Rouvinen., D. Johansson., T. Finnbjornsson, E. Solberg., and K. Pedersen. 2013. Nordic growth entrepreneurship review 2012. Nordic Innovation, June 2013. http://www.nordicinnovation.org/no/publikasjoner/nordic-growth-entrepreneurship-review-2012/

OECD. 2014. OECD economic surveys: Norway. OECD, Mar 2014. France. http://www.oecd.org/eco/surveys/economic-survey-norway.htm

Rugland, E. 2009. Taking in Norway. Forskning, 8 Apr 2009. http://www.forskning.no/artikler/2009/april/216403

The Economist. 2013. Norway: The rich cousin, in special report: Nordic countries. The Economist, 2 Feb 2013. http://www.economist.com/news/special-report/21570842-oil-makes-norway-different-rest-region-only-up-point-rich

TV2. 2014. TV2 sell out of StormGeo. TV2. Press Release, 27 Mar 2014. http://www.tv2.no/a/5448358

WEF. 2013. The global competitiveness report 2013-2014. World Economic Forum. http://www.weforum.org/reports/global-competitiveness-report-2013-2014

World Bank. 2013. Doing business 2014. http://www.doingbusiness.org/reports/global-reports/doing-business-2014.

World Bank. 2014. Research and development expenditure (% of GDP). The World Bank. http://data.worldbank.org/indicator/GB.XPD.RSDV.GD.ZS

11

24symbols in Madrid: Leveraging Cultural Links

24symbols is an online platform for streaming books from the cloud. It treats books as a service rather than as a product. With e-books widely available online, it was only a matter of time before an online platform that provided e-books as streamed content was launched. In 2010, four Spanish entrepreneurs in Madrid experienced in the information technology (IT) industry decided to form a company to develop a platform to stream and provide e-books for download. The team consisted of ÁngelLuengo, AitorGrandes, both of whom graduated from the Instituto Superior para el Desarrollo de Internet (ISDI), and David Sánchez and Justo Hidalgo, who graduated from the Universidad Politécnica de Madrid.

The four co-founders met while working at the Madrid office of software company Denodo, which was headquartered in Palo Alto, California, but originally founded in Spain in 2000 (Brunelli 2013; Hidalgo 2014). Experienced technology entrepreneurs, the team members discovered they shared an interest in technology and how it affected economies. They also shared a love of books. Meeting over coffee they discussed ideas for business ventures which linked technology with culture.

© The Editor(s) (if applicable) and The Author(s) 2016   **177**
S. Mahroum, *Black Swan Start-ups*,
DOI 10.1057/978-1-137-57727-6_11

E-Book History

The first e-book was created in 1971, when the US Declaration of Independence was typed as a document file that could be viewed on a computer screen in an initiative called Project Gutenberg, which advocated the creation of more electronic books. Early versions of e-readers were introduced as early as 1992, with the launch of the Sony Discman and other similar products. Two years later, Amazon.com was launched as an online bookstore and established the presence of books on the Web. However, it was not until 2004 that modern e-readers debuted with the launch of Sony's LIBRIe, which used the patented E-ink technology (Pilato 2004). It took Amazon less than 3 years to follow up with its own e-reader model, the now famous Kindle.

Along with the rising popularity of the Kindle and other e-readers which use the E-ink technology, the years 2008 and 2009 saw dramatic annual growth in e-book sales of 354 % and 198 %, respectively (Milliot 2013). In April 2011, the Association of American Publishers announced that, for the first time, more e-books had been sold than print books. By 2012, e-books made up 22.6 % of all US publishing revenue; however, the growth rate of e-book sales was slowing while sales of e-readers were declining as customers shifted to multifunction tablets (Franzen 2013).

Hence, it was becoming increasingly apparent that the way people consumed books would also change. While books had been partially replaced by e-books, the consumption style had remained the same. Moreover, books were becoming more specialized, and the market was becoming flooded with new content. Hence, the founders of 24symbols felt that it was time to offer a subscription service to a catalogue of books where subscribers could stream books without having to purchase copies or download content.

After discussing this idea with publishers and other industry stakeholders, the team soon recognised the opportunity before them. The team reasoned that, with various kinds of digital content being made available through online portals, such as Netflix for movies and television series to Spotify for music, it seemed a logical extension to create a platform for reading digital books online without having to download files or pay for content. Not surprisingly, 24symbols is sometimes referred to as the 'Spotify' for books (24symbols 2011; Galaria 2013).

Madrid as Home Base

The founders of 24symbols all graduated from two Madrid-based universities: two from ISDI and two from the Universidad Politécnica de Madrid. Both schools specialised in new technologies. Founded in 1971, the Universidad Politécnica de Madrid is the largest technological university in Spain, established when technological innovation gained prominence and based on the pre-existing engineering schools in the city (Leon 2013). Madrid's Institute for Internet Development (ISDI) is also a leading university.

Overall, Madrid does not lack for tertiary education and research institutions. The city is home to 15 universities and more than 20 public research institutions, with much of the country's research activity concentrated in the capital. Moreover, the city hosts 48 research institutions out of a nationwide total of 121.

Madrid also boasts a number of business schools, including the IE Business School, which is consistently ranked in the top 15 business schools in the world.[1] The quality of Spain's universities is high by international standards, with Spain ranked 22nd out of 142 countries based on the average score of its top three universities in QS university rankings (Cornell et al. 2013).

Perhaps not surprising given the high levels of youth unemployment, Spain has experienced a sharp increase in the number of students admitted to higher education institutions in recent years, with enrolments in higher education rising from 66 % in 2004 to 83 % in 2012. Hence, the supply of tertiary educated talent is not an issue in Madrid and provides a large talent pool from which start-ups can recruit, as well as a supply of potential entrepreneurs.

What has been lacking, however, has been a culture of entrepreneurship and risk-taking (ESADE 2011).

Spanish society is often criticized for its lack of innovation and entrepreneurial culture. According to the Global Entrepreneurship Monitor (GEM) 2013, close to half of Spanish adults surveyed indicated that they believed they possess the requisite skills, knowledge and experience to

---

[1] http://rankings.ft.com/businessschoolrankings/ie-business-school.

start a business. However, more than one-third cited a fear of failure as preventing them from starting a business, while only 16 % believed that opportunities existed to start a business where they lived.

Not surprisingly, only 8 % of Spanish adults surveyed indicated entrepreneurial intentions compared to a European Union (EU) average of closer to 14 % (Amorós and Bosma 2014). Some credit this lack of entrepreneurship to factors such as the country's risk-averse culture, poor perceptions towards entrepreneurship, the stigmatisation of business failure, political corruption, the enduring effects of civil war and years of political dictatorship, and the profound impact of the global financial crisis (GFC) and Eurozone crisis on the Spanish economy (Riggins 2013; Weverbergh 2013).

Despite Madrid's concentration of excellent schools, Spain's education system has failed to encourage independent and critical thinking or decision-making skills among Spanish youth. In a country where the expected route after graduation has been to seek salaried employment, the Spanish education system has not equipped students with basic entrepreneurial skills (Riggins 2013). Indeed, a study by the Spanish business school ESADE found that the preference of young Spaniards for salaried work over self-employment actually increased from 34 % in 2001 to 52 % in 2009. Many students spend years studying with the primary motivation of passing the highly competitive civil service exam.

A study by Coduras et al. (2008) found no significant statistical relationship between the level of support provided by universities to entrepreneurial training and the actual level of entrepreneurial activity in the country. The study did find, however, that the probability of entrepreneurial intentions was higher for people who knew someone who had started a business, had developed entrepreneurial skills, could recognise entrepreneurial opportunities and believed their university would provide positive support to their entrepreneurial endeavours. It was therefore evident that higher education had an important role to play in influencing the entrepreneurial intentions of future generations of Spaniards and in the socialisation of attitudes towards entrepreneurship in the country.

A white paper on entrepreneurship in Spain by ESADE Business School estimated that entrepreneurs represented only 5.1 % of the Spanish population compared to 8.5 % in Norway and 8.0 % in the

USA. Moreover, an increasing number of young Spaniards preferred sala-ried employment—52 % in 2009, up from 34 % in 2011. The study determined that young Spaniards felt they had not been taught adequate entrepreneurial skills and called for teachers to be given better tools and materials to teach business acumen and initiative and to foster greater interaction with local entrepreneurs (ESADE 2011).

Risk-Taking Is Not Encouraged

Individual workers do not appear to be ambitious when it comes to expan-sion, and many are happy to work on their own as freelancers rather than start an actual business. When businesses fail, there is no culture of learn-ing from their mistakes. Rather, failure is viewed negatively. This also acts as a deterrent to entrepreneurship (ESADE 2011; Weverbergh 2013).

Professor Albert Fernandez, a professor at Barcelona's IESE business school, attributes the lack of entrepreneurship in Spain not only to cul-tural barriers but also to the country's low levels of English proficiency and the failings of government policies (PRI 2013). Overall, risk tolerance for entrepreneurs in Madrid is considered to be much lower than in ecosys-tems such as Silicon Valley, with entrepreneurs estimated to be 24 % less likely than their peers in Silicon Valley to commit to their start-up ventures on a full-time basis (Start-up Genome and Telfonica Digital 2012).

Juan Angel Hernandez, founder of the financial portal Estrategias de Inversion, estimates that around 70 % of Spanish students want to work for a large corporation, while the same percentage of American students prefer to start their own businesses (Weverbergh 2013). Hernandez contends: 'We should instill a culture where people want to work for themselves—where they at least consider it' (Hernandez 2012).

Sourcing Risk Capital

A study by Start-up Genome and Telefonica Digital (2012) investigating locations where entrepreneurship has occurred outside of Silicon Valley concluded that while the overall performance of start-ups in Madrid was not significantly different from those in Silicon Valley, the funding of start-ups was insufficient both before and after product market fit owing to the limited availability of risk capital.

When 24symbols was launched in 2010, the amount of seed capital available to tech start-ups in Spain was limited. The founders were nevertheless able to obtain around 250,000 euros in seed capital within 6 months by reaching out to both business angels and seed capital investors.

In the first instance, Borja Hormigos, a Spanish entrepreneur, supported the team both by providing capital and sharing his entrepreneurial experience and knowledge of the publishing and media industries. They also approached a newly formed seed capital company called Sidkap which invested in the start-up. This investment was further supported by a soft loan provided by the Ministry of Industry of Spain under its NEOTEC programme, which provided an interest-free loan of up to 70 % of 24symbols' budget (based on its business plan) and was repayable once the company was cash-flow positive. This funding enabled the start-up to build an initial team of nine people (24symbols 2014).

While the team found it relatively easy to raise seed capital to fund the early start-up phase of their venture, raising growth capital was much harder in Madrid. Hidalgo claimed that financial institutions were reluctant to support tech start-ups, while international investors were weary of Spanish companies.[2]

How They Coped

The founders believed that mobile devices would become the key place where reading would take place in the future (Hidalgo 2013). They developed the 24symbols platform—which they launched in July 2011 (24symbols 2014)—which enabled users to access e-books on the cloud, thereby allowing readers to switch devices and continue to enjoy the same reading experience anywhere without having to download a file and with all content related to the reading process residing on an Internet service (e.g., what they were reading, the page they were up to, all highlights and annotations they had made).

---

[2] From interview with Justo Hidalgo, Co-Founder of 24symbols, on 4th June 2014.

The team developed a business model for 24symbols that was based on a vision of how they considered readers and authors would interact in the future. They felt that since books had become digital, conventional publishing practices were less attractive and the time was ripe for disruptive changes to the publishing industry (24symbols 2014).

Piracy, shrinking consumer attention spans and rising competition have also forced media distributors to rethink how they charge for content. The distributors of online content such as Audible, Netflix, Amazon Prime and Spotify have responded by adjusting their revenue models from charging customers per purchase to charging flat fees regardless of content accessed.

Adopting a Freemium-Based Subscription Model

In developing the company's business model, Hidalgo also explained that the founders aimed to deliver 'books as a service' rather than as a product (i.e., involving physical ownership). Hence, like many other media Websites, 24symbols streamed content rather than delivering ownership of a product. This was a model similar to that followed by other streaming services such as Netflix, Spotify, Spuul and Pandora which provided an alternative to purchasing products such CDs and DVDs (Webb 2011).

24symbols' founders followed an approach similar to that of other online services by adopting a subscription-based business model. Reflecting the founders' mantra when they started the company of 'bringing books to everyone, everywhere', they adopted a freemium service that allowed subscribers to read as many books as they liked by streaming them from the cloud for free while selling paid advertising space to generate revenue (Hidalgo 2013). However, free access only allowed readers to choose from a limited, albeit reasonably large, range of books. Premium subscribers who paid a fee were provided access to a broader catalogue of books that could be read both online and offline (through downloads) and through a service that was free of advertisements. It was hoped that premium subscriptions would eventually become 24symbols' main source of revenue.

The Value Added for Publishers

The founders of 24symbols contended that the benefits to publishers of using the new platform to publish e-books were manifold and included the following (Sanchez 2011):

* Generating real-time statistics dashboards with information such as what users read, the volume of traffic, the number of unique users, the number of users per book and the number of comments per book; data could be used for marketing and promotional purposes, including for the promotion of books on the 24symbols platform during searches and by issuing new reading options to targeted subscribers;
* Making it easier and less expensive for publishers to experiment with publishing new content with minimal investment required as printing and distribution costs were removed. Similarly, old books could be re-released at little cost;
* Providing a new way for publishers and authors to interact with readers;
* Providing publishers with the ability to better tackle the growing problem of e-book piracy. Streaming books through the cloud meant that books were not illegally downloaded; only premium subscribers who paid a fee could download book. Hidalgo argued that if provided 'with a convenient, unified and affordable way to access content, people will use it'. He explained that 'Once that's achieved, piracy doesn't matter that much' (Webb 2011);
* Paying publishers each month for the number of pages read by subscribers, with publishers paid a 70 % share of all advertising and subscription fee revenues. Consequently, the 24symbols platform was designed to facilitate 'social reading' by allowing subscribers to interact with other readers before, during and after reading a book, including sharing comments, passages and book recommendations. Moreover, a reader's profile could be used to crowd-source reviews and recommendations. In this way, and like several other content-streaming services such as Netflix, YouTube and Spotify, the application was designed to provide suggestions for books based on a reader's profile; and

* Importantly, by creating a community of people who believed in the project, social media also helped 24symbols grow its user base. This in turn enabled the start-up to gain the interest of publishers and grow the content available on the platform (24symbols 2014).

Growing Pains

Luis Rivera Gurrea-Nozaleda, investor and founder of Okuri Ventures, described the funding situation in Madrid as follows:

> Madrid is a great place to launch thanks to its cheap resources and talent availability (>50 % of <30 unemployed). But it is [an] extremely challenging place to scale given how long it takes for customers to adopt and pay, and how risk averse most local investors are. There aren't too many investors ready to make big leaps of faith in the over >30 K round and the equity gap for 0.5–5 M rounds pushes most start-ups towards early monetization. A common pattern is that out of the first 500 K, 100 K is invested in product and 400 K in advertising.

With limited equity the company found it difficult to scale because this required the start-up to acquire content, which meant establishing contacts and developing a rapport with publishers internationally. To do this, they needed to build brand recognition so that everyone in the industry would know that 24symbols represented the 'Spotify' for books. London was a key market in the publishing world, but with limited funds they could not afford to establish an office in the city. It made economic sense to base the company in the relatively lower-cost Madrid, which also provided them with a convenient base from which to travel regularly to London to meet with industry representatives and develop a network of contacts within the UK publishing industry.[3]

24symbols could also ill afford expensive marketing and promotional activities, so the team decided to attend the London Book Fair in April 2011. In a relatively inexpensive strategy the team set up a booth at the book fair and delivered a presentation to over 100 people to announce

---

[3] From interview with Justo Hidalgo, Co-Founder of 24symbols, on 4th June 2014.

the launch of the alpha version of the 24symbols platform. In doing so they managed to create a lot of buzz about 24symbols (24symbols 2014).

The company's efforts to expand into international markets were aided in early 2012, when it won the European Micro Seed Fund for Internet tech start-ups at the London SeedCamp event. SeedCamp is a leading start-up accelerator which provides start-ups with access to capital, mentorship and networking opportunities. Winning the London event brought 24symbols much-needed recognition and valuable access to venture capital (VC) investors and enabled the 24symbols team to expand their network throughout Europe and the USA. This helped the company gain faster traction for growing its user base and securing high-quality content from publishers not only in Spain but also in the UK. The company also established a presence at the main international book fairs not only in London but also in New York and Frankfurt (24symbols 2014).

Over time, the centre of the global publishing industry had also shifted from London to New York[4] as leading publishing houses established a presence in the city in order to be closer to US-based companies such as Amazon, the leading publisher worldwide. As a result, establishing contacts and a presence in New York became an increasing priority for the 24symbols team. By May 2013 it was able to secure an A round of VC funding from Zed, a multiplatform digital media company that bought a 32 % stake in 24symbols for two million euros; this meant that 24symbols was valued at 6.25 million euro (US$8.1 million) (Wauters 2013).

This deal was particularly significant as Zed, which had also been founded in Spain in 1996, was one of the most prominent mobile content, services and technology providers in the world. The company's operations spanned more than 60 countries, and it had forged partnerships with around 200 mobile carriers worldwide (Wauters 2013). Not only did the Zed deal provide 24symbols with much-needed growth capital, but it also gave it an exclusive distribution agreement with Zed which allowed 24symbols to leverage Zed's salesforce and marketing-savvy team to secure introductions to mobile carriers around the globe (24symbols 2014). In discussing the deal with Zed at the time, the company's co-founder,

---

[4] By 2012, the United States represented almost one-third of total revenues of the global publishing industry (based on market values at consumer prices) (24symbols 2014).

Hidalgo, explained that having what he considered to be the most important content distributor in the world as an investor meant that 24symbols now had the 'strategy, tactics, know-how, contacts and a sales force that we could only have imagined just a few months ago' (Hidalgo 2013).

Hidalgo claimed the company was on track to expand its worldwide user base to 200,000 subscribers (Wauters 2013). At the time, it had content from more than 120 publishers and offered readers access to more than 15,000 books in Spanish, English and other languages. The partnership with Zed meant that 24symbols also had access to Zed's extensive network of telecommunications operators. For example, users could now pay for a premium subscription through this expanded network of operators, thereby increasing the potential number of paying subscribers to which 24symbols had access. The amount of the investment provided by Zed would also help the company enrich its team and diversify the company offerings.

Aided by its deal with Zed, 24symbols continued to expand, and by 2014, Hidalgo claimed the company had over 500,000 users and had made inroads into new markets, including Mexico, Latin America and Russia. To develop the company's presence in the Spanish publishing industry, 24symbols was also able to successfully recruit leading talent from Argentina to act as the company's Director of Publisher Relations. 24symbols also had its eyes set on pursuing opportunities in new markets in Africa, the USA, Asia and across Europe. At the same time, the number of books in its catalogue was growing, as were the languages in which its books were being published.[5]

The Place Surplus of Madrid

Madrid's geographical location in the middle of the Iberian Peninsula, which itself is located far into the Atlantic, has resulted in the city's historically being an Iberian hub and connection point between the old and new worlds. The city's location has allowed it to serve as a bridge between Latin America, Europe and North Africa. Madrid is the main destination

---

[5] From interview with Justo Hidalgo, co-founder of 24symbols, on 4 June 2014.

for people immigrating to Spain. A significant flow of skilled immigrants come to Spain each year from the South American continent, the majority of whom are native Spanish speakers.

As the economies of Latin America mature, their economic relationship with Spain—their biggest former colonising power—is experiencing a shift. With over 2.3 million people of Latin American origin living in Spain at the beginning of 2009, cultural and linguistic similarities between the two regions have attracted Latin American investors. Latin America has helped to reinvigorate the Spanish economy during its time of need. In 2013, Latin American companies invested more in their Spanish counterparts than the other way around (The Economist 2014). Moreover, Latin American investment banks are reported to have begun extending credit to Spanish companies. This reversal in trend follows two decades during which Spain accumulated 145 billion euros (US$200 billion) worth of assets in Latin America. The number of Spaniards heading to Latin America is also rising as young Spaniards pursue job opportunities in the region, while the flow of people entering Spain from Latin America is falling. The city also draws talent from around the country and Europe. In fact, in the past decade, the rate of non-Spanish residents in Madrid has risen to 19 % of the total population. An OECD report on Madrid claimed the city was 'an emerging hub in the global economy' and attributed this, in part, to the availability of skilled labour through immigration (OECD 2007).

The Role of Government

Madrid is also the country's capital and seat of government. Not surprisingly, Madrid's economy has been orientated towards the service sector, including banking, real estate, business services, transportation and communications. Moreover, the city is home to many multinationals.

Madrid has enjoyed one of the highest rates of population growth in Europe and is Europe's third largest city. Madrid experienced an average annual growth rate of 3.7 % in the two decades before the GFC and Eurozone crisis, making it one of the strongest regional economies in Europe until 2008. In addition, Spain offers start-ups a relatively low cost base. Not only are labour costs relatively low (although social security contributions are high and partially offset this benefit), the cost of living is also much lower, with Madrid ranked 185th by the Numbeo Cost of Living Index 2014, which ranks cities around the world.

The government has also tried to encourage entrepreneurial activity amongst Madrid's unemployed by offering to pay up to 80 % of the equivalent of 2 years of unemployment benefits upfront for approved business plans for small businesses and start-ups. However, few of Madrid's unemployed have been reported to take up this offer (Riggins 2013). This has occurred despite Spain's youth unemployment rate peaking at more than 56 % in mid-2013 (Ham 2014). And while the government has proposed a number of other initiatives aimed at making it easier to launch start-ups, including a reduction in taxation and reducing the cost of hiring employees, these measures are taking a long time to be implemented (PRI 2013).

Despite the tendency towards risk aversion and difficulties raising VC, a nascent start-up hub would appear to be emerging in the capital. A report on global entrepreneurship by Start-up Genome and Telefonica Digital (2012) investigated locations where entrepreneurship has taken hold outside of Silicon Valley and developed a Global Start-up Ecosystem Index that rated various start-up ecosystems. Madrid was ranked as one of the 20 'runner-up' cities for entrepreneurship globally—after the top 20 cities—and is considered an up-and-coming start-up ecosystem and the strongest in Spain. Nevertheless, Madrid's entrepreneurial ecosystem remains in its infancy, as noted by Josep Amoros, Vice President of Wayra Spain—an ICT accelerator with operations spanning Latin America and Europe—who claimed: 'In fact I would say that here there is not such an ecosystem yet but an embryo of [an] ecosystem'.

As a sign of the improving ecosystem for start-ups in Madrid, the city is now home to numerous co-working spaces, incubators and accelerators. One of those accelerators is Chamberi Valley, which is a non-profit platform that acts as a shared platform to improve connections between entrepreneurs in Silicon Valley and Madrid in general. Since 2012, the Madrid-based IE University has hosted the Spain Startup & Investor Summit, the largest start-up conference in Spain. The summit, also called the South Summit, invites investors and important figures from local, regional and global countries.

Start-up activity has been strongest in the ICT sector, with many Spanish tech start-ups launching online businesses which have enabled them to operate globally. Many of these business ventures have been established on the premise that the Internet lacks Spanish content. While Spaniards typically have a low level of English proficiency (PRI 2013), something that is viewed by many as a challenge to starting businesses with global reach, with Spanish the third most popular language on the Internet, online businesses do not lack a user base whether for distributing content or sharing user-generated content. This can be attributed to the large number of Spanish speakers in Latin America, with many online Spanish companies having more online traffic from Latin America than from Spain.

How Did 24Symbols Do It?

In launching 24symbols, the start-up's co-founders were able to clearly identify and effectively leverage the unique resources and characteristics offered by Spain's capital, Madrid. This enabled them to derive the competitive advantage they required to successfully develop a platform for streaming high-quality books serving primarily the large global Spanish-speaking market and, later, the company's International expansion. Hidalgo explains that by leveraging the surpluses of Madrid, 24symbols was able to derive competitive advantage in three key areas, namely:

* Convenience,
* Calibre,
* Cost.

These 'place surpluses' were sufficient to offset the deficits caused by the country's high taxation regime, challenging business environment and weak entrepreneurial culture.

Convenience

A key advantage of basing 24symbols in Madrid was that the city served as a major hub between Latin America, Europe and Northern Africa, explained co-founder Hidalgo. Thus Madrid provided an excellent base for serving key Spanish-speaking markets, a factor which became increasingly important as the company expanded into new markets outside of

Spain. The city's geographic location and transportation connections also meant that the founders were able to travel regularly to London, including attending the London Book Fair and London Seedcamp, in order to forge important ties with the international publishing industry while taking advantage of the relatively lower cost base of Madrid. As 24symbols expanded globally, however, servicing markets outside of the Spanish-speaking world in Asia and America were becoming more difficult from the company's Madrid headquarters.

24symbols was also founded in the city where the founders lived, worked and graduated university. Hence, Madrid afforded them the convenience of familiarity and established social and professional networks, an important factor in the locational choices of many company founders. Experienced entrepreneurs, the founders were closely connected with the educational and start-up ecosystem in Madrid. Each teaches at one or more of the city's universities and collaborates with Madrid's start-up incubators and accelerators. Hidalgo, for example, is a board member of the Tetuan Valley Start-up School and collaborates with the start-up accelerator, UEIA. Ángel Luengo, co-founder and Chief Technology Officer, regularly delivers talks at events promoting technology entrepreneurship and collaborates in the development of a master's degree in entrepreneurship at Madrid's University of Technology, Art and Design.

Madrid is also the services hub in Spain and home to many multinational companies; hence, 24symbols is within close proximity to a range of potential service providers, suppliers and technical support. And while Spain's publishing industry is concentrated in Barcelona, the founders did not consider that this presented a serious obstacle for the start-up.

Madrid's universities and business schools provide the company with convenient access to a pool of skilled talent from which it could draw, especially in the fields of technology, finance and administration (24symbols 2014). The fact that the company's founders also teach at a number of these universities has meant that they are well positioned to identify and recruit local talent. The size of Madrid's talent pool is also bolstered by the number of immigrants drawn to the city.

Countering some of the convenience factors provided by Madrid, and despite the fact that 24symbols had found it relatively easy to raise seed capital in the Spanish capital, sourcing growth capital was much harder.

According to Hidalgo, Spanish financial institutions were reluctant to support tech start-ups, while Spanish companies were not well regarded by international investors. The severe impact of the GFC and Eurozone crisis on the Spanish economy had tarnished the country's reputation as a place for investment. Partly offsetting this disadvantage, however, was the support provided by the Spanish government in the form of public funding initiatives such as the soft loan 24symbols received when it was first launched. Winning the London SeedCamp competition in 2012 also enabled the founders of 24symbols to expand their networks, make valuable connections with international investors and raise the company's profile globally. This in turn enabled 24symbols to gain traction in the global marketplace, acquire content and grow its user base. It also meant that 24symbols was able to secure a first round of VC funding and an exclusive distribution deal with Zed. This enabled 24symbols to fund the expansion of its international operations while leveraging Zed's global salesforce and connections with mobile carriers around the world.

On returning to Madrid from Silicon Valley in 2008 Hidalgo had also noticed the small size of the city's entrepreneurial ecosystem, a factor that challenges entrepreneurs and start-ups as they try to establish and scale. Nevertheless, Hidalgo claimed the ecosystem had improved later with an increasing number of events and greater levels of collaboration between universities and other stakeholders which were trying to develop an entrepreneurial culture and support start-ups.[6]

Calibre

The quality lifestyle Madrid afforded the founders also made the city a more attractive location to base their start-up. In 2012, Madrid was ranked 49th out of 205 cities by the Mercer Quality of Living Survey, reflecting the relatively attractive quality of life offered to residents of the city. Spain also ranked well in terms of the quality of its infrastructure and placed 10th out of 148 countries by the World Economic Forum's Global Competitiveness Index 2013–2014 (WEF 2013).

---

[6] From interview with Justo Hidalgo, co-founder of 24symbols, on 4 June 2014.

The company also benefitted from having access to a large pool of highly talented students from the city's universities. However, 24symbols encountered difficulties recruiting people with strong English-language skills, which were considered particularly important for the company since it was operating in a global environment. Moreover, a lack of entrepreneurial culture in Spain challenged the company as it tried to expand and attract early adopters to the service. Nevertheless, Hidalgo believed that the population's English-language skills were improving and that changes to the Spanish education system were slowly improving the entrepreneurial spirit in the country (24symbols 2014).[7]

Cost

Hidalgo argued that operating out of Madrid had afforded the founders a relatively low-cost base as Madrid's cost of living was low while still offering a high standard of living. Wage costs were also low and allowed the company a low burn rate. Nevertheless, this cost advantage was in part offset by the relatively high cost of starting a business as well as the high level of taxes and fees companies are required to pay in Spain. For example, 24symbols indicated that Spanish companies were required to pay 250 euros per month to the government regardless of how much revenue they generated (24symbols 2014). Hidalgo claimed that the tax situation was especially challenging for start-ups, and though politicians claimed they were working to improve the situation, little had been achieved.

References

24symbols. 2011. 24symbols: The spotify model for eBooks— presentation. SlideShare, 16 Mar 2011. http://www.slideshare.net/24symbols/ 24symbols-the-spotify-model-for-ebooks-presentation

24symbols. 2014. The black swan start-up—24Symbols: Business plan. 24symbols, updated 23 May 2014.

---

[7] From interview with Justo Hidalgo, co-founder of 24symbols, on 4 June 2014.

Amorós, J. E., and N. Bosma. 2014. Global entrepreneurship monitor 2013 global report. GEM Consortium: Babson College (US), Universidad del Desarrollo (Chile), Universiti Tun Abdul Razak (Malaysia) and London Business School (UK). http://www.gemconsortium.org/docs/download/3106

Brunelli, M. 2013. Denodo technologies aims for a broader approach to data virtualization. Search Data Management, 21 June 2013. http://searchdatamanagement.techtarget.com/news/2240186649/Denodo-Technologies-aims-for-a-broader-approach-to-data-virtualization

Coduras, A., D. Urbano, A. Rojas, and S. Martínez. 2008. The relationship between university support to entrepreneurship with entrepreneurial activity in Spain: A GEM data based analysis. *International Advances in Economic Research* 14: 395–406.

Cornell, INSEAD, and WIPO. 2013. The global innovation index 2013. Johnson Cornell University, INSEAD, and World Intellectual Property Organization (UN). http://www.globalinnovationindex.org/content.aspx?page=GII-Home

ESADE. 2011. White paper on entrepreneurship in Spain: Executive summary. ESADE Business School. http://itemsweb.esade.es/wi/research/eei/Investigacion/Executive%20Summary.pdf

Frannen, C. 2013. Ebooks made up 22.55 Percent of all US publishing revenue in 2012. *The Verge*, 12 Apr 2013. http://www.theverge.com/2013/4/12/4216862/ebooks-made-up-22-55-percent-of-all-us-publishing-revenue-in-2012

Galaria, F. 2013. Publishing crisis? Time to create a spotify for books. *The Guardian*, November 13. http://www.theguardian.com/media-network/media-network-blog/2013/nov/13/publishing-crisis-spotify-books-music

Ham, A. 2014. The lost generation of Spain's unemployed youth *Sydney Morning Herald*, Feb 27. http://www.smh.com.au/world/the-lost-generation-of-spains-unemployed-youth-20140226-33i8e.html

Hernandez, J. A. 2012. Spain does not need mini-jobs, requires 5,000 Steve jobs. *Actibva*, Feb 14. http://www.actibva.com/magazine/mercado-laboral/espana-no-necesita-minijobs-necesita-5000-steves-jobs-por-juanangelher

Hidalgo, J. 2013. Why 24symbols partnered with Zed and what our future holds. *DigitalBookWorld*, 9 May. http://www.digitalbookworld.com/2013/why-24symbols-partnered-with-zed-and-what-our-future-holds/

Hidalgo, J. 2014. The black swan start-up—24symbols: Business plan. 24symbols, updated 23 May 2014.

Leon, G. 2013. Analysis of university-driven open innovation ecosystems: The UPM case study. Universidad Politécnica de Madrid, August. http://www.upm.es/sfs/Montegancedo/documentos%202013/documentos%20finales/UPM-driven%20open%20innovation%20ecosystem_ok2.pdf

Milliot, J. 2013. BEA 2013: The e-Book boom years. *Publishers Weekly*, 29 May. http://www.publishersweekly.com/pw/by-topic/industry-news/bea/article/57390-bea-2013-the-e-book-boom-years.html

OCED. 2007. *Madrid, Spain. OECD territorial reviews*. Paris: OECD. http://browse.oecdbookshop.org/oecd/pdfs/free/0407111e.pdf

Pilato, F. 2004. Sony LIBRIe – The first ever e-Ink e-Book reader. *Mobile Magazine*, 25 Mar. http://www.mobilemag.com/2004/03/25/sony-librie-the-first-ever-e-ink-e-book-reader/

PRI. 2013. Spain trying to combat joblessness by promoting entrepreneurship. PRI,8May2013.http://www.pri.org/stories/2013-05-08/spain-trying-combat-joblessness-promoting-entrepreneurship

Riggins, J. 2013. 'Why the Spanish aren't entrepreneurs. SmartPlanet, Blog, 17 Feb2013.http://www.smartplanet.com/blog/global-observer/why-the-spanish-arent-entrepreneurs/

Sanchez, D. 2011. 24symbols: One-click reading. Trends & Technology, 2 Oct 2011. http://www.slideshare.net/clustergrafico/1-david-snchez-24symbols

Start-Up Genome, and Telfonica Digital. 2012. Start-up ecosystem report 2012. Start-up Genome & Telefonica. http://cdn2.blog.digital.telefonica.com.s3.amazonaws.com/wp-content/uploads/2013/01/Start-up-Eco_14012013.pdf

The Economist. 2014. Shoe on the other foot. *The Economist*, 25 Jan 25. http://www.economist.com/news/americas/21594985-spains-crisis-and-latin-americas-cash-prompt-gradual-rebalancing-relations-shoe

Wauters, R. 2013. Zed buys 32% stake in seedcamp-backed 24symbols, the Spanish 'spotifyforbooks'. *TheNextWeb*,10May.http://thenextweb.com/insider/2013/05/10/zed-buys-32-stake-in-24symbols-the-spanish-spotify-for-ebooks/

Webb, J. 2011. Books as a service: How and why it works. TOC, 28 July 2011. http://toc.oreilly.com/2011/07/books-as-a-service.html

WEF. 2013. The global competitiveness report 2013–2014. World Economic Forum. http://www.weforum.org/reports/global-competitiveness-report-2013-2014.

Weverbergh, R. 2013. Why Spain has an entrepreneurship problem (and why there'shope).*WhiteboardMagazine*.http://www.whiteboardmag.com/why-spain-has-an-entrepreneurship-problem-and-why-theres-hope/

12

Bayt.com in Dubai: Taking Nepotism Out of 'Wasta'

Bayt.com, an Internet company and leading recruitment Website, was established in 2000, coinciding with the collapse of the dot-com boom, in a place lagging in Internet adoption: Dubai, in the United Arab Emirates (UAE). At the time, less than 2 % of the population in the Arab world was using the Internet, compared to rates of 28 % in OECD countries and 44 % in North America. E-recruitment was at a nascent stage of development in general, with job Websites such as Monster.com in the USA and Jobserve.com in the UK having launched only a few years earlier.

Hence, the launch of Bayt.com in the Middle East and North Africa (MENA) region appears to be a bold decision by the company's founders, though it seemed to fit a need: when Bayt.com was founded, countries in the MENA region were not creating sufficient jobs to meet the needs of their growing populations, resulting in high rates of unemployment by international standards. The man behind the company was a Kuwait-born Lebanese citizen, Rabea Ataya, who returned to the Middle East in 1995 after studying and working abroad, an aspiring entrepreneur looking for opportunities.

© The Editor(s) (if applicable) and The Author(s) 2016   **197**
S. Mahroum, *Black Swan Start-ups*,
DOI 10.1057/978-1-137-57727-6_12

In originally naming the online recruitment Website, the founders had settled upon the name Bayt, the Arabic word for *home* or *house*. The choice of name was no accident, explains Ataya, but rather a deliberate choice reflecting the company's vision of improving the quality of life for people in the region. Assisting jobseekers in finding new or better employment opportunities meant that Bayt.com was achieving what the founders considered to be the most important determinant of quality of life, namely getting better jobs. They were able to leverage the fast-growing popularity of the Internet to roll out e-recruitment services in local markets. In doing so they identified opportunities to deliver technology solutions which would assist regional employers in candidate-selection processes. Bayt.com also provided a bilingual recruitment platform (i.e., Arabic and English) to meet the differing needs of clients across the MENA region.

Eventually, the company also ventured into the group buying market with the launch of GoNabit, providing shoppers with the ability to purchase goods and services online at significant discounts through bulk buying opportunities, which attracted large discounts from suppliers. The popularity of the Website grew quickly, and it was sold to LivingSocial.com in 2011, a year after it was launched, for a price many times the cost of its development. Other ventures incubated within Bayt.com included a Website which provides advice on car purchases called YallaMotor and a successful online shopping Website for children's clothing and toys, MumzWorld. By the end of 2013, Ataya estimated that business from core search and postings represented around 70 % of the company's revenues, with the remaining revenue generated from innovative solutions offered by the company, including advertising, premium subscriptions and brand career channels. Approximately 20 % of all traffic to the Website was estimated to have come from mobile users through the Bayt.com mobile apps.

Why Dubai?

Few dispute Dubai's status today as an international hub which provides an essential base for companies wishing to develop markets in the region and abroad. The Emirate's close ties in the region and globally have aided its development as a regional information and communications technology (ICT) hub. A large expatriate community has also helped to develop strong networks which facilitate greater levels of regional and international collaboration. Many of the most talented students in the wider MENA region study and work overseas (Mahroum et al. 2013) and are drawn to Dubai on their return to seek work or start their own businesses, having developed core technical and business skills as well as international networks.

Dubai's free zones have also promoted the growth of strong global networks which benefit the country's ICT industry through business links, investment flows and knowledge transfers. The general view in the region is that the talent comes from the Levant and the money from the Gulf. But when Bayt.com was founded at the turn of the millennium, large-scale construction projects were overshadowing entrepreneurship and small business enterprises in Dubai.

By 2000, Dubai's construction industry was booming, fuelled by investments financed by oil revenue and foreign direct investment. Investments were directed into infrastructure, such as ports, airports and roads, as well as large residential and commercial projects. Growth in Dubai's construction industry was underpinned by its ability to attract both skilled and unskilled expatriate labour. This in turn compensated for a relatively small indigenous labour pool, with the expatriate workforce estimated to represent around 90 % of the total workforce.

Not surprisingly, early-stage start-ups often struggle with the relatively high costs associated with attracting and hiring expatriate labour with little in the way of local ICT talent available in Dubai.[1]

Cultural barriers to risk-taking in the Arab world constrain new business ventures and innovation by national and Arab expatriate entrepreneurs: business failure involves not only financial loss but also loss of face for the individual and family as a whole (King 2013b; Mahroum et al. 2013). It is not surprising, then, that the national population prefers to take on well-paid jobs with the government. The Emirate's legal system presented strong disincentives to risk-taking and entrepreneurship. Business failure is a crime under local law, and matters such as bounced

---

[1] From interview with Fadi Ghandour on 30th April 2014.

cheques result in company directors being apprehended while the matters are being investigated in the courts, effectively precluding them from pursuing opportunities to keep their business going and setting matters right. A lack of transparency in the court system and the long time necessary to resolve disputes further hinder the development of an entrepreneurial culture.

The UAE limits foreign ownership to 49 % of companies incorporated outside of business free zones, thereby requiring non-nationals to handover a controlling interest to a national partner through joint-venture agreements. And while the Dubai government opens up industry-specific free zones which allow 100 % foreign ownership, these zones restrict operations outside of free zones in mainland Dubai in the absence of a local commercial agent (ITR 2000; Rahman 2012). Free zone business licences also restrict the range of activities a company can undertake within a specific free zone, and the zones typically charge high rents as they are also driven by the Emirate's growth model, which includes revenue generation from large-scale property developments of which the free zone developments arguably form a part.

Expatriate entrepreneurs also face challenges in terms of immigration. The inability of most expatriates to obtain permanent or long-term residency (let alone citizenship) in the UAE, regardless of their length of stay or the amount of money they invest in the country, has reduced the overall attractiveness of Dubai as a location for business ventures (Tong et al. 2012). While this is a common hindrance across much of the Middle East, more immigration-friendly countries, such as Australia and Canada, have benefitted from an influx of highly skilled and wealthy immigrants from the UAE.

Additionally, geopolitical instability in the MENA region has also amplified levels of risk aversion. Further constraining entrepreneurship is local investors' reluctance to invest in start-ups, especially those in the ICT sector which lack both an established track record and tangible assets.

The MENA region presented a challenging environment for companies like Bayt.Com seeking to establish Pan-Arab operations. On the one hand, the Arab World is united by a shared cultural heritage, with the Arabic language and largely Islamic religion tying the countries together. On the other hand, the laws, regulatory systems and customs vary widely between countries. Unlike trading blocs that exist in other regions—such as the European Union (EU) and Association of South-East Asian Nations (ASEAN)—companies wishing to operate in the MENA region confront numerous market barriers that prevent free and open trade across borders. The introduction of a common market by the Gulf Cooperation Council (GCC) for member countries (i.e. Bahrain, Kuwait, Oman, Qatar, Saudi Arabia and the UAE) whose *raison d'être* was to remove barriers to trade and allow free movement, employment and residency of GCC citizens, did not occur until several years later, in 2008. Furthermore, Arab countries outside of the Arabian Peninsula were not included in the agreement. Hence, for start-ups like Bayt.com seeking to establish regional reach, market barriers presented a significant challenge.

Furthermore, when Bayt.com was launched in 2000—the first Website to cater specifically for the needs of employment markets in the region—few Arabic speakers were using Internet services, though the UAE stood out as an exception with the highest Internet penetration rate at 23.6 %. Thus, despite the growing popularity of online recruitment in international markets, limited use of the Internet in the MENA region at the turn of the millennium presented a major hurdle for companies wishing to introduce this method of recruitment to the Arab world. Before Bayt. com, prevailing recruitment practices typically involved the use of intermediaries and introductions which were often ineffective in matching talent with opportunities. This mismatch was holding back the development and prosperity of both the regional workforce and industry alike.

How They Did It

Unsure at first of how to launch his own business, Ataya initially accepted a position with US-based investment bank Alex Brown & Sons, where he helped to structure mergers and acquisitions and public offerings of technology companies. Ataya maintains this experience provided him with the opportunity to gain valuable insights from successful technology entrepreneurs who were either going public or acquiring or selling other companies. As part of the team working on the initial public offering (IPO) of Remedy Corporation, a software development company, he was especially inspired by CEO Larry Garlick, who had left a high-paying job with Hewlett-Packard to found Remedy. Garlick had canvassed industry contacts and identified a gap in the market; in establishing Remedy, he successfully leveraged this opportunity. When Remedy went public a few years later, Garlick grew wealthy from the proceeds of the sale. Ataya asserts Garlick's success and his determination and commitment to building an institution which would last and add value inspired him to follow suit.

In deciding to return to the Middle East to pursue his goal of starting his own business, Ataya's decision to settle in Dubai was influenced by a close Emirati friend from his Stanford days, as well as by Ataya's father, who had relocated the family business from Kuwait to Dubai and offered his son a position with the company. Ataya was also attracted by the quality of life and the opportunities offered by the fast-growing Emirate of Dubai.

After working for his family's construction company for a period, Ataya left to pursue his first business venture. In 1997, he founded InfoFort, a records and information management company. The business was highly successful, grew rapidly and generated what Ataya claims were healthy profits. Nevertheless, while his bank account grew, Ataya felt the need to find a new venture which would not only be profitable but also have a social impact and in doing so 'pay it forward' in his home region.

In early 2000, with some seed capital behind him, Ataya set about building a team to establish the first online recruitment company in the MENA region. Ataya states that the vision of the company was to empower people in the region with the tools and information necessary to build a better lifestyle and future. He also aspired to building a sustainable company which would become a global brand and, unlike many leading companies in the Gulf region, was not government-owned. He was also looking to develop a company with strong growth potential which was a good long-term investment rather than a company which would achieve short-term profits and provide quick exit opportunities through an IPO or sale.

In establishing and growing InfoFort, Ataya had observed the difficulties employers in the MENA region encountered recruiting staff, with traditional recruiting sources failing to deliver the services employers were looking for. There was a reliance on word of mouth and intermediaries to source skilled staff. This system did not work effectively and stood as an impediment to the growth of companies in the region. Ataya had also observed that employers at the time were often reluctant to openly advertise vacant positions owing to the likelihood that people would try to leverage *wasta* (connections) to secure positions for their friends or relatives. This sometimes hindered recruitment processes and the appointment of the most suitable candidates to a position. Equally, Ataya had noted the large number of talented people in the MENA region seeking employment but who were frustrated by existing hiring processes.

Over a period of 6 months Ataya formulated a strategy to launch an online recruitment portal which would become Bayt.com, which he believed would have a positive social impact by providing jobseekers, including the large number of Arab unemployed, with a tool to improve their quality of life by improving their access to jobs and employers. Ataya felt that online recruitment would remove the need for intermediaries and empower employers and jobseekers to communicate directly. His vision was to reduce geographic boundaries, promote labour force mobility, better match job opportunities to available talent and, in doing so, transform regional recruitment practices.

By mid-2000 Ataya had pulled together a core team and was ready to launch the company. One of the greatest challenges was finding world-class talent to drive the technology behind the Website. Ataya approached Akram Assaf, a Jordanian who at the time was working for Oracle, and invited him to join Bayt.com as a co-founder and Chief Technology Officer (CTO), and Dany Farha, who was appointed Chief Operating Officer. Ataya also convinced his sister, Mona Ataya, to join Bayt.com as a fellow co-founder and Chief Marketing Officer.

Dubai Internet City

From the outset, Bayt.Com chose the Dubai Internet City (DIC) as its home. Plans to establish DIC had been announced in October 1999, and the ICT business park and free zone was formally launched in October 2000. At the time it was claimed to be the world's first free trade zone for e-commerce (Sundaram 2002).

Designed to promote the development of the Emirate's ICT sector, DIC allows companies full foreign ownership, tax-free status, 100 % repatriation of capital and a relatively business-friendly regulatory environment vis-à-vis mainland Dubai (ITR 2000). Advanced ICT infrastructure and office space are also provided to companies operating within the business park, as are services to expedite incorporation, obtaining visas and work permits, as well as other support services. By drawing together a large concentration of ICT companies, DIC creates networking opportunities which are further supported by organised events. DIC's close proximity to Dubai Media City (a free zone for media companies[2]) and Dubai Knowledge Village (a free zone for education and training companies) were meant to provide 'a thriving, pulsating milieu where thoughtful minds meet', proclaimed DIC CEO Dr Omar Sulaiman in 2002. Close proximity means that people bump into each other over coffee or lunch or by simply walking around. This increases connectivity, promotes the flow of ideas with suppliers, talent and other related companies within the digital community. The business park's geographic location also aimed to provide ICT companies with a strategic base for targeting emerging markets in the MENA region, Africa and the Indian subcontinent.

Bayt.com established the core of its technology development team in the Jordanian capital of Amman. Ataya explains that this choice of location reflected the combined calibre of ICT talent in Jordan and the lower-cost base offered by the location. Jordan was actively promoting its ICT sector as a development strategy aimed at boosting economic growth and export revenues while tackling high levels of youth unemployment. Unlike other capital-intensive industries such as manufacturing, the ICT sector was labour-intensive, making it a perfect fit for this resource-poor country and its young, tech-savvy population (Mahroum et al. 2013). Nevertheless, the core management team remained in Dubai.

Dubai has a strong employment market from which companies located in the Emirate can leverage to their advantage. Dubai, as well as the wider UAE, has undoubtedly benefitted from the brain drain experienced by its

---

[2] Including broadcasting, publishing, advertising, public relations, research, music and post-production services.

neighbouring countries as a result of the tumultuous Arab Spring and by other countries around the world.

Finding the Money

In establishing Bayt.com, the founders had estimated that they would require around US$3.5 million. 'We decided that if we burnt through this money but failed to succeed we would leave the business', remarked Ataya. The founders initially raised US$500,000 of seed capital, contributing half from their personal funds and the balance from several private investors. Over the ensuing months the company struggled with cash flow and its cash balance fell to zero and salaries had to be paid from the founders' pockets. Fortunately, they were able to successfully lobby several key suppliers, including Oracle and Sun Microsystems, which supported the start-up by providing short-term credit plans. These two strategies enabled the start-up to survive the early days of operation. The company subsequently managed to successfully raise the remaining US$3 million in a single round of funding from the Jordanian-based Inter-Arab Management Fund (no longer in operation).

The company adopted a business model in which revenue was generated by selling subscriptions to employers for posting job advertisements and for using its search engine to access and assess candidates' curriculum vitae (CV). These services leveraged the company's advanced filtering systems, which were in turn supported by its ongoing investment in research and development (R&D). This strategy helped the company sidestep the lack of spending on online advertising in the region at the time.

Bayt.com recognised that staying ahead of the market and retaining its first-mover advantage required that it continue to invest in cutting-edge technology. In doing so, it managed to maintain a leading market share, attracting large numbers of people to the site, which enabled it to connect users to opportunities better than any other recruitment Website.[3]

---

[3] In 2014, the Web analytics site Alexa.com ranked Bayt.com 46th in the UAE in terms of traffic to its Web site, well ahead of its major competitors, including JobsInDubai.com, GulfTalent.com and NaukriGulf.com. Source: http://www.alexa.com/siteinfo/bayt.com

Bayt.com grew rapidly, partly driven by a strong battle for talent in key regional markets such as the UAE, Saudi Arabia and Qatar. Between 2000 and 2009 the company grew at an estimated compound average growth rate of over 90 %. Rapid growth in Internet penetration rates in the MENA region, together with technological developments which significantly increased what companies could do with the Internet, underpinned this growth. Strong profits enabled the company to self-fund future expansion without having to go to the market for additional funding.[4] Bayt.com also remained focused on growing the Website's e-recruitment services while at the same time paying careful attention to its bottomline to make sure the company had money in the bank. Ataya asserts that this strategy stood in contrast to that of many other dot-com companies in the region, which were funded by wealthy business people in the Middle East who wanted to make quick profits through Internet companies. He argues that many Internet companies tried to focus on too many things and as a result lost direction and failed.

In general, as start-ups become established, their growth can be constrained by relatively low levels of bank lending to small and middle-sized enterprises (SMEs). A report by the World Bank and the Union of Arab Banks found that loans to SMEs represented less than 8 % of total loans by MENA banks. Of note, bank lending to SMEs in GCC countries was particularly low at 2 %. The report attributed this to the dominance of large enterprises and relatively small non-oil-related sectors in GCC countries. Bank lending to SMEs in the UAE was higher than the GCC average at 3.9 % but still well below the average for the MENA region. The study also noted that while state banks partly compensated for the low level of involvement of private banks in SME financing, lending to SMEs in the region was noticeably lower than in OECD countries, where bank lending to SMEs stood at close to 27 % of total bank loans (Rocha et al. 2011).

---

[4]Tiger Global Management acquired a growing interest in Bayt.com as several early shareholders, including CEO, Dany Farha, divested their shareholdings over time.

Financial Crisis, Re-Grouping

When the global financial crisis hit the region in early 2009, the employment market collapsed and the company experienced a massive decline in revenues. While Bayt.com's strong focus on e-recruitment had enabled it to grow quickly in the boom years, following the crisis the company realised that it needed to diversify so that it would no longer be overly exposed to a single industry. It responded by also reframing what it wanted to achieve and returned to its original vision of promoting quality of life for people in the region.

Additional free and paid-for products and services were added to the Website. For example, Bayt.com posted the results of a regular salary survey and a variety of research reports which it had either conducted or sponsored, as well as career information and self-assessment tools. It also offered users a range of paid-for services, including CV writing and evaluation, psychometric evaluations and workshops teaching job search strategies. As part of a CSR initiative the company offered unemployed jobseekers a free CV-writing service. Additionally, the Website leveraged the growing popularity of social networking by including features which allowed jobseekers to post public profiles and network with other registered professionals online.

To leverage its ongoing investments in R&D and technological innovations, in 2010, Bayt.com also launched a subscription-only premium service which enabled companies to link the career pages on their Websites directly to the Bayt.com platform. In this way, when jobseekers clicked on the *Careers* button of corporate Websites, they were redirected to a branded career channel operated by Bayt.com. Ataya claimed that the key advantages Bayt.com's platform offered customers included the avoidance of high up-front investment costs in developing in-house platforms and associated infrastructure requirements, as well as ongoing development and maintenance costs.

Bayt.com has continually invested in R&D as the size of the database grew and as technology advanced. The company progressively developed its recruitment platform by including new features which, for example, allowed companies to search a greater number of fields in order to filter candidates (approximately 27 different fields by 2014), as well as features which allowed employers to annotate candidate CVs and directly schedule candidate interviews via e-mail.

Its large registered user base and the high level of traffic on the Bayt. com Website also enabled the company to generate additional revenue by offering customers targeted advertising opportunities through banners, sponsorship, e-mail, SMS and postal services, a revenue stream the company has begun to pursue more actively. Advertisements could be targeted according to a wide range of criteria, including industry, nationality, gender, education, age, income, employment status, career status and language. In recent years, Bayt.com has also released mobile applications for Android, iPhone, Blackberry and Windows.

The UAE Today

In the years since Bayt.com was launched, the UAE has taken the lead in the ICT sector in the Gulf region. Overall it was ranked a relatively favourable 29th out of 120 countries in terms of entrepreneurial attitudes, aspirations and activity by the 2014 Global Entrepreneurship and Development Institute Index. Further to this, World Bank data indicate an improvement in the level of start-up activity since 2010. Samih Toukan, co-founder of Jordan-based Arabic portal Maktoob, claims that one of the good things about Dubai is that you can tap into resources from around the world (King 2013a). Companies locating in Dubai benefit from the Emirate's attractiveness as a preferred destination for talent from around the MENA region as well as from its being a strong draw for talent sourced more widely from around the globe (EIU 2013). Standing testament to this is Dubai's large expatriate community, which is estimated to account for around 90 % of the UAE's population (Tong et al. 2012). A benchmarking study conducted by the Economist Intelligence Unit (EIU) in 2013 identified Dubai's economic strength, low-tax and pro-business policies as key factors attracting businesses and people to the Emirate (EIU 2013).

Many of the Arab working class are eager to relocate to Dubai in pursuit of the opportunities it offers them and their families. Molavi (2004) cited a Dubai-based engineer who declared: 'In Dubai, the rulers create opportunities for everyone. Arab leaders all talk about dignity, but it is very hard to maintain dignity when you don't have enough money to support your family.' The 2014 edition of ASDA's Burson-Masteller Arab Youth Survey, which included 16 countries and 3500 face-to-face interviews, found that Arab youth named the UAE as the country they would most like to live in (Badam 2014); similar results were found in a survey of fresh graduates in the Middle East conducted by Bayt.com in 2010. These results illustrate the drawing power of the UAE in the Arab world.

Reflecting the attractiveness of the UAE as an employment destination, the WEF's Global Competitiveness Index (GCI) 2013–2014 ranked the UAE 7th out of 148 countries for its capacity to attract talent and 6th for its ability to retain talent (WEF 2013). The UAE also ranked a relatively strong 13thglobally for the availability of scientists and engineers, an important factor for the development of the nation's ICT industry.

In fact, the DIC free zone grew rapidly following its launch in 2000 (Sundaram 2002). It is now home to the regional headquarters of many of the world's leading ICT companies including Microsoft, Oracle, HP, IBM, Dell Siemens, Canon, Sony Ericsson, Schlumberger and Cisco. In 2011, DIC launched its first ICT incubator, the Majid bin Mohammed Innovation Centre, or in5. The stated aim of in5 is to promote entrepreneurship and technical innovation in the UAE by accelerating the development of new start-ups, fostering entrepreneurship, driving technology innovation, contributing to the ICT ecosystem and promoting Dubai as a location for tech start-ups. By 2013, the incubator was reported to be home to 33 tech start-ups and entrepreneurs.

How Did Bayt Do It?

It can be argued that in launching Bayt.com in 2000, the company's founders were able to clearly identify and effectively leverage the unique resources and characteristics presented by the start-up's Dubai location and the access this location afforded the start-up to the wider MENA region in order to derive a competitive advantage. In analysing the case of Bayt.com, Ataya argues that four areas of competitive advantage underpinned the success of the company, namely community, cost, convenience and calibre surpluses.

Community

A key factor behind Bayt.com's co-founder and CEO Ataya's initial decision to select Dubai as the base from which to launch his career as a technology entrepreneur reflected the community surpluses the location offered. The young entrepreneur was initially drawn by family connections and the offer of work at the family's construction business. He also had a community of friends in the Emirate, including alumni from Stanford. Moreover, Dubai offered an attractive lifestyle that aligned with his cultural preferences as a member of the community of the Arab diaspora. After Ataya successfully launched his first start-up, InfoFort, in Dubai in 1997, Dubai became the obvious choice of location for his next venture owing to the business connections Ataya had developed in the Emirate and MENA region. Added to this was the launch of DIC, first announced in 1999, which promised access to an important community of related businesses which would support the Internet start-up as it was established and grew.

Cost

Ataya asserts that the ability to establish a fully owned company in one of Dubai's free zones was of key importance to the founders of Bayt. com, claiming that Dubai was the first in the region that offered this form of company ownership. Had the company been required to offer a 51 % ownership stake in Bayt.com to a local sponsor, this would, Ataya posits, have represented a significant additional cost of doing business in the Emirate.

Convenience

Locating Bayt.com in Dubai afforded the online recruitment start-up convenient access to the strong growth market of Dubai and placed it within close proximity to fast-growing job markets across the MENA region. When Bayt.com was first launched in 2000, Ataya explains that the MENA region's population of just over 300 million was the fastest growing in the world. Moreover, he estimated that almost six million new jobseekers were entering regional job markets each year. The Middle East's rapidly growing young population was also becoming better educated and seeking attractive employment opportunities, especially in Dubai. At the same time, a large number of migrant workers were seeking employment opportunities in the MENA region, providing both opportunities and challenges for regional recruiters. Selective recruitment practices used by employers in the MENA region also meant that the advanced filtering systems offered by Bayt.com aligned well with the needs of regional markets.

Ataya and his fellow co-founders believed these factors combined to provide enormous growth potential in the MENA region going forward. This in turn provided Bayt.com, as a Dubai-based start-up, with immense opportunities for providing online recruitment services tailored to the needs of employers both in Dubai and across the region, despite low Internet penetration rates and the bursting of the dot-com bubble at the time. 'Dubai was young and showed a huge amount of promise. In deciding to launch Bayt.com I chose a business that suited Dubai and the MENA region', asserts Ataya.

From the early 2000s, fast-growing Internet penetration rates in Arab countries, especially in the UAE, were also transforming the way companies were doing business. Combined with the region's young and tech-savvy populations, being located in the MENA region provided Internet companies with ready access to enormous growth opportunities in what was a relatively untapped market.

Dubai's position as a regional and international business hub in the Arab world with a strong policy focus on developing its ICT sector also meant that the choice of location afforded Bayt.com considerable place surplus. The Emirate's ability to access talent from across the region and the globe further added to the attractiveness of the location.

Ataya also acknowledges the important advantages the start-up's original location in the newly launched DIC provided Bayt.com in its early days. As he explains, DIC provided access to good infrastructure and a good legal framework, together with the ability to register the company quickly and with 100 % foreign ownership. The free zone also provided Bayt.com with convenient access to a large network of suppliers which were important to its growing business. This and the strong support provided to the company as it first established operations, especially by the then head of DIC, HE Mohammed Al Gergawi, were important factors contributing to the place surplus offered by Dubai. In 2000, Ataya remarks, Dubai was 'a very welcoming business place'.

Expanding its operations across the different markets in the MENA region meant that Bayt.com needed to deal with a range of disparate laws and regulations as well as differing cultures and client needs and preferences. 'Almost every city state has a different set of legal and economic frameworks that you most operate within', explained Ataya. He recalls: 'Understanding what every city requires and how each differs is of key importance to success in region. The region is not uniform, and beyond a commonality of language and religion there is little that ties it together. However, there is an affinity of culture and language. As a business trying to tackle the region you really need to get into the nitty-gritty and understand the specific requirements of each location.' Further elaborating, Ataya explains: 'This offers both a challenge and an opportunity. If you can set up shop in each market and effectively deal with the legal and economic frameworks and conditions in each market then you have an almost insurmountable competitive advantage.'[5] Bayt.com responded by opening offices across the region in a strategy which enabled it to effectively navigate the differing legal and regulatory frameworks in each market and tailor its services to meet the needs of its diverse client base.

And while entrepreneurs in Dubai and its neighbours across the MENA region suffered from a lack of venture capital funding, the founders of Bayt.com were able to raise a first round of funding of US$3 million, which, combined with initial seed capital of US$500,000, was sufficient to launch the company. Cash-flow positive from the early days of operation, the start-up was subsequently able to self-fund growth going forward, thereby circumventing a key challenge presented by its MENA location.

---

[5] http://www.youtube.com/watch?v=E0BrYIRiuCo

Calibre

Bayt.com's Dubai headquarters not only provide it with convenient access to a large network of suppliers critical to its growth, including IT companies, advertising agencies and other support services, but Ataya opines that the calibre of companies located in Dubai was of critical importance to the development and growth of the company. Dubai boasted regional offices of many leading companies, including Oracle, Microsoft and others, which he contends provided a vital and high-quality support infrastructure. Further, Bayt.com was also able to leverage an advantage from the Emirate's strong drawing power, which enabled it to attract high-calibre talent and develop a strong management in its head office. The strength of Dubai's businesses community and its quality lifestyle contributed to the Emirate's drawing power.

By 2014, Bayt.com's revenue was growing by more than 30 % per annum, employed around 300 staff (with approximately 80 people at its Dubai headquarters and a similar number in its Jordan office) and remained very profitable. As well as continuing to incubate new Internet-based start-ups, Bayt.com was setting its eyes on new growth opportunities in the North African markets. Ataya expressed pride in the fact that instead of growing Bayt.com quickly and opting for a quick exit, the founders had gone a long way towards achieving their original vision of developing a start-up into a successful privately held company in the Middle East which invests in new businesses and supports entrepreneurship and job creation in the region.

References

Badam, R. T. 2014. UAE most popular country to live in, Arab youth survey. *The National*, 7 Apr. http://www.thenational.ae/uae/government/20140407/uae-most-popular-country-to-live-in-arab-youth-survey-reveals

EIU. 2013. Hot spots 2025—benchmarking the future competitiveness of cities. *The Economic Intelligence Unit*. file:///F:/1%20Innovation%20-%20IPI%20Sami%202013/1%20Silicon%20Valley%20Project/1%20Bayt/Lit%20Review/EIU%20hotspots2025.pdf

ITR. 2000. Dubai makes a bid for e-business. *International Tax Review*, 1 Dec, UK. http://www.internationaltaxreview.com/Article/2610904/Dubai-makes-a-bid-for-e-business.html

King, N. 2013a. Building an entrepreneurial ecosystem. *Arabian Business*, 30 Mar. http://www.arabianbusiness.com/building-entrepreneurial-ecosystem-495633.html

King, N. 2013b. Mona's world. *Arabian Business*, 1 Sept. http://floost.com/arabianbusiness-post-monas-world--arabianbusinesscom-6655925

Mahroum, S., J. M. Al-Bdour, E. Scott, S. Shouqar, and A. Arafat. 2013. Jordan: The Atlas of Islamic world science and innovation case study. Royal society & organisation of the Islamic conference. http://royalsociety.org/uploadedFiles/Royal_Society_Content/policy/projects/atlas-islamic-world/Atlas_Jordan.pdf

Molavi, A. 2004. Dubai dispatch: City on A Hill. *The New Republic*, 9 Feb.

Rahman, S. 2012. Doing business in the Mainland of Dubai through a free zone entity. UAE: Al Tamimi & Co., Nov. http://www.tamimi.com/en/magazine/law-update/section-6/november-3/doing-business-in-the-mainland-of-dubai-through-a-free-zone-entity.html

Rocha, R., S. Farazi, R. Khouri, and R. Pearce. 2011. The status of bank lending to SMEs in the Middle East and North Africa region: Results of a joint survey of the Union of Arab Bank. Policy research working paper 5607, The World Bank and The Union of Arab Banks, Mar. http://elibrary.worldbank.org/doi/pdf/10.1596/1813-9450-5607

Sundaram, V. 2002. Dubai Internet City: Distant destination? *Silicon India*, Nov. http://www.siliconindia.com/magazine_articles/Dubai_Internet_City__Distant_Destination-GEY401598954.html

Tong, Q., D. McCrohan, and M.S. Erogul. 2012. An analysis of entrepreneurship across five major nationality groups in the United Arab Emirates. *Journal of Development Entrepreneurship* 17: 4.

WEF. 2013. The global competitiveness report 2013–2014. *World Economic Forum*. http://www.weforum.org/reports/global-competitiveness-report-2013-2014

13

Atlassian in Sydney: Beating the Tyranny of Distance

Atlassian is an enterprise software company providing collaborative software for product teams founded in Sydney, Australia, in 2002, by Scott Farquhar and Mike Cannon-Brookes—then both in their early 20s—who first met in 1998 when they were recipients of the Business IT Co-op Scholarship at the University of New South Wales (UNSW). A little more than a decade after Atlassian's launch, the company had almost 40,000 customers worldwide, close to 1000 employees across 6 offices around the globe, annual turnover nearing US$250 million, and an estimated valuation in the vicinity of US$3.3 billion (Michal 2014; Schetzer 2014). Atlassian's large market size, high growth rate, its approach to marketing and its ability to maintain profitability from the outset had made it unique amongst software companies. The company's client list also read like a business who's who and included NASA, BMW, Pfizer, Samsung, eBay, Harvard, MIT, Visa, Procter & Gamble, Shell, American Express, Cisco, Honeywell and the New York Stock Exchange, to name just a few.

© The Editor(s) (if applicable) and The Author(s) 2016   **215**
S. Mahroum, *Black Swan Start-ups*,
DOI 10.1057/978-1-137-57727-6_13

Australia as a Place for Entrepreneurs

Historically, Australia's economy has been driven by its manufacturing, mining and agricultural sectors. However, as the country entered the new millennium, it confronted the need to transition to a knowledge-based economy where the Internet and technology would take a front seat in driving future growth. 'We can no longer rely on the land, through minerals and agriculture in particular, or the heavy lifting done by previous generations of manufacturing. We can no longer rely on that to sustain our quality of life in the future', said Australian Treasurer Joe Hockey (Coorey and Tingle 2014).

Atlassian stood at the forefront of tech start-ups looking to take this leap and push the economy forward. Historically, Australia's distance from the major trading hubs of Europe and America had proved problematic for local companies and caused many to focus on domestic markets, thereby limiting their potential for growth. A study of Australia's start-up ecosystem by Deloitte (2012) concluded that Australia's small population and geographic distance from major markets had shaped the country's business culture, leading companies to take fewer risks and instead focus on the domestic market rather than build global businesses. Indeed, Australian's early tech start-up success stories, such as SEEK.com.au and realestate.com.au (established in Melbourne in 1995), had initially targeted customers in the domestic market before expanding globally.

An initial analysis of international indicators suggests a relatively favourable environment for innovation and entrepreneurship in Australia. The Global Entrepreneurship and Development Index 2013 ranked Australia 4th out of 121 countries and highlighted Australia's strengths in terms of its entrepreneurial ability (e.g. quality of human resources and technology sector) (GEDI 2013). The Global Innovation Index 2014 also placed Australia at a relatively strong 17th out of 143 countries based on a multifaceted assessment of innovation drivers and outcomes (Cornell et al., 2014; GEDI 2013). In 2010, expenditure on research and development (R&D) was equivalent to 2.4 % of GDP in Australia, a level that compared favourably to countries including the USA (2.7 %), the UK (1.8 %), Germany (2.8 %) and China (1.8 %) but that lagged noticeably behind countries such as Israel (3.8 %), Japan (3.3 %) and Korea (3.7 %). In terms of ease of doing business—an important factor for new business ventures—Australia was ranked 11th out of 189 countries by the World Bank (World Bank 2014). Sydney also offered entrepreneurs an attractive lifestyle, with the Economist Intelligence Unit (EIU) ranking it the fifth most liveable city in the world (EIU 2012).

In 2012, an in-depth study of the Australian start-up ecosystem released by Deloitte Private et al. ranked Sydney's start-up hub 12th globally. Hubs were ranked according to the number of companies they produced, the availability of funding and other support, start-up performance, talent availability, community mindset, how quickly the community learnt and adapted and the diversity of ecosystems (Deloitte 2012).

Despite the favourable picture painted by these indicators, areas of weakness were also evident. Of particular importance was the country's high cost structure, with Australia ranked 113th out of 148 countries based on the extent to which pay is related to worker productivity (WEF 2013a). Australia also ranked a poor 107th out of 144 countries for its high total tax rate (WEF and INSEAD, 2014). In mid-2014, Numbeo, the world's largest user-contributed database, ranked Australia 6th out of 119 countries (and Sydney 23rd out of 446 cities) for its cost of living. This high-cost environment presented a challenge for entrepreneurs trying to bootstrap their start-ups in Sydney. Additionally, and according to the World Economic Forum, Australia also ranked a low 124th out of 140 countries for ease of hiring foreign labour (WEF 2013b), the result of the country's strict immigration laws.

A review of the Australian start-up ecosystem by StartupAus—an organisation representing key leaders in the local start-up community—claimed that Australian culture failed to celebrate or promote an entrepreneurial mindset (StartupAUS 2014). Compared to their Silicon Valley counterparts, Australian entrepreneurs also considered themselves less likely to succeed and were more cautious before launching a start-up, according to 'Silicon Beach', a recent study of the Australian ecosystem conducted by Deloitte Private et al. (2012). Nevertheless, the study determined that Australian entrepreneurs were more committed to building great products and long-term businesses and were less likely to be motivated by monetary rewards.

Jono Herrman, co-founder of StartNest, a co-working space located on Sydney's North Shore, says 'People don't typically establish start-ups in Sydney because of the start-up ecosystem. They establish start-ups here because of the lifestyle and personal and family connections'.[1]

Many stakeholders also point to insufficient government support of the tech start-up sector. Atlassian's founders were especially outspoken in calling for reforms to Australia's strict immigration laws and in particular the relaxation of restrictions applying to the country's 457 visas to enable start-ups to employ sufficient skilled information and communications technology (ICT) talent from overseas to address the talent gap in the local market (Fitzsimmons 2014a; StartupAUS 2014).

A post on the Website of Pollenizer, a Sydney-based start-up incubator and accelerator and consultancy practice, provided a good overview of Sydney's start-up scene: 'The startup scene in Sydney is definitely growing but there is still a need for more government funding and education and capital investment. The general population are starting to look towards innovation and entrepreneurship as there is a stronger belief towards these areas being key drivers of the economy in the near future.'[2, 3]

Sydney's strong Asian connections also worked to the advantage of start-ups wishing to gain a foothold in Asia. Sydney had a growing Asian immigrant population and a large number of Asian students studying at its universities, and Mandarin and Cantonese were the most commonly spoken second languages. In addition to strong networks across Asia, Sydneysiders could also leverage the city's historic links with the UK, Europe and the USA, which provided local start-ups with extensive global networks to leverage.

Additionally, Australia's clear rule of law proved attractive to start-ups. Melissa Ran of New South Innovations (NSi), an initiative of the UNSW aimed at encouraging students to become entrepreneurs, added that a high degree of social order, including low levels of corruption and low

---

[1] From interview with Jono Herrman, co-founder, StartNest, on 5 November 2014.

[2] http://pollenizer.com/sydney-startup-scene/.

[3] Cooper estimated that that the east coast of Australia was in the same time zone as almost two-thirds of the world's online population.

barriers to entry (e.g., the low cost of registering a legal business entity), provided a favourable environment for starting a business in the city.[4]

While the tech sector remained small, start-up activity had increased significantly in recent years, with around two-thirds of Australia's estimated 1500 tech start-ups located in Sydney (PwC 2013). In addition to Atlassian, a growing number of Australian tech companies, such as Freelancer, BigCommerce and 99designs, had begun to achieve a significant global scale. Modelling conducted by PwC (and sponsored by Google) estimated that the economic contribution of high-growth technology companies could grow as high as 4 %of gross domestic product (GDP) by 2033 (PwC 2013).

Although the ecosystem for tech start-ups has changed and improved drastically since the company first launched, Sydney has yet to achieve the critical mass necessary for a tech hub to generate the types of symbiotic relationships and interactions that underpin the success of more established start-up hubs (Heber 2014).

How They Did It

Farquhar and Cannon-Brookes both had been inspired by the Internet boom and the international success stories of high-tech companies such as Microsoft and Hewlett-Packard (Zalan et al. 2009).

Cannon-Brookes eventually dropped out of university and, still in his late teens, founded a start-up with fellow student Niki Scevak which developed an Internet bookmark management tool named Bookmark Box. After some initial success they sold the start-up to US Internet company Blink.com just before the dot.com crash (Fitzsimmons 2014c). Cannon-Brookes then went on to work for a research firm and travelled extensively around Asia evaluating Internet start-ups. During this time he claimed to have learnt 'a lot of lessons about how not to run a business'. When the research firm closed its Asian office in 2001 owing to the

---

[4] From interview with Melissa Ran, Associate, New South Innovations, UNSW, on 7 November 2014.

dot-com crash, Cannon-Brookes returned to university to complete his studies (Zalan et al. 2009).

By late 2001, he had teamed up with Farquhar, who was also finishing his tertiary studies at UNSW. Unsatisfied with the employment options on offer in Sydney to graduates and eschewing the notion of working for large corporations—the most popular career path for graduates at the time—the duo made the decision to establish their own start-up.

Cannon-Brookes claimed they complemented each other; he was the 'ideas man' while Farquhar turned his ideas into a structure and steered the ship (Lacy 2013). In 2002, the pair established a software consultancy company, registering the business name Atlassian, after the Greek titan Atlas (Zalan et al. 2009; Fitzsimmons 2014a; Tay 2014). 'Our original goal as founders for the company was just to earn as much money as our friends were earning working for soul destroying consulting companies like IBM or PWC', explained Farquhar (Moses 2010).

The Vision

The founders' goal was to provide everything customers needed online. Atlassian's Website was designed to be the company's primary sales and marketing tool and to provide ongoing customer support and maintenance. They reckoned that with improving Internet speeds, the Internet would provide an effective distribution channel for their products (Tay 2014). 'We felt if we could sell something at a reasonable price, and sell it on the Internet, then we'd be able to find a market there. And that's what worked out', explained Farquhar (Morrell 2014).

Cannon-Brookes recalled: 'We were determined to prove we could sell enterprise software through the Internet. You have to cast your mind back to 2002, and that was a very foreign notion compared to today' (Lacy 2013). This meant that Atlassian was able to avoid the high costs associated with hiring dedicated sales and support staff. Instead, resources were directed towards engineering efforts to develop a user-friendly platform.

This strategy enabled them to overcome the tyranny of distance that Australian businesses had struggled with for generations and provided the start-up with a competitive edge in the market for enterprise software.

Enterprise software was regarded as the 'bread and butter' of Silicon Valley, yet Atlassian was able to beat Silicon Valley companies at their own game (Lacy 2013). It had done this by effectively addressing several of the key weaknesses of the enterprise software market at the time, namely: (1) user hostility, (2) high licensing and support costs and (3) a lack of flexibility and agility (McLellan 2013). Instead of selling the expensive, multiple-component systems offered by other enterprise software companies, which included costly add-ons and tied companies into pricey service agreement contracts, Atlassian was able to develop a suite of products which customers could add on to at any time at a fraction of the cost of competitor products, as well as provide ongoing customer support and maintenance, all from a user-friendly online platform.

The founders also worked on the premise that once software was developed, it could be cheaply replicated. Adopting a lean start-up model, they were able to successfully develop and sell software that was much cheaper than other products available on the market at the time. Importantly, Atlassian's low-cost online software model made it accessible to small teams which could sign up for its products without the need for lengthy authorisation processes. This strategy meant that Atlassian's sales often grew virally through a company (Geron 2012).

Early sales were to friends and through word of mouth via the company's networks. Atlassian's first UK customers, for example, came through their connections in the Java developer community. A critical development which validated the founders' business model was when it received a purchase order from American Airlines, one of Atlassian's earliest customers. American Airlines purchased Atlassian's software directly from its Website without any personal interaction with the company; the first they knew of the sale was when they received a facsimiled purchase order from the airline (Lacy 2013). 'Customers could install the product themselves and figure out how to use it simply by trying it or reading online documentation', claimed Cannon-Brookes (Geron 2012). At this point, they realised: 'We can have a huge number of customers that pay a very low price and change the way enterprise software is sold to large organisations. We don't need armies of sales people running around the globe' (Lacy 2013). In the first year of operations, the company generated revenues of $1 million (Tay 2014).

Dual Headquarters

From the early days, Atlassian had established dual head offices in Sydney and San Francisco. For a long time Cannon-Brookes split his time equally between the two locations, although over time this dropped to around 1 week in 4 spent in the USA. Having a presence in both places enabled Atlassian to build strong networks in both ecosystems (Lacy 2013). Cannon-Brookes claimed that Silicon Valley gave them access to people who were building 'amazing companies that change industries and the planet because they have this vision'.

Nevertheless, Sydney provided a relatively cheaper base from which to operate (Gardner 2012). By retaining a presence in Sydney, Atlassian also had direct access to 'a large community of corporate customers who want to do better at what they do', posited Cannon-Brookes. Having a base in each location afforded Atlassian a unique perspective of what customers wanted; Cannon-Brookes argued that Australian companies did not want to be lectured that 'Facebook does it this way, therefore you should do this too' (Lacy 2013).

Most of the company's engineering, R&D, customer support and corporate functions remained in Sydney, while the San Francisco office gave it access to marketing talent not available in Australia; other offices were established largely for time-zone considerations to facilitate customer support (Zalan et al. 2009). As the company grew, a shortage of software engineers in the developed world saw Atlassian also establish an engineering office in South-East Asia (Smith 2012). By 2014, Atlassian had offices in Amsterdam, Austin, Manila, San Francisco, Sydney and Yokohama, employed a small number of developers in Poland, and had small sales offices in other markets (Fitzsimmons 2013).

Shifting Its Domicile to the UK

While Atlassian considered itself an Australian company, in early 2014 it announced that it was shifting its legal headquarters to the UK (Fitzsimmons 2014c; Wallbank 2014). While the company planned to retain a large number of people in Sydney and indicated that it would continue to collect all of its revenue through Australia, after some soul-searching the founders decided that it would be in the best interests of the company to be domiciled in the UK. The founders reasoned that this would move the company closer to a global investor base which was more used to investing in UK companies (Waters 2014). The British government had worked with the tech community in the implementation of a range of initiatives aimed at making London a global tech centre by attracting entrepreneurs and small businesses. For example, London offered companies certain advantages, including favourable taxation arrangements for employee share options, the UK Entrepreneur Visa and the Small Enterprise Investment Scheme (Wallbank 2014). These initiatives were particularly important to Atlassian as it moved towards an IPO (Tay 2014). Cannon-Brookes and Farquhar indicated that other factors influencing their decision to move included where the company's customers were located, where the team wanted to live and treaties between Australia and the UK (Waters 2014).

Adopting a Long-Term View for Growth and the Decision to Raise Venture Capital

Farquhar and Cannon-Brookes bootstrapped Atlassian for 8 years before they decided to raise venture capital. The year 2009 was a turning point for the founders; both had turned 30 and were getting married and felt the need to re-evaluate their lives (Tay 2014). They started asking themselves what the future held, including whether they should sell the company. It was at this point they concluded that Atlassian still had its best years ahead of it. Farquhar and Cannon-Brookes decided that a good measure of their success would be whether or not Atlassian was still around in 50 years' time.

They also believed that many companies often hit a ceiling when they reached annual revenues of around $80 million to $100 million. While access to venture capital (VC) was reported to have improved over recent years,[5] start-ups still encountered difficulties in sourcing funding from local investors, especially as they entered their growth phase. Despite often being able to access some level of seed capital, the funding necessary for start-ups to take the next step was limited (Twemlow 2014).

---

[5] From interview with Jono Herrman, co-founder, StartNest, on 5 November 2014.

Freelancer's Matt Barrie described the situation for start-ups seeking VC funding in the $1 million to $5 million range as like being in the Valley of Death in Australia.[6] And while Barrie noted that some superfunds were looking to invest directly in local start-ups, deal values for seed and early-stage capital were generally too low for most superfunds, which usually made much larger investments on the order of $100 million.[7]

Stuart Richardson, founder and managing partner of Australian VC firm Adventure Capital, argued that 'Private investors are equally risk-averse taking safety in passive investments such as property and cash'. 'There is no denying that our risk-aversion and short-sightedness is holding us back as a smart country failing at innovation on the grandest scales', lamented Richardson.

And while crowd-sourced equity funding had gained increasing popularity in overseas markets, legal restrictions in Australia prevented start-ups from offering equity through crowdfunding platforms. Consequently, crowdfunding remained a relatively untapped market, although a review of legislation was underway (Fitzsimmons 2014b). Barrie (2013) contended that crowd-sourced equity funding had 'the potential to disrupt the entire venture capital industry and turn GPs into stock pickers'. He advocated a model whereby crowdfunding was run through a regulated stock exchange in order to protect the rights of crowd-funded equity holders.

Accordingly, the founders decided to bring in an experienced outside investor who could act as mentor, provide access to important networks and help build a great board and a strong management team to guide the company's future growth. Like many Australian tech companies, Atlassian looked to the USA and, in July 2010, sold a 20 % stake in the company and raised $60 million in growth financing from leading Silicon Valley VC firm Accel Partners. This move marked a new growth trajectory for the company (Fitzsimmons 2014c; Lacy 2013; Tay 2014).

In early 2014, Atlassian raised a further $150 million from US-based T. Rowe Price and Dragoneer Investment Capital. This amounted to a 4.5 % stake and valued Atlassian at $3.3 billion, eight times higher than

---

[6] From interview with Matt Barrie, founder of Freelancer.com, on 6 November 2014.
[7] From interview with Matt Barrie and Peter Cooper, Freelancer, 6 November 2014.

in 2010 (Fitzsimmons 2014a). Cannon-Brookes claimed that this second deal marked the next stage in the company's life. Whereas the Accel deal had been undertaken so they could learn about scale and growth, the second deal was designed to bring in an equity partner who knew about public markets and to prepare Atlassian for an initial public offering (IPO). At the same time, the deal enabled past and present employees to liquidate shares (Lev-Ram 2014). 'As we head towards an initial public offering we've now got one of the largest tech investors in the US on board and with their public market experience they will really help us set up', asserted Farquhar (Waters 2014).

Recruiting and Retaining Talent

Atlassian had initially recruited staff through personal contacts and networks, especially classmates from UNSW; Cannon-Brookes states: 'We knew they were smart' (Fitzsimmons 2014c; Tay 2014). The founders considered Sydney engineering talent to be highly skilled, while the country's developers were also considerably cheaper and more loyal than their counterparts in Silicon Valley (Gardner 2012). Cannon-Brookes attributed the greater levels of loyalty to a lack of competition in the Sydney marketplace, with local ventures competing against banks, retailers and resource companies rather than tech giants such as Google and Facebook when recruiting talent. Cannon-Brookes felt it was easier in Sydney to 'be cool' and a preferred employer than in Silicon Valley.

However, as Atlassian grew, it was challenged by a shortage of skilled ICT talent. 'There are not enough good graduates coming out of university [in Australia]', opined Farquhar (Smith 2012). He claimed they were 'turning over every rock we can find to find talented people in Australia' (Whyte 2014). Added to this, the country's nascent start-up scene lacked people with experience growing technology companies. Cannon-Brookes noted: 'We have very smart engineers in Australia but we don't have very experienced engineers.'

Growing competitiveness in the global recruitment market also saw Atlassian open offices in new locations. Cannon-Brookes explained: 'That's one of the reasons we're opening an office in Austin [Texas] and most of our engineering is in Sydney—to give us multiple hiring centers.' Christian Macolino, a senior recruiter with Atlassian, indicated that the company relied heavily on foreign nationals. 'There are only a few thousand Java developers in Australia, and assuming we go for the top 1 %, that doesn't give us a huge amount of talent to pull from', he opined (Cottell 2014). Fortunately, international talent was attracted to Australia for a number of reasons, including its beaches, good education and lifestyle, claimed Macolino. By 2014, Atlassian was recruiting around 40 % of its staff in Australia from abroad (Cottell 2014).

Graeme Smith, director of IT recruiter Network20, argued that Atlassian refined its recruitment processes over time and were more realistic than competitors in the recruitment market, with companies such as Google often demanding many interviews and taking prolonged periods to make hiring decisions. He posited that the Atlassian recruitment team was 'more realistic and don't ask people to jump through as many hoops' (Smith 2012). Atlassian recognised that key to its success was its ability to attract and retain the best tech talent and experience from around the world. To do this, it needed to stand out from the competition as a place to work. Cannon-Brookes explained: 'We need the best minds to work for us to make amazing products that compete on the world market. We do what it takes to attract, nurture and retain those incredibly talented people'. Farquhar added: 'I want to ruin employees so they never want to work anywhere else. I want them to rue the day they left Atlassian' (Smith 2012).

How Did Atlassian Do It?

Addressing a group of investors in 2013, Jonathan Teo, former Managing Director of Silicon Valley venture capital firm General Catalyst, opined that successful Australian start-ups such as Atlassian and 99Designs were 'one-offs' (Khadem 2013). The development of a vibrant start-up ecosystem in Australia, Teo argued, required the country play to its strengths in mining, health care or agriculture in order to develop a start-up 'niche' or a 'brand' that would in turn create an ecosystem that could support 'a multitude of companies that do well globally'.

Community Surplus

For Atlassian, it was the founders' personal and professional networks that tied them to Sydney and maintained their loyalty to the city. From the onset, they have, for example, started the company using desks in the offices of a company owned by a friend from university. This 'community' aspect of the place gave it an important sense of surplus to the owners, something that might not be the same had they been from out of town. But in addition, voted continuously as one of the most liveable places in the world, the quality lifestyle offered by Sydney which the founders valued proved conducive to attracting talent to Sydney from overseas.

Cost Surplus

Other factors also played to Sydney's advantage, such as the relatively low cost structure vis-à-vis Silicon Valley. This is an important observation since, although Sydney is still a relatively high-cost location versus other locations in Asia and parts of Europe, for Atlassian the comparison was always with the other most suitable location for their business, namely Silicon Valley. This comparison also characterised the nature of the short-comings, such as low access to quality talent—while quality was high, it was in short supply, resulting in a talent gap in the local labour market. Also, in comparison with Silicon Valley or London, there was a lack of VC, with local investors risk adverse and unfamiliar with investing in tech start-ups and large superfunds reluctant to invest in tech start-ups.

Unlike Silicon Valley, Sydney and Australia in general lacked established success stories and mentors with a 'pay-it-forward' mindset. Other problems Atlassian's founders had to overcome by expanding and branching out overseas were strict migration laws impeding the hiring of skilled talent from overseas to bridge shortfalls in the supply of talent in local markets and the taxation of employee share options—introduced in 2009, after Atlassian was established.

Nevertheless, despite the decision to domicile Atlassian in London, the founders were adamant that they would continue to live in Sydney and that it would remain Australian in terms of its physical presence

(Fitzsimmons 2014a). Farquhar asserted, 'We still bring all our revenue through Australia', while acknowledging that the company's global tax rate was likely to be slightly lower as a result of incorporating in the UK (Fitzsimmons 2014c).

References

Barrie, M. 2013. Crowdfunding. Influencer article, Linkedin. http://www.linkedin.com/pulse/article/20130407082610-921366-crowdfunding. Accessed 10 Nov 2014.

Coorey, P., and L. Tingle. 2014. Hockey lays grounds for cuts. Australian Financial Review, 5 Feb 2014. http://www.afr.com/p/national/hockey_lays_ground_for_cuts_KF85IKpfopp7oyN79jDn5H

Cornell, INSEAD & WIPO. 2014. The global innovation index 2013. Johnson Cornell University, INSEAD, & World Intellectual Property Organisation (UN). http://www.globalinnovationindex.org/content.aspx?page=GII-Home

Cottell, C. 2014. Global spotlight on Australia Recruiter magazine, Sept 2014. http://www.recruiter.co.uk/analysis/2014/09/global-spotlight-on-australia/

Deloitte Private, Pollenizer and Startup Genome. 2012. Silicon beach—building momentum: A study of the Australian startup ecosystem [WWW]. Available from:http://www2.deloitte.com/content/dam/Deloitte/au/Documents/technology-media-telecommunications/deloitte-au-tmt-silicon-beach-031014.pdf.

EIU. 2012. Best cities ranking and report. Economist Intelligence Unit. 2012. http://pages.eiu.com/rs/eiu2/images/EIU_BestCities.pdf

Fitzsimmons, C. 2013. Tech growth star revs up: Atlassian to add 100 staff in next three months. BRW, 6 June 2013. http://www.brw.com.au/p/tech_growth_star_revs_next_atlassian_IVOrGq78Q1708BKyUXD6nN

Fitzsimmons, C. 2014a. Accidental billionaires: Why Atlassian's Mike Cannon-Brookes and Scott Farquhar are so admired in the start-up sndustry'. BRW, 12 Apr 2014. http://www.brw.com.au/p/tech-gadgets/accidental_billionaires_admired_pWZSTvYYXQWnZe91atJY6K

Fitzsimmons, C. 2014b. Equity or rewards-based, how start-ups harness crowd-funding. Australian Financial Review, 2 May 2014. http://www.brw.com.au/p/entrepreneurs/equity_or_rewards_based_how_start_g7UUnd5BKhzeZLoWzk2JjM

Fitzsimmons, C. 2014c. How Atlassian's Scott Faraquhar and Mike Cannon_ Brookes became software titans. Australian Financial Review, 25 July 2014. http://www.afr.com/p/lifestyle/afrmagazine/titans_atlassian_scott_ farquhar_DA1hhVu8LaPJkQChS0OnrO

Gardner, J. 2012. Greetings from a start-up nation. BRW. 23rd – 29th Aug 2012, pp. 22–27.

GEDI. 2013. GEDI index. The Global Entrepreneurship and Development Institute. http://www.thegedi.org/research/gedi-index/

Geron, T. 2012. We're all coders: Atlassian opens up the engineering sandbox. Forbes, 12 Mar 2012. http://www.forbes.com/sites/tomiogeron/2012/02/22/ were-all-coders-atlassian-opens-up-the-engineering-sandbox/

Heber, A. 2014. Atlassian founder Mike Cannon-Brookes says Sydney should be Australia's tech hub. Business Insider Australia, 3 Sept 2014. http://www. businessinsider.com.au/atlassian-founder-mike-cannon- brookes-says-sydney-should-be-australias-tech-hub-2014-9

Khadem, N. 2013. Start-up nation: Australia needs specialisation and tax breaks, says leading US investor Johnathan Teo. BRW, 28 Oct 2013. http:// www.brw.com.au/p/entrepreneurs/start_leading_nation_australia_ needs_Tjal2sjQy15rqqBCFzeQ0I

Lacy, S. 2013. A fireside chat with Atlassian's Scott Farquhar and Mike Cannon-Brookes. PandoDaily, 3 Oct 2013. https://www.youtube.com/watch?v= pty1LR-XtuU

Lev-Ram, M. 2014. Atlassian: The $3.3 billion company you've never heard of. Fortune, 10 Apr 2014. http://fortune.com/2014/04/10/atlassian-the-3-3- billion-software-company-youve-never-heard-of/

McLellan, C. 2013. The evolution of enterprise software: An overview. ZDNet. com, 1 May 2013. http://www.zdnet.com/the-evolution-of-enterprise -software-an-overview-7000014006/

Michal, L. 2014. Atlassian: The $3.3 billion software company you've never heard of. Fortune.com, 11 Apr 2014. http://fortune.com/2014/04/10/ atlassian-the-3-3-billion-software-company-youve-never-heard-of/

Morrell, A. 2014. Two 34-year-old Aussies are latest techies to become billion- aires thanks to sky high financing round. Forbes, 9 Apr 2014. http://www. forbes.com/sites/alexmorrell/2014/04/09/new-financing-round- for-australian-software-company-atlassian-turns-founders-into-billionaires/

Moses, A. 2010, From uni dropouts to software magnates. Sydney Morning Herald, 15 July 2010. http://www.smh.com.au/technology/enterprise/from-uni-dropouts-to-software-magnates-20100714-10bdh.html

PwC. 2013. The start-up economy: How to support tech start-ups and accelerate Australian innovation. PWC Digital Pulse, Apr 2013. http://www.digitalpulse.pwc.com.au/wp-content/uploads/2013/04/PwC-Google-The-startup-economy-2013.pdf

Schetzer, A. 2014. Atlassian sales leap 44% as revenue hits $242 million. Australian Financial Review, 13 Sept 2014. http://www.afr.com/p/technology/atlassian_sales_leap_as_revenue_7HYwjBcYr0BZzL0pDn6N4O

Smith, F. 2012. Is Atlassian the coolest company in Australia? BEW, 8 Nov 2012. http://www.brw.com.au/p/sections/features/is_atlassian_the_coolest_company_877SCYxXLwl7N9cNiMF6vJ

StartupAus. 2014. Crossroads: An action plan to develop a vibrant tech startup ecosystem in Australia. StartupAUS, Apr 2014. http://startupaus.org/crossroads/

Tay, L. 2014. Atalssian – The untold story: How two Australian young guns built a company headed for a billion-dollar IPO, BusinessInsider, 7 Feb 2014. http://www.businessinsider.com.au/atlassian-the-untold-story-how-two-australian-young-guns-built-a-company-headed-for-a-billion-dollar-ipo-2014-2

Twemlow, G. 2014. Australia's unregulated tech incubator scene could be doing more harm than good. Sydney Morning Herald, 17 June 2014. http://www.smh.com.au/it-pro/it-opinion/australias-unregulated-tech-incubator-scene-could-be-doing-more-harm-than-good-20140616-zs97u.html

Wallbank, P. 2014. Atlassian's move to the UK exposes Australia's tech investment black hole. SmartCompany, 8 Jan 2014. http://www.smartcompany.com.au/technology/35070-atlassian-move-to-london-exposes-australia-s-tech-investment-black-hole.html

Waters, C. 2014. The long-term view is the secret to Atlassian's success. StartupSmart, 10 Apr 2014. http://www.startupsmart.com.au/growth/atlassian-co-founder-scott-farquhar-on-how-he-became-australias-newest-billionaire/2014041012093.html

WEF. 2013a. The global competitiveness report 2013-2014. World Economic Forum. http://www.weforum.org/reports/global-competitiveness-report-2013-2014

WEF. 2013b. The travel and tourism competitiveness report 2013. World Economic Forum. http://www.weforum.org/reports/travel-tourism-competitiveness-report-2013

WEF & INSEAD. 2014. The global information technology report 2014. http://www3.weforum.org/docs/WEF_GlobalInformationTechnology_Report_2014.pdf

Whyte, J. 2014. Government doesn't understand technology: Atlassian co-founders. BRW, 26 May 2014. http://www.brw.com.au/p/business/mid-market/government_doesn_understand_technology_vlN3H1L cnw7OinSQT8ilPN

World Bank. 2014. Doing business 2014. http://www.doingbusiness.org/~/media/GIAWB/Doing%20Business/Documents/Annual-Reports/English/DB14-Full-Report.pdf

Zalan, T., O. Muzychenko., and S. Burshtein. 2009. Atlassian: Supporting the world with legendary service. Case study. *Journal of International Business Education* 4 (Ref. No. JIBE4-0CS2, 2009).

14

All Unhappy Start-ups Are Alike, Each Happy Start-up Is Unique

In *Anna Karenina*, Leo Tolstoy cautions us that *'All happy families are all alike; each unhappy family is unhappy in its own way'*. The so-called Anna Karenina Principle suggests that reasons for failure are manifold and complex, and only one of them is needed for a company to fail. This is true of start-ups; a recent survey by CB Insights found that the number one reason for start-up failure (42 %) was having a product buyers did not want, followed by running out of cash (29 %). But what about the causes of success? As we have seen in the 11 cases examined in this book, every successful (happy) start-up was successful in its own way. It is the Anna Karenina Principle again, only in reverse, whereby all unhappy start-ups are alike, but *every happy start-up is happy in its own way*. Peter Thiel, co-founder of PayPal, in his book *Zero to One: Notes on Startups, or How to Build the Future*, echoes a similar conclusion that 'all happy companies are different because they found something unique that defines their mission and their purpose in this world, whereas all unhappy companies are alike because they somehow failed to escape the essential sameness that is competition'.

© The Editor(s) (if applicable) and The Author(s) 2016
S. Mahroum, *Black Swan Start-ups*,
DOI 10.1057/978-1-137-57727-6_14

Indeed, the conditions of success seem to be more intricate than those of failure and are often identified only in hindsight. People can only speculate about what will lead them to success and hope that they are right, but there are many things that people know which will surely lead them to failure. Nevertheless, it is tempting to look for patterns or shared observations amongst the rich insights derived from the 11 cases studied in this book. Hence, in this final chapter, we go back to where we began to explore the conditions which mattered for success. And though we are not able to generalise, we can identify these and survey them every time they are observed to have played a role. Applying the light format of grounded-theory coding, I use the materials derived from the interviews and the literature review to extract and generate structured information which can be used to derive insightful observations. More specifically, I search for the 15 conditions outlined in Chap. 2 across the 11 cases to examine their relevance and importance in every case. I ask how many of the 15 start up supporting ecosystem conditions were actually relevant to the success of our black swans, and how many of these factors were actually present. Is it possible to identify a set of 'domestication conditions', to use Jared Diamond's term, as critical conditions for start-up survival in a particular place?

The 15 Conditions That Were Observed to Be Relevant Across the 11 Cases

Examining the materials we have at hand, we find that 4 of the 15 ecosystem conditions appear as relevant to the success of all 11 companies (Fig. 14.1). These include access to global networks of knowledge and information, access to a variety of professional business services, access to professional social and professional networks and access to risk capital. These four conditions appear critical in every one of the 11 cases. Furthermore, with the exception of Red Bull, access to highly skilled talent emerges as a fifth critical condition of success.

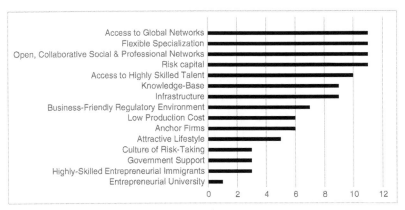

Fig. 14.1 Factors cited as most relevant for success

What Else Is Important?

The interview data reveal the importance of certain other aspects which might not be as critical but potentially very conducive to success, such as the availability of entrepreneurial universities, skilled immigrants, anchor firms and an attractive lifestyle. These conditions enhance what I referred to as the calibre and convenience factors of a place. They add to the quality of doing business in places which have them in abundance as they directly impact some of the critical conditions identified earlier, such as access to professional networks. They also enhance the quality of the surrounding local community, which is often cited as a key aspect of what makes Silicon Valley succeed in high-tech entrepreneurship. In Table 14.1, I provide an overview of how often a relevant mention of one of the five Cs was made in interviews.

From these observations one can infer that calibre- and convenience-enhancing conditions are the most important factors in locations for technology start-ups, whereas cost and creativity appear less important. But overall, different conditions appear to matter more than others in each case. For example, in the case of Red Bull, to manufacture and market a

Table 14.1 Frequency of observations of relevant supporting conditions distributed along the five Cs

Cost (total observations: 9)	Calibre (total observations: 39)	Convenience (total observations: 37)	Creative destruction (total observations: 4)	Community (total observations: 17)
Low-cost production (6) Government support (3)	Infrastructure (9) Access to highly skilled talent (10) Flexible specialisation (11) Knowledgebase (9)	Access to global networks (11) Business-friendly regulatory environment (7) Highly skilled entrepreneurial immigrants (3) Risk capital (11) Attractive lifestyle (5)	Entrepreneurial university (1) Culture of Risk-taking (3)	Open and collaborative social and professional networks (11) Anchor firms (6)

lifestyle-targeted beverage, there was little need for it to be located in a city with skilled immigrants or an entrepreneurial university. Fuschl am See, near Salzburg, Austria, the home town of Red Bull, lacks most of the 15 ecosystem conditions identified with start-up success. For Red Bull, there was no particularly important factor or condition in Austria or its local region apart from its relevance as a place for extreme outdoor supports where the company brands itself as the number one drink for its community. Another interesting example is the case of Sofizar, which, as we saw, despite the fact that it is located in an area that lacks most of the 15 needed ecosystem conditions, the founder—Zafar Khan—was concerned only with one missing factor—local access to global networks.

The overall picture from the 11 cases looks like this: the importance of the various 15 conditions differed widely across the 11 cases, with Bayt in Dubai and 24 symbols in Madrid citing 10 or more of them as being relevant and important for their success, but Sofizar in Lahore, Pakistan, and Red Bull citing only 6 of the 15 as being relevant and important (Fig. 14.2).

Eight out of the fifteen conditions were absent in at least half of the 11 cases. Access to talent was available in all 11 locations, whereas access to risk capital was absent in all cases. In two cases, Madrid and Amsterdam, it was noted that access to small seed capital of between 50,000 euros and €300,000 euros was not a problem, but access to growth capital was a real problem. One informant from Amsterdam observed that 'There are

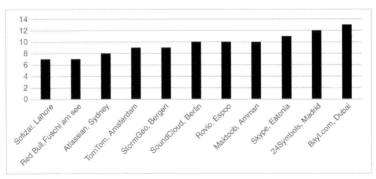

Fig. 14.2 Availability of supporting conditions at 11 locations

a lot of "wannabe" investors but they are only small and short of funds. There is not a lot of follow-up finance available'. In almost all cases, a strong local knowledge base was relevant to the start-up. Helsinki had a strong gaming and IT knowledge base which supported the technical and content needs of Rovio, Berlin and Madrid offered a strong local knowledge base in music and literature, respectively, whereas Bergen had a long tradition and a strong knowledge base in meteorology.

On the whole, the home locations of the 11 successful start-ups were deemed by their founders to have offered enough of the supporting conditions to enable them to succeed at a global level. There was agreement across all companies about the importance of having access to talent, a supporting knowledge base, an environment which offers a multiplicity of specialisations to draw on, and opportunities to access international networks.

Deficiencies Are Not Necessarily Important

Two of the most important conditions for start-up growth and success— risk capital and access to global networks—were often missing (Fig. 14.3). In fact, ecosystem conditions we relate to the convenience of starting a business were identified as the most undersupplied. Risk capital was

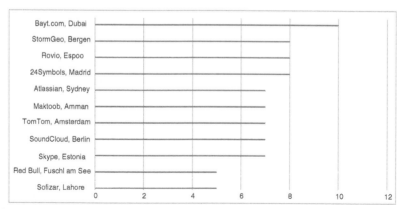

Fig. 14.3 Conditions availability across 11 locations

absent across all 11 locations, and access to global networks was absent in half of the cases. And yet what is interesting here is not that these factors were lacking but that the start-ups examined managed to grow or scale up without those conditions in their home locations.

What Can We Learn from These 11 Cases?

In all 11 cases, the entrepreneurs developed strategies to maximise the advantages of their locations and to mitigate their various shortcomings. In a way, the entrepreneurs created their own place-specific comparative advantage. Though calibre-supporting conditions were deemed to be available across a majority of locations, in one instance (Sofizar), the entrepreneur chose to relocate from the high-calibre conditions of California to the seemingly lower-calibre conditions of Pakistan in order to avoid the strings typically associated with seed and venture capital (VC) and to be able to self-finance his business.

Nevertheless, the 11 locations had an undersupply of each of the 15 conditions that were deemed critical by a majority of informants. Risk capital, global networks, domestic networks, business-friendly regulation, a culture of risk, anchor firms and flexible specialisation in local industry are all more often missing than available in the 11 cases. Interestingly, government support was cited as present more often than relevant across the 11 cases. Less relevant in the 11 cases was the presence of skilled immigrant entrepreneurs, infrastructure, an attractive lifestyle, skilled talent and a knowledge base. This does not mean that these conditions are unimportant or irrelevant from the perspective of a given region or location, but that in these particular instances they were not especially important for success. Thus in some cases, these positive conditions were present but were not deemed relevant.

Sometimes the presence of government support was viewed negatively. In Norway, an informant observed that 'governmental funding has become a "sleeping pillow" to many aspiring entrepreneurs. Instead of hunting customers, too many founders put their efforts and existence in chasing governmental grants.' In Austria, one informant said that 'If entrepreneurs fail in Austria the social welfare system will catch them.

This tends to make entrepreneurs less aggressive as they don't have so much to lose'. These observations seem to go against recent research from Finland, by Erkko Autio and Heikki Rannikko (2015), which shows a positive link between government support and start-up success. The study found that start-up firms which have received government support enjoyed higher growth rates than those that did not over a 6-year period.

Government support thus emerged as a somewhat controversial factor; in that, it was seen as an enabler or a distractor. Government support was favourable in Dubai and Madrid, but less so in Bergen. In Estonia, government's role was both direct and indirect. It was noted by one informant that 'the pressure to make public administration as efficient as possible forced our government to look for opportunities to take advantage of modern technology and turn Estonia into eEstonia'. In Dubai, the founder of Bayt.com said that 'Bayt.com would not have existed if not for the auspicious announcement by the Dubai Government of a new Dubai Internet City', whereas in Madrid, the founder of 24symbols pointed out that 'Spain has strong public funding initiatives. We got a soft loan from the Ministry of Industry when we started'. Autio and Rannikko (2015), in the aforementioned study from Finland, ascribe the success of government support to the design features of the intervention, particularly the need to integrate performance-based conditions in it.

Successful Entrepreneurs Actively Customise Their Locational Comparative Advantages

The response of entrepreneurs in places missing many of the 15 start-up supporting conditions, such as Amman, Bergen, Estonia, Fuschl am See, Lahore and Sydney, was not uniform. With Sofizar, SoundCloud and Skype, the decision by their respective founders to exit certain places in order to relocate elsewhere was based on personal beliefs about a cost—benefit advantage. The cost of doing business was the most important factor for Zafar Khan because he believed that addressing this would allow him the time and flexibility to build his business into a success.

Khan found that the lower cost of doing business in Lahore represented a greater advantage than the abundance of VC in California.

The founders of SoundCloud believed that they needed to be nearer music producers and users and that Berlin would be a much richer and vibrant place for lead-music producers. We also saw start-ups emerging and scaling up in locations traditionally stymied by high taxation regimes, together with challenging climates and geographies, and highly homogenised societies with very low appetite for risk, such as Rovio in Helsinki, Finland, and StormGeo in Bergen, Norway. Note that these countries rank low on the Bohemian Index popularised by Richard Florida owing to their high levels of ethnic homogeneity.

Across all 11 cases, only half of what was needed in terms of supporting ecosystem conditions was available. Skype in Estonia, Atlassian in Sydney and Maktoob in Jordan are the three companies which had to look most beyond their locations to compensate for conditions absent in their home locations. In this regard, successful entrepreneurs actively customise their locational comparative advantages. They assess the local conditions in terms of (1) their needs, (2) how much value can be leveraged locally and (3) how much value can be leveraged globally, and then they seek to compensate for any missing critical factors by reaching out beyond their locations, mostly overseas. They look for resources within their own personal and professional networks to lessen the disadvantage of the place, especially with regard to risk capital.

This is why in all 11 cases, start-ups opened offices in other countries to access relevant resources which were absent locally, but the home location of the start-up was identified by opportunity. Mona Ataya, co-founder of Bayt.com, puts it succinctly when she says 'the place identifies the opportunity'. This is true to a large extent, and what varies is the perception of the opportunity. Bayt.com took advantage of Dubai's rapid development and modernisation, reflected in both an exponential growth in its job market and free trade zones. StormGeo, in Bergen, also took advantage of the liberalisation of broadcast media and, later, energy markets and leveraged the strong local community of meteorology and geophysics scientists which dates back to 1917 when Vilhelm Bjerkness founded the Geophysical Institute at the University of Bergen. Rovio, the company behind the computer game Angry

Birds, took advantage of Helsinki's strong knowledge base in mobile telephony and IT and an existing long tradition in game development.

Thus, entrepreneurs appear to make assessments of their local conditions based on what they perceive as being most important for their success. This is in line with some of the research findings outlined earlier in Chap. 2 (particularly the work of Lafuente et al. 2010). On paper, both Lahore in Pakistan and Fuschl am See in Austria look like the least desirable places for start-up activity, and yet in both cases the founders decided that those locations had greater place surpluses than they would find elsewhere. These entrepreneurs made a positive evaluation of the suitability of the locations for their particular businesses.

The 11 cases examined in this book show that, though start-ups may not have all the recommended 15 factors and conditions traditionally required for them to grow and succeed in technology hubs, they have managed to succeed with a minimum set of conditions deemed most critical for them. Though other places may have offered plenty of other goodies and positive attributes, these were not deemed sufficiently important for the success of a specific type of business. Amongst all 11 cases of pioneering start-up success, what emerges as an important tool for leveraging a place surplus and overcoming a place deficit is networking. The opportunity and the ability to reach out, connect, showcase and raise interest in one's venture through conferences, expos, festivals, competitions and other platforms emerge as critical factors in making a place work for an entrepreneur. This is an important lesson for governments and other players interested in supporting technological entrepreneurship in their regions. Creating the opportunities and providing the means to enable local entrepreneurs to connect with potential investors, partners, markets and their peers in other regions and countries is more important than providing seed capital and office space. What entrepreneurs need most is the opportunity to tap into supporting business networks where relationships are driven by mutual interest and the shared objective of creating new value. In this respect, peers and profit-centred networks can be more effective than networks centred on government support, where goals are not as aligned and the strings and conditions attached create incentives for firms to help the region rather than the way around. A prime example here is seed capital made available by local or national governments for start-ups with the condition of recruiting locally. The goal of the government here is to create jobs locally through the start-up rather than to support the growth strategy of the start-up. Thus, governments, business associations, chambers of commerce and other players keen on creating successful global start-ups would do well to support networking and match platforms and opportunities where local entrepreneurs can find the needed seed capital, the talent and the market rather than having these delivered to them by a government or other supporting agency. The government's role as an enabler is ultimately superior in delivering the government's own goals in terms of creating jobs and economic growth. For entrepreneurs, it is important to understand the surpluses and the deficits of the local place and to think globally to match and complement partners in order to achieve a local-global positive.

On this note, I end the book with the following remark. Places which have experienced the emergence of black swan start-ups are now in the advantageous position of having successful pioneer entrepreneurs who can serve as nodes for local networks of entrepreneurial activity. They provide mentorship, coaching, investment and access to global networks. In this respect, one expects the emergence of a black swan to be the beginning of an ecosystem which will generate so many more black swans that they are no longer greeted with surprise.

References

Autio, Erkko and Rannikko, Heikki. 2015. Retaining winners: Can policy boost high-growth entrepreneurship. Imperial College Business School Innovation and Entrepreneurship Working Series. May.

CB Insights. The top reasons startups fail. https://www.cbinsights.com/research-reports/The-20-Reasons-Startups-Fail.pdf

Lafuente, Esteban, Yancy Vaillant, and Christian Serarols. 2010. Location decisions of knowledge-based entrepreneurs: Why some Catalan KISAs choose to be rural? *Technovation* 30(11): 590–600.

Index

Note: Page number followed by 'n' refers to footnotes.

© The Editor(s) (if applicable) and The Author(s) 2016
S. Mahroum, *Black Swan Start-ups*,
DOI 10.1057/978-1-137-57727-6